a–z o

Every field of practice has its own methods, terminology, conceptual debates and landmark publications. The *Professional Keywords* series expertly structures this material into easy-reference A to Z format. Focusing on the ideas and themes that shape the field, and informed by the latest research, these books are designed both to guide the student reader and to refresh practitioners' thinking and understanding.

Available now

Mark Doel and Timothy B. Kelly: *A–Z of Groups & Groupwork*
Jon Glasby and Helen Dickinson: *A–Z of Inter-agency Working*
Richard Hugman: *A–Z of Professional Ethics*
Glenn Laverack: *A–Z of Health Promotion*
Neil McKeganey: *A–Z of Addiction and Substance Misuse*
Steve Nolan and Margaret Holloway: *A–Z of Spirituality*
Marian Roberts: *A–Z of Mediation*

Available soon

Jane Dalrymple: *A–Z of Advocacy*
David Shemmings, Yvonne Shemmings and David Wilkins:
   A–Z of Attachment Theory
Jeffrey Longhofer: *A–Z of Psychodynamic Practice*
David Garnett: *A–Z of Housing*
Fiona Timmins: *A–Z of Reflective Practice*

a–z of
mediation

Marian Roberts

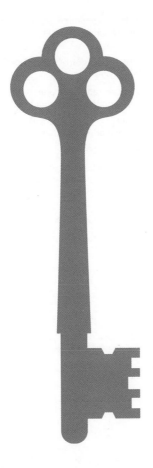

palgrave
macmillan

First published 2014 by
PALGRAVE MACMILLAN

Palgrave Macmillan in the UK is an imprint of Macmillan Publishers Limited,
registered in England, company number 785998, of Houndmills, Basingstoke,
Hampshire RG21 6XS.

Palgrave Macmillan in the US is a division of St Martin's Press LLC,
175 Fifth Avenue, New York, NY 10010.

Palgrave Macmillan is the global academic imprint of the above companies
and has companies and representatives throughout the world.

Palgrave® and Macmillan® are registered trademarks in the United States,
the United Kingdom, Europe and other countries

ISBN: 978–1–137–00298–3

This book is printed on paper suitable for recycling and made from fully
managed and sustained forest sources. Logging, pulping and manufacturing
processes are expected to conform to the environmental regulations of the
country of origin.

A catalogue record for this book is available from the British Library.

A catalog record for this book is available from the Library of Congress.

Printed in China

For Jacob, Beatrice and Grace – students of the future

contents

acknowledgements

The collegiality of mediators contributes significantly to the knowledge about mediation that this work aspires to pass on. Therefore I would like to acknowledge how much I have learned from colleagues with whom I have worked over many years – those at the South East London Family Mediation Bureau and within the College of Mediators especially. The mediators who contributed their rich and diverse practice experience and reflections to the project that resulted in *Developing the Craft of Mediation: Reflections on Theory and Practice* (London: Jessica Kingsley Publishers, 2007) also crucially informs this work, in particular in understanding the commonalities and differences across different fields of mediation practice. The insight and enthusiasm of my students, both at LSE and at SOAS, have also enriched my understanding of this field. I would like to thank Nikki McVeagh for all the help she gave me to better inform myself in preparing the entry on Church Mediation, especially about mediation practices within the Anglican Church in this country. Catherine Gray, editor at Palgrave Macmillan, has been a great support and constructive presence throughout. The encouragement, guidance and scholarship of Simon Roberts has been as invaluable as ever. Responsibility for the limitations of this book and any errors remain mine.

An article on 'Specialist Child Care Mediation', from which the entry Specialist Child Care Mediation is derived was first published in *Family Law Journal*, June 2013, Volume 43, Issue 6.

how to use this book

Mediation is both a scholarly discipline, informed by its own history, debates, theory and research, and a field of practice, widely applied and of increasing importance in everyday life. This book aims to capture and clarify the concepts, themes, ideas and challenges which describe and inform mediation in all its complexity. My aim is to build a coherent and systematic picture of the subject for readers – students, practitioners and the interested public alike.

The entry content is wide in scope and made up both of analytic and descriptive categories. Arranged alphabetically, each entry is self-contained and concise, intending to get to the heart of the subject matter clearly and precisely. At the same time, for those wishing to enhance their understanding and expand their knowledge base, the entries signpost readers to related further reading, supported by a full bibliography at the end of the book. So this book is more than a glossary or dictionary of words and definitions. It covers concepts, theories, debates, critiques, contextual frameworks and institutions, principles, processes, practice fields and their applications, and adjacent interventions.

As a resource and reference text with an alphabetical structure of compact entries, this book may be approached in several different ways, depending on the interests, needs and requirements of the reader. These various routes of navigating this book include the following:

- **The alphabetical approach**: this is helpful for those wanting to gain an overview of the whole terrain of the subject of mediation and its relationship to other disciplines and interventions.
- **Central theories and processes**: for readers completely new to the subject and wanting to gain an understanding of the nature of mediation as a distinctive process, the navigation route could begin with the key entry on mediation and encompass related

entries on the mediation process, negotiation, principles of mediation, the mediator, attributes, party control, etc.

- **Subject areas:** for those who have some knowledge of the subject and want to expand their understanding of its relationship with/to other processes and applications in a variety of subject areas, you can find discussion, for example, on adjudication; arbitration; international mediation; restorative justice; workplace mediation, etc.
- **Concepts:** for students and those wishing to understand theoretical concepts that inform mediation, see, for example, entries on authority; confidentiality; conflict; craftsmanship; disputes; fairness; party control; power, etc.
- **Debates and critiques:** for those wishing to locate mediation in a developmental, historical and political context, see, for example, entries on critiques of ADR; informal justice; domestic abuse; power; professional regulation; theory, etc.
- **Specific fields of mediation practice:** for those who want to expand their knowledge of specific applications of mediation, see entries on the different areas of mediation practice such as civil and commercial mediation; family mediation; environmental mediation; international mediation, etc.

Readers will also find entries on models, skills, styles and processes (for example, *the Bromley Model of family mediation* and *the caucus,* etc.) and applications of mediation practice. I have included both adjacent interventions (for those wishing to compare and contrast different interventions such as *conciliation, collaborative law, Early Neutral Evaluation,* etc.) and traditional interventions (for students wishing to understand the differences between mediation and traditional forms of dispute resolution such as *adjudication* and lawyer negotiation).

A list of statutes provides the legislative framework that informs different fields of practice and a list of organizations offers information about organizations operating in the field of mediation, including training providers, service providers, regulatory bodies, professional and support bodies, etc. I have also included a list of abbreviations, given the number of acronyms that crowd this field.

All the entries are linked in a four-fold referencing system, which offers the reader a variety of navigational tools for accessing the material:

- The contents list offers a complete overview of all the 'keywords' discussed in the text in order of appearance.
- Each substantive entry is accompanied by a 'see also' listing of other entries to which it might be useful to turn to next.
- The use of italics type in the narrative identifies terms on first mention in a given entry which have an entry in their own right in the book.
- The index provides an important supplement to the book's 'keywords', allowing the reader to gain access to terms and ideas which could not be allocated an entry in their own right.

table of statutes and statutory instruments

Access to Justice Act 1999
Arbitration Act 1996
Child Abduction Act 1984
Children Act 1989
Children Act 1975
Children Act 2004
Children (Scotland) Act 1995
Children and Adoption Act 2006
Children and Families Bill 2013
The Civil Evidence (Family Mediation) (Scotland) Act 1995
Civil Procedure Act 1998
Civil Procedure Rules 1998
Conciliation Act 1896
The Crime and Disorder Act 1998
Criminal Justice Act 2003
Domestic Violence, Crime and Victims Act 2004
Draft Mediation Bill (Ireland) 2012
Education Act 1996
Education Act 2002
Employment Act 2002
Employment Protection Act 1975
Equality Act 2010
Family Law Act 1996
Family Procedure Rules 2010
Housing Act 1996
Housing, Grants, Construction and Regeneration Act 1996
Human Rights Act 1998
Industrial Courts Act 1919
Legal Aid Act 1988
Proceeds of Crime Act 2002
Roman Catholic Code of Canon Law 1446 (Western Church)

list of abbreviations

ACAS	Advisory Conciliation and Arbitration Service
ADR	alternative dispute resolution
CEDR	Centre for Dispute Resolution
COM	College of Mediators
DA	Disqualification Agreement
DCA	Department of Constitutional Affairs
DWP	Department for Work and Pensions
ENE	Early Neutral Evaluation
FGC	Family Group Conference
FJC	Family Justice Council
FMC	Family Mediation Council
ICRC	International Committee of the Red Cross
ICT	Information and Communications Technology
LEAs	Local Education Authorities
MIAM	Mediation Information and Assessment Meeting
MoJ	Ministry of Justice
NADRAC	National Alternative Dispute Resolution Advisory Council
NAO	National Audit Office
NFM	National Family Mediation
ODR	Online Dispute Resolution
OFDR	Online Family Dispute Resolution
PPC	Professional Practice Consultancy
SCCM	Specialist Child Care Mediation
SEN	Special Educational Needs
UKCFM	UK College of Family Mediators

list of organizations

Aasha Gang Mediation Project
ADRGroup (ADRg)
Capital Conflict Management (CCM)
Centre for Dispute Resolution (CEDR)
Chartered Institute of Arbitrators (CIArb)
Civil Mediation Council (CMC)
College of Mediators (COM)
Family Justice Council (FJC)
Family Mediators Association (FMA)
Family Mediation Council (FMC)
Family Mediation Scotland (FMS)
In Place of Strife (IPOS)
Mediators Institute of Ireland (MII)
National Centre for Restorative Justice in Education
National Family Mediation (NFM)
Resolution (formerly Solicitors Family Law Association)
Reunite International Child Abduction Centre
Scottish Mediation Network
Standing Conference of Mediation Advocates (SCMA)
Transforming Conflict (TC)
West Midlands Mediation and Transformation Service (WMMTS)

introduction

A radical transformation

The modern revival of mediation, as an established pathway in the landscape of dispute resolution processes, represents the rediscovery of an ancient and universal mode of intervention, as old as human-kind itself. This is a process of consensual joint decision-making in which a third person, the mediator, exercising a non-aligned role and without authority to impose a decision, assists those in dispute to negotiate together and to reach their own agreements.

Beginning in the 1970s, the re-emergence of mediation as a mode of settling quarrels introduced a radically different approach to the resolution of conflict and dispute to that prevailing. This came at the end of a long period during which judges had acted as principal official agents of dispute resolution and lawyers had established themselves as virtually the sole means of access to the courts. This powerful and pervasive legal and judicial bias was one that long conditioned thinking about dispute resolution in Western society.

An important aspect of the transformation that occurred was the new significance accorded to the views of disputants themselves. The affirmation of the 'person-oriented perspective', which distin-guishes mediation from the 'act–orientation' of litigation, chal-lenged traditional attitudes and values in the context of dispute resolution (Fuller, 1971). Writings now demonstrated that courts and legal professionals, inevitably constrained by general rules and limited knowledge, had failed to respond to the needs and inter-ests of disputants who not only cared about the process by which decisions were reached, but who were perfectly able, in most cases, to devise their own, more satisfactory solutions to their disputes (Galanter, 1981; Menkel-Meadow, 2004).

The values of mediation exemplified the spirit of the time – the fundamental importance attached to respect, dignity, fairness, justice, reciprocity, individual participation, consensus and party control (Fuller, 1971; Rubin and Brown, 1975; Davis, 1984). The resurrection of these values countered a dominant legal system characterized by adversarial processes, confrontation, impersonality, lawyer control and rule-centred authoritarian command.

The radical ideological and institutional changes that have transformed civil disputing arrangements at the close of the twentieth century, across the common law and civilian worlds of the West, also reflected this cultural transformation of approach to dispute resolution (Menkel-Meadow *et al.*, 2005, 2012; Roberts, 2006; Roberts and Palmer, 2005; 3rd edn forthcoming 2014). Negotiation leading to consensual decision-making first challenged then superseded traditional entrenched primary reliance on the competitive processes of litigation and of imposed third-party decision-making (Woolf, 1996; Roberts and Palmer 3rd edn, forthcoming 2014). In domains other than civil justice, there have been parallel developments of innovative alternative approaches to dispute resolution: in the spheres of criminal and restorative justice, the environment; the workplace, the community, education and other specialist areas such as disability and medical negligence. These fields now join the international arena and labour relations where mediatory interventions have long been practised and endorsed.

So this work seeks to record a contemporary ascendancy that mediation has achieved as an institutionalized and expanding mode of dispute resolution across many areas of social life and across jurisdictions. That this has occurred in so short a time and despite the opposition (in some areas of practice) of powerful professional vested interests and some academics, is nothing short of remarkable. That this transformation, with its significant social, cultural, legal and political ramifications, has also generated contradictory and problematic consequences, is not surprising.

Critiques and challenges

Two themes, often intertwined, have been identified as informing the impetus behind official enthusiasm for mediation (Galanter, 1984). The 'warm theme' has celebrated mediation not only as the embodiment of a new way of thinking about disputes but also its larger purpose, the self-conscious aspiration to seek 'a better way' of addressing quarrels, one intended to bring parties into 'mutual accord' (Galanter, 1984, p. 2). The 'cool theme', on the other hand, has emphasized different objectives – cost-savings, diversion from the courts and the reduction of court hearings, and administrative efficiency. Early writings, initially in the USA, raised important concerns about the growth of private ordering (see, for example, Abel, 1982; Auerbach, 1983; Freeman, 1984; Davis and Bader, 1985; Matthews, 1988; Rifkin, 1994). An important dimension of the powerful political critique about 'informal justice' focused on debates about justice, fairness, neutrality and power. A feminist critique, based on assumptions about power inequalities in the family, raised fears about mediation damaging women's interests (Bottomley, 1984, 1985).

Another influential critique not only highlighted concerns about the impact of power disparities on settlement processes, but also affirmed the predominant *social value* of the court. Courts were public institutions, devoted primarily to the goal, not of resolving disputes, but of explicating and giving force to the values of society – liberty, equality, due process and freedom of speech. Alternative processes, on the other hand, could be seen to operate as attempts to privatize the courts, trivializing their role and avoiding public accountability (Fiss, 1984).

Nowadays, with mediation an established, even mainstream, process in many fields, the focus of concern has shifted away (though not entirely) from those broad, theoretical and ideological critiques about informal justice, to a new focus of concern specifically about the nature and quality of mediation practice. Questions about *whether* alternative processes serve the public interest have been replaced by questions about *whither* – in what direction and to what degree – mediators themselves are prepared to recognize the necessity of meeting, in the public interest, objective, national, uniform standards of professional practice. Even regulatory independence, acknowledged to be the safest means of ensuring an effective, safe and constructive process and of protecting the public, still meets with only qualified acceptance.

The imperatives of the professionalization project ground attention on the importance of informed understandings about:

- the nature of the mediation process and its core principles;

- the independence of mediation as a discrete, autonomous form of intervention distinct from any other forms of intervention (therapy, counselling and welfare, on the one hand, or legal process and refurbishing court process on the other);
- constituents of ethical and competent practice;
- safeguards of fairness, transparency and accountability.

These understandings, which this book foregrounds, assume even greater significance in the light of current developments that give rise to a range of serious concerns (of which I have direct experience, both as a practising mediator and via my engagement, over many years, in collegiate efforts to create a professional regulatory framework for family mediators). For example, the core principles of mediation that safeguard the public and the integrity of the process can be distorted and undermined by pressures towards mandatory participation in mediation or where mediators adopt manipulative strategies (derived from other interventions such as lawyer negotiation or family therapy). Early criticisms of alternative processes have current relevance in contexts where mediation has been co-opted for ulterior objectives (for example, a local housing authority's deployment of mediation to avoid fulfilling statutory responsibilities for the homeless young) or where there is ideological or over-zealous governmental promotion of mediation, regardless of its suitability, with the purpose of diverting or deterring applicants from courts or statutory child maintenance schemes. Commercial interests (of training providers, for example) tend to conflict with efforts to raise practice standards. The proliferation of commercial training programmes, the ever-expanding growth of a body of inexperienced practitioners overcrowding the market, and the variety of different accreditation schemes are likely to cause public confusion and an increase in the prevalence of bad practice.

These problems are compounded where mediation is muddled up with other interventions and attempts are made to combine, in the same practitioner, mediation with advisory, guidance and counselling functions (as envisaged, in so-called 'therapeutic justice' – see DWP Report 2013).

Where mediation 'success' is defined as diversion of the case from legal process, quicker, more evaluative and directive forms of settlement approaches, such as those traditionally practised by lawyers, appear more likely to meet governmental expectations of 'cost effectiveness' (for example, in respect of legal aid provision for mediation). Finally, there are the dangers posed by the legal profession itself, in seeking to dominate the development of alternative processes – as was witnessed a decade or so ago in North America where lawyers 'tumble(d) over each other in their enthusiasm for non-legal dispute resolution alternatives' and where 'the relentless force of law in modern American society can be measured by its domination, and virtual annihilation, of alternative forms of dispute settlement (Auerbach, 1983, p. 15 and p. 139).

The importance of the knowledge base for learning and practice
This book gives prominence to the foundational principles, core characteristics and ethical values that lie at the heart of mediation. Their realization in the process is essential for safe and effective practice. One of the main objects of this work is to provide knowledge and understanding of the importance of this dimension of the subject, and of how, paradoxically, these features can be both protected on the one hand but also potentially undermined, on the other.

Mediation has the potential, in appropriate cases, to achieve considerable benefits for those who participate (and for those outside the process such as children and other family members), not only in the resolution of their dispute, but also of improved communication, reduced conflict and stress, and an increased capacity to negotiate together in the future. With aspirations as ambitious as these to fulfil, and in circumstances as difficult, the scale of the task requires the mediator to adopt a modest approach, with full awareness of the limits, boundaries and inherent tensions of the process. In many instances mediators can do no more than provide disputing parties with a calm, safe forum for reasonable exchange, enabling them to have the conversation that they are unable to have on their own.

In the current world, mediation, as a practice intervention across many fields, and as a subject of scholarly study, is characterized by variety, ambiguity, contradiction, structural and institutional tensions and conflicts of function and interest, as well by the adoption of a multiplicity of practice approaches, models and styles (all labelled 'mediation'). This situation gives rise to a corresponding need for a knowledge base that can provide clarity, consistency and concision on the fundamental precepts of mediation and its applications.

Conceptual clarity is necessary for the delineation of the discrete autonomous nature of mediation and its distinctive features. Conceptual clarity on the nature of the mediation process (its analytically identifiable negotiation stages and patterns of expectations in particular) is of particular importance given the dynamic reality and the powerful emotions, and turbulent political and social circumstances, that characterize situations of conflict. Conceptual congruence on fundamental principles and purposes is essential for professionals who, without an unequivocal understanding of *what* they are doing and *why* they are doing it, cannot know *how* to realize their role and function effectively. Fully informed consent to participate in mediation requires clarity of understanding too. Congruence of purpose is bound up crucially with expectations as to what does or does not constitute success or failure of the process (vital for funding bodies' ability to support projects in the field) and with officially sanctioned ethical and professional codes of practice and approved standards of training, practice and evaluation. Terminological accuracy can prevent definitional slippage and vague and contradictory usages that give rise to muddled practices that compound public misunderstanding and ignorance on vital aspects, especially those relating to the location of power and authority.

Contemporary complexities and confusion may be contrasted with the greater clarity of an earlier period when leading theorists of the past century were agreed on the defining characteristics of mediation, observable across cultures and across times. These were distinguished clearly from other interventions and in particular from the other primary form of third-party decision-making, namely adjudication. This is why the classic texts assume central significance in this work (see, for example, Simmel, 1908; Douglas, 1962; Fuller, 1971 and Gulliver, 1979).

The narratives, key texts, and additional reading references reflect the historical depth, breadth, complexity and inter-disciplinarity of the literature (both classic texts and current works) on the subject of mediation and its relationship to other interventions. This is a field richly informed by many disciplines – anthropology, economics, history, industrial relations, international relations, law, philosophy, psychology, social psychology and sociology – which all expand perspective and widen understanding.

Mediators today can be conceived of as contemporary practitioners of an ancient and universal craft where expertise is gained from experience and largely in association with others working in the field, in the tradition of the guildhall mode – the apprenticeship model for acquiring skills, for example, and the continuing educational development and support provided by informal networks of peers. This collegiality contributes its own vital source of learning and expertise. New and expanding areas of application – from the most intimate and personal to the large-scale and international – are making a significant contribution to the advancement of understanding about conflict resolution in general and the benefits and limits of mediation in particular. Every fresh mediation, bringing an opportunity to respond to the unique richness of each predicament, increases experience and understanding.

Knowledge, combined with scholarly research, practice experience and resources of expertise derived from practitioners' own contributions to their field (in teaching, training and writing), can provide the sure foundation for the freedom that is necessary to nourish innovation and creativity.

This work seeks to contribute a measure of enhanced understanding of mediation to that varied and growing fund of knowledge.

a

adjudication

SEE ALSO arbitration; decision-making; judicial mediation; justice; law

What distinguishes adjudication (and *arbitration*) from *mediation* is the location of *decision-making authority*. In mediation this lies with the parties themselves, whereas in both adjudication and arbitration, there is an appeal to a third party to impose a decision. In arbitration the parties consent to this imposed decision. In adjudication the parties surrender this authority to a neutral third party who derives authority, not by invitation of the parties but by virtue of the office s/he holds. Adjudication usually follows a hearing (though there may be a determination on the basis of submitted documents) attended by formal rules and procedures where the parties are represented by professional advocates. The role of *lawyers* is closely linked to the courts in the Anglo-American common law world providing an indispensable function in an adversarial legal system. They act on behalf of their opposing client(s), each presenting evidence, arguments and challenges so that the judge is enabled to reach a fully reasoned and deliberate decision. The determination made by the judge is in the form of an order in favour of one of the parties who is regarded as the winner, and the other the loser. Both parties are legally bound by the order, the implementation of which carries all the authority of the court. The courts' claim to legitimacy lies in their link to the apparatus of state power, to the long established convention of 'the rule of law', and in the hierarchical appellate structure of most judicial systems (Roberts and Palmer, 2005). This gives the losing party the opportunity to seek an alternative outcome.

Adjudication (as the culmination of litigation) as a method of legal conflict resolution has been vividly depicted a century ago as 'the most merciless type of contestation because it lies wholly outside the subjective contrast between charity and cruelty' (Simmel, 1908a,

p. 85). While the disadvantages of the modern adversarial system – its cost, delay, inaccessibility and increased *conflict* – are well recognized (see Interim Woolf Report, 1995), it may be that an adjudicated decision based on a full assessment of all the facts would be the best solution to a genuinely irreconcilable conflict of interest. The benefits of adjudication in appropriate cases include, for example, where an immediate decision is necessary in the interests of either of the parties and/or a child, where there are serious disparities of *power* and resources, or where an issue of public importance requires an authoritative ruling.

Roberts and Palmer (2005) chart the dramatic transformation that has occurred over the past three decades – from an entrenched culture of public disputing with courts delivering justice and the legal profession using the litigation process as a vehicle for securing late settlement, to a new 'culture of settlement', one promoting early settlement and *alternative dispute resolution (ADR)*, and mediation in particular. The powerful and coercive impact (implicit and explicit) of litigation and adjudication on out-of-court negotiation remains, nevertheless, profound (see Mnookin and Kornhauser's seminal North American article which describes all such negotiations as 'bargaining in the shadow of the law' (1979, pp. 978–979)).

A specific example of adjudication used as a method of alternative dispute resolution can be found under the Housing, Grants, Construction and Regeneration Act 1996, Part II. This confers on parties the statutory right to insist upon the statutory adjudication of construction disputes, formerly only resolvable through court-based litigation or arbitration. Owing to the main advantages of this approach – its speed, flexibility, simplicity and informality – statutory adjudication has become the main approach to resolving disputes in the construction industry (Dolder, 2008).

KEY TEXTS
- Cane, P. and Conaghan, J. (eds) (2008) *The New Oxford Companion to Law* (Oxford: Oxford University Press)
- Dworkin, R. (1986) *Law's Empire* (London: Fontana)
- Dworkin, R. (2005) *Taking Rights Seriously* (Boston: Harvard University Press)
- Hart, H.L.A. (1961) *The Concept of Law* (Oxford: Clarendon Press)

- Palmer, M. and Roberts, S. (forthcoming, 2014) *Dispute Processes: ADR and the Primary Forms of Decision-Making.* 3rd edn (Cambridge: Cambridge University Press)
- Shapiro, M. (1981) *Courts: A Comparative and Political Analysis* (Chicago: University of Chicago Press)

Advisory Conciliation and Arbitration Service (ACAS)

SEE ALSO **arbitration; industrial relations mediation; workplace mediation**

Industrial Relations has the longest practice history of an official conciliatory process in Britain. The Conciliation Act 1896 provided the recognizably modern statutory framework for state-sponsored conciliation and *arbitration* of collective labour disputes, although other forms of intervention existed for several decades prior to the Act of 1896. The Advisory, Conciliation and Arbitration Service (ACAS) was originally set up as the Conciliation and Arbitration Service in 1974, becoming a statutory body in 1976. The current legal framework is contained in Section 212 of the Trade Union and Labour Relations (Consolidation) Act 1992. Within this legal framework, the public agency, ACAS, sponsors voluntary 'third party' services, namely, *conciliation, mediation* and arbitration to employers and their associations on the one hand and workers and trade unions on the other. This long-established, dominant institutional context determines the way its practitioners enter the field.

ACAS provides conciliation services, conducted by conciliation officers directly employed by ACAS, in collective disputes where both parties agree to this. The conciliation officers also have a legal duty to try to resolve disputes between individual workers and employers which involve workers' legal rights – such as the right not to be unfairly dismissed or discriminated on various grounds including sex or race (New Oxford Companion to Law, 2008). The conciliator follows the dispute carefully and, if appropriate, seeks to intervene to promote settlement – a non-directive process termed 'running alongside a dispute' – in order to avoid the dispute having to go to an employment tribunal for adjudication. ACAS does this on an entirely voluntary basis within the legal framework.

For its arbitration and mediation work, on the other hand, ACAS has a Panel of Independent Persons, which is mostly made up of former academics. However more recently ex-consultants and lawyers have also been appointed to act as arbitrators and mediators.

Whereas the terms 'mediation' and 'conciliation' were often used interchangeably in the context of their early application to family disputes, their definitions in a labour-relations context are distinct and different with mediation being associated with the making of formal recommendations (ACAS publication n.d., para. 29).

In the 1970s and 1980s, ACAS' work focussed on collective disputes involving actual or threatened strikes. This century, in addition to the work of its conciliation officers, ACAS' advisory role has expanded through the provision of a helpline and its published codes of practice (for example, on Disciplinary and Grievance Procedures) and good practice guidelines on industrial relations.

KEY TEXTS

- ACAS (Advisory, Conciliation and Arbitration Service) (n.d.) *The ACAS Role in Conciliation, Arbitration and Mediation* (London: ACAS Reports and Publications)
- Douglas, A. (1957) 'The Peaceful Settlement of Industrial and Intergroup Conflict', *The Journal of Conflict Resolution*, 1 (1): pp. 69–81
- Douglas, A. (1962) *Industrial Peacemaking* (New York: Columbia University Press)
- Latreille, P. (2011) *Mediation: A Thematic Review of the ACAS/CIPD Evidence*. Research Paper ACAS Ref. No 13/11. www.acas.org.uk/researchpapers
- Lewis, R. and Clark, J. (1993) *Employment Rights, Industrial Tribunals and Arbitration: The Case for Alternative Dispute Resolution* (Liverpool: Institute of Employment Rights)

alternative dispute resolution (ADR) (includes appropriate and proportionate dispute resolution)

SEE ALSO **critiques of ADR and mediation; informal justice**

Alternative dispute resolution is an umbrella term usually used to describe processes of *dispute resolution* other than formal judicial determination. The first use of the term 'alternative dispute resolution' (ADR) is attributed to Professor Frank Sander in a paper to the Pound Conference (Sander, 1976) attended predominantly by lawyers and judges concerned, ironically, with renovating court processes. ADR in a narrow sense originated therefore as something lawyers, encouraged by judges, intended to achieve (Palmer and Roberts, forthcoming, 2014).

The processes most commonly covered by this term, or its abbreviation, ADR, are *negotiation, mediation* and *arbitration* but can include additional hybrid processes such as *Med-Arb, conciliation,* conferencing, *ombudsmen* and *Early Neutral Evaluation.* The ADR practitioner intervenes in an impartial way in relation to the parties assisting them to resolve the issues in dispute by means of one of several approaches, depending on the location of *decision-making authority* – facilitative (as in mediation where the parties have decision-making authority) or determinative (as in arbitration where decision-making authority rests consensually with a third party) – or in some cases, a combination of these approaches (for example, advisory or expert determination). Mediation is the primary mode of ADR intervention and the most wide ranging in the scope and variety of fields it covers – for example, *commercial, community* and *neighbourhood, education, environmental* matters; *family* disputes; housing; *medical negligence, industrial, international* and *cross-border* disputes; and the *workplace.*

Complexity characterizes the terminological implications of ADR (see National Alternative Dispute Resolution Advisory Council (NADRAC Definitions Paper, 2002)). ADR may not always be an *alternative* to judicial determination or any alternative at all. It may be resorted to because it is the only realistic approach available where other options are themselves unsatisfactory or untenable – for example, having to tolerate conflict, or withdraw from the issue in dispute, or having to take industrial or even violent action. Some prefer to replace the 'A' of 'alternative' with either 'assisted' or *'appropriate' dispute resolution* or replace the 'alternate' with *'proportionate' dispute resolution.*

The Beldam Committee on Alternative Dispute Resolution as early as 1991 'was convinced that the case was made out for the courts *themselves* to embrace the systems of alternative dispute resolution' (emphasis added, p. 1).

Following Lord Woolf's recommendations (1995), the Civil Procedure Rules introduced two main alternative processes into the formal civil justice system – forecasting devices such as the *mini-trial* and *Early Neutral Evaluation (ENE)*; and interventions that directly facilitate negotiations such as mediation. The degree to which the formal justice system further intends to integrate 'alternative processes' in the context of the Family Justice System in England and Wales is exemplified in its most recent radical review which recommends that 'alternative dispute resolution' should be re-branded as 'dispute resolution services' in order 'to minimize a deterrent to its use' (The Family Justice Review Final Report, November, 2011, p. 162, 4.115).

Further complexity is apparent in respect of the assumption in ADR that there is a *dispute* to resolve for there may well not be any dispute (yet) or a dispute may be of secondary significance. For example, mediation can occur in situations where re-establishing communication, negotiating, consensual joint decision-making or problem-solving may be the predominant objective. ADR also covers many other practices that include consensus-building, dispute prevention and conflict transformation, going further therefore than the resolution of specific issues between disputing parties.

Furthermore, while the *resolution* of the matter may be highly desirable, it may not be achievable realistically. The object of the exercise may be either less ambitious, such as clarifying the issues, disposing of the legal issue through settlement, or narrowing the scope of difference, or it may be more ambitious, such as improving communication and future negotiating capacity or achieving 'transformation' through 'recognition and empowerment' (Bush and Folger, 2005).

Alternative dispute resolution refers therefore not only to a variety of modes of intervention or processes. Its emergence in the West in the early 1970s reflected a new way of thinking about dispute and embodied a self-conscious aspiration to find 'a better way' of dealing with civil disputes and addressing quarrels (Burger, 1982; Davis, 1984). One major influence (among others) that stimulated this early growth, in the USA and the UK, of mediation in particular, was the idealism of its early pioneers. This idealism embodied the hope that consensual and participatory dispute resolution processes, more attuned to human values and needs (compared to the traditional adversarial, hierarchical formal justice system), would transform not only disputing individuals but also 'nudge' society in the same direction (Chase, 2005, p. 135). These are the motivations that still inspire practising mediators, not only those who mediate in the international arena with direct experience of the violence of political conflict but also those working in the less dramatic situations of *workplace* or *family* conflict (Roberts, 2007)

Since the early 1980s, developments associated with ADR and mediation in particular have been the subject, to an unusually large extent, of a rich body of scholarly study and cross-disciplinary research which encompass a range of perspectives and conclusions.

KEY TEXTS

- ADR Bibliography (n.d.) London: Standing Conference of Mediation Advocates (SCMA). website@mediationadvocates.co.uk.
- Davis, A.M. (1984) 'Comment' in *A Study of Barriers to the Use of Alternative Methods of Dispute Resolution* (South Royalton: Vermont Law School Dispute Resolution Project)
- Menkel-Meadow, C. (ed) (2012) *Foundations of Dispute Resolution,* Vol. 1 (Aldershot, Hants: Ashgate)
- Palmer, M. and Roberts, S. (forthcoming, 2014) *Dispute Processes: ADR and the Primary Forms of Decision-Making.* 3rd edn (Cambridge: CUP)
- Sander, F.E.A. (1976) 'Varieties of Dispute Processing', *70 Federal Rules Decisions,* pp. 11–134

applications of mediation

SEE ALSO **alternative dispute resolution; decision-making; Early Neutral Evaluation; Med-Arb**

Mediation is deployed primarily in the service of joint *decision-making* with the objective of *alternative dispute resolution.* The application of *mediation* in pursuit of additional objectives has characterized innovative developments in the context of commercial and construction projects. One new objective of mediation, for example, has been *dispute avoidance,* an extension of dispute resolution, in the creation of mechanisms for pre-empting disputes and their costs and delay. Another new and ambitious objective has been the application of mediation in the design and management of transactions.

This form of third party facilitation involves mediators in being both involved in the formation of a complex transaction and 'on call' to assist in the continuous monitoring of that transaction, by means of the creation of a collaborative and inclusive work/staff environment. This can achieve the commercial advantage of hitting project targets on time and within budget. An early successful example of such a transaction was the project designed by ResoLex to alter the alignment of the taxi-way at Jersey Airport.

'Neutral risk monitoring' (ResoLex) or 'project mediation' (CEDR) are descriptions of the kinds of approaches that have been designed to integrate conflict management and dispute resolution techniques into contracts for projects which are distinguished by their distinctive collaborative contracting approach. These endeavours aim to reduce the risk of serious problems arising in the teams that deliver projects or contracts by providing a neutral and confidential forum for identifying and addressing potential problems, over payment or delay, for example, *before* they become disputes. The creation of a mechanism for fast access to a 'safe environment' (i.e. neutral and strictly confidential) with expert assistance on hand to address concerns or areas of risk, often difficult to recognize from within project teams, is considered to be one of the keys to the success of this approach. The main benefits of this application of mediation are as follows:

- The focus on dispute prevention/avoidance;
- The demonstration to parties that collaborative working is being taken seriously;
- The savings involved in the use of more flexible and cost-effective management techniques compared to other conflict or dispute resolution mechanisms;
- Costs can be budgeted for in advance;
- The integration of conflict prevention and management design into the contract.

ResoLex as the pioneer of Neutral Risk Monitoring has developed, additionally, a web-based risk monitoring tool, the 'X-Tracker', that creates a virtual and 'safe arena' for the regular and anonymous reporting, from all stakeholders, of any risk perceptions about a programme, project or contract. Its major benefit is that it provides the opportunity to identify and reduce potential risk, whether on a project or relationship basis, by building on an early-warning and collaborative approach.

The design and delivery of risk management, dispute prevention and dispute resolution systems are the objectives of this form of contracted and 'bespoke' mediation. As an imaginative application of mediation, it can boast considerable success and the support all parties involved.

KEY TEXTS

- CEDR: www.cedr.com
- Palmer, M. and Roberts, S. (forthcoming, 2014) *Dispute Processes: ADR and the Primary Forms of Decision-Making.* 3rd edn (Cambridge: CUP)
- ResoLex: www.resolex.com

aptitude

SEE ALSO **attributes of the mediator; craftsmanship; the mediator; professional regulation of mediation**

The *attributes* of the good mediator, both personal qualities and qualifications, have long been recognized (see Goethe's description of his character Mittler in his evolutionary progress as a mediator, 1809, *Elective Affinities*, pp. 31–44). Yet very little has, in fact, been written about the personal qualities of a mediator precisely because these are often elusive and idiosyncratic and therefore not easily susceptible to analysis. What does emerge is a consensus that a combination of attributes, intellectual, moral and personal, go towards the making of the ideal mediator. There is also consensus that no particular type or degree of prior education, job experience or qualification has been shown to be an effective predictor of success as a mediator or any other professional 'neutral' (Society of Professionals in Dispute Resolution Report, 1989).

Professional standards for family mediators now incorporate quality requirements for selection as well as for training, practice and accreditation on the basis of competence. Selection criteria for eligibility for mediation training have been devised based not on prior educational or professional qualifications of the candidate but on the primary requirement of *aptitude* for mediation (see National Family Mediation Selection Criteria, 1991). Aptitude has been analysed in terms of specific personal attributes relating to four main areas – intellectual attributes, interpersonal attributes, ethical and personal attributes, and motivation attributes. It is the combination of these attributes constituting aptitude that are seen to be necessary for the effective practice of mediation.

KEY TEXTS
- Bowling, D. and Hoffman, D. (2000) 'In Theory: Bringing Peace into the Room: The Personal Qualities of the Mediator and Their Impact on the Mediation', *Negotiation Journal,* 5: pp. 5–27
- Raiffa, H. (1982) *The Art and Science of Negotiation* (Cambridge, MA: Belknap, Harvard University Press)
- Roberts, M. (2007) *Developing the Craft of Mediation: Reflections on Theory and Practice* (London: Jessica Kingsley Publishers),Chapter 10
- Roberts, M. (2008) *Mediation in Family Disputes: Principles of Practice.* 3rd edn (Aldershot, Hants: Ashgate), Chapter 6
- Society of Professionals in Dispute Resolution (SPIDR) (1989) *Qualifying Neutrals: The Basic Principles* (Washington, DC: National Institute for Dispute Resolution)
- Stulberg, J. (1981) 'The Theory and Practice of Mediation: A Reply to Professor Susskind', reprinted in S.B. Goldberg, E.D. Green and F.E.A. Sander (eds), *Dispute Resolution* (Boston and Toronto: Little, Brown)

arbitration

SEE ALSO **adjudication; decision-making; dispute resolution; Med-Arb**

What distinguishes different forms of dispute resolution is the location of *decision-making authority.* In *mediation*, authority for decision-making lies with the parties themselves. *Arbitration* and *adjudication*, on the other hand, both involve an appeal to a third party to impose a decision because the parties themselves cannot agree. In arbitration, the parties voluntarily invite the arbitrator to make this decision and agree to honour the decision even though it is not legally binding.

The difference between arbitration and mediation has been described in this way:

Mediation is a form of peacemaking in which an outsider to a dispute intervenes on his own or accepts the invitation of disputing parties to assist them in reaching agreement. Whereas under arbitration the parties agree in advance to accept the decision of the arbitrator, no matter how unpalatable his judgment may appear when it is rendered, in mediation the parties maintain at every point in the proceedings, up to the very end, the prerogative of declaring the mediator 'persona non grata'. (Douglas, 1957, p. 70)

Another way of summing up the differences between the processes is as follows:

- Mediation 'involves helping people to decide for themselves';
- Arbitration and adjudication 'involve helping people by deciding for them' (A.S. Meyer, Chairman, New York State Mediation Board, 1960, p. 164).

The process of arbitration, which dates back to the ancient Greeks and has been in use in Britain for over three centuries, has seen a significant revival in recent years in a wide variety of settings such as international disputes (either inter-state arbitration or arbitration between a state party and another entity, corporation or individual) and disputes between major corporations as well as in employment and consumer disputes (Dolder, 2008). This revival was part of the search for alternatives that were less adversarial, cheaper, simpler and speedier than court adjudication, benefits particularly for commercial organizations and in consumer disputes.

Arbitration involves an impartial third party, independent and chosen by the parties, hearing both sides of the issue in dispute and making a final, binding decision in order to achieve resolution of the disagreement. The arbitrator's final decision may be based on 'reasonableness', 'good practice' or legal precedent. Although arbitration is the most formal and structured of *ADR* processes and is conducted within a legal framework, its process and outcome are not bound by the rules of litigation (for example, rules of evidence) and its procedures can be flexible – for example, a documents-based procedure (common for resolving consumer disputes) may replace a hearing. Nevertheless arbitration proceedings can be slow and expensive replicating those aspects of adjudication it was designed to remedy. Also, under the Arbitration Act 1996, there is very limited scope for appeal to a court against an arbitrator's decision.

The more directive, interventionist style of the labour relations mediator may reflect not only a positive approach appropriate to the tough circumstances of labour negotiations, but also an approach consistent with the link to the arbitration role where mediators in this context may act in either capacity depending on the terms of reference (Roberts, 2007, p. 139). One of the advantages of mediation and one of the major factors distinguishing mediation from arbitration is 'the latitude a mediator has to move beyond the issue of who is right and who is wrong' (William Hopgood quoted in Kolb *et al.*, 1994, p. 159).

KEY TEXTS
- Backaby, N., Partasides, C., Redfern, A. and Hunter, M. (eds) (2009) *Redfern & Hunter on International Arbitration*. 5th edn (Oxford: Oxford University Press)
- Baldwin, J. (2008) 'Arbitration' in P. Cane and J. Conaghan (eds), *The New Oxford Companion to Law* (Oxford: Oxford University Press)
- Moses, M. (2012) *The Principles and Practice of International Commercial Arbitration*. 2nd edn (Cambridge: CUP)
- Paulsson, J. (2013) *The Idea of Arbitration*. 2nd edn (Oxford: Clarendon Law Series)
- Roebuck, D. (2001) *Ancient Greek Arbitration* (Oxford: Oxford University Press)
- St John Sutton, D., Gill J. and Gearing, M. (forthcoming) *Russell on Arbitration*. 24th edn (London: Sweet and Maxwell)

artistry

SEE ALSO **aptitude; craftsmanship; ethics of mediation; the mediator; styles of mediation**

Mediation has been perceived variously as an 'art', a science, a 'craft', the skilled exercise of a technique, and as a combination of all these. In the mid-20th century some North American mediators described their practice as a 'subtle art' (Douglas, 1962, p. 108; quoting Meyer, 1950, p. 6). This notion highlighted the significance of inspiration and timing essential to responding to the uniqueness of the parties, the particular issues and the requirements of each mediation session. The concept of the freedom of artistry where 'timing is everything' was a shared one particularly among labour mediators in the USA but it was also a controversial one because it appeared to preclude any general formulation about the nature of mediation practice except as one of continual improvization on an ad hoc basis.

More recently the concept of the artistry of the mediator has taken on a different dimension of meaning, one that is considered to reflect the highest level of professional practice. Lang and Taylor (2000) postulate, for example, that artistry of this kind can be attained in two ways: first as a level of practice competence, resourcefulness and effectiveness resulting in the attainment of an elegant and effortless 'flow'; and second as the summation of mediator professional development, the culminating achievement through progressive stages from novice to apprentice, to practitioner and finally to artist. (Lang and Taylor, 2000, pp. 11, 14).

This later view of artistry, as the achievement of professional excellence, is both more complex and more specific than the earlier conception of artistry. It involves a new conceptual framework and a practical methodology which consist of the realization in practice, over time, of the integration of three essential elements that make up artistry – practice skills, theoretical knowledge and the ability to connect the two. It is not inspiration therefore that defines artistry of practice, according to this analysis, but rather a sound foundation of theory which establishes the basis for making choices about timing and the implementation of strategies and techniques (Lang and Taylor, 2000, p. 20).

KEY TEXTS

- Douglas, A. (1962) *Industrial Peacemaking* (New York: Columbia University Press)
- Lang, M.D. and Taylor, A. (2000) *The Making of the Mediator: Developing Artistry in Practice* (San Francisco: Jossey-Bass)
- Roberts, M. (2007) *Developing the Craft of Mediation: Reflections on Theory and Practice* (London: Jessica Kingsley Publishers)

attributes of the mediator

SEE ALSO **aptitude; artistry; craftsmanship; impartiality; the mediator; principles of mediation**

Traditionally, certain core attributes have been acknowledged to characterize the practice of the 'good' mediator. These are: substantive

knowledge of the subject matter in dispute; skills of analysis and problem-solving; an awareness of the moral dimension of the problem;
and wisdom and compassion in dealing with people (as exemplified
in the character of Mittler, the distinguished mediator in Goethe's
Elective Affinities, 1809).

The personal qualities of the mediator have received far greater
attention historically than the processual aspects of the mediator
role. Yet because these qualities are often elusive and idiosyncratic
and therefore less susceptible to analysis, early studies have been
anecdotal rather than scientific. Early approaches to understanding
the necessary qualities of the good mediator adopt the perspectives
of *the parties* to the dispute for cataloguing exemplary attributes (for
example, Landsberger, 1956; Douglas, 1962; Stulberg, 1981; Raiffa,
1982). A typical list of attributes (not always consistent) includes the
following (Raiffa, 1982):

- Originality of ideas;
- Sense of appropriate humour;
- Ability to act unobtrusively;
- The mediator as 'one of us';
- The mediator as respected authority (i.e. with personal prestige);
- Accumulated knowledge;
- Persistence;
- Physical endurance;
- The hide of a rhinoceros;
- The wisdom of Solomon;
- The patience of Job;
- Intelligence and the ability to understand quickly the
  complexities of a dispute;
- Control over feelings;
- The capacity to appreciate the dynamics of the environment.

What emerges from all these studies is a consensus that a combination of attributes – intellectual, moral and personal – goes towards
the making of the ideal mediator.

The views of mediators themselves expand understanding
further. For example, in a unique collaboration of mediators with
occupational psychologists, aimed at devising a selection procedure
for trainee family mediators, the *aptitude* of the mediator, rather

than any prior professional qualification, was recognized to be the primary attribute of effective mediation practice. The constituents (essential and desirable) of personal aptitude were identified in a specification of attributes. These intellectual, personal, interpersonal, ethical and motivational attributes informed a rigorous selection procedure made up of a range of exercises designed to elicit the strengths and weaknesses of each candidate (Blacklock and Roberts, 1995).

In a small study, mediators, irrespective of their professional background, field of mediation practice or gender, shared similar views about which personal qualities are essential for effective practice. These highlight intellectual capacity (analytic and creative) and the capacity to listen attentively (Roberts, 2007). Additional qualities identified include a genuine interest in, liking and concern for people (recognized to be hugely demanding in practice), personal warmth and approachability, toughness in the face of conflict, and self-knowledge of one's own failings.

These reflections also provide fresh practitioner insight into the nature and function of that highly prized attribute of the good mediator, patience, and the relationship of patience to the very purpose of mediation (Roberts, 2007). If the primary objectives of mediation is to enable *the parties themselves* to reach their own mutually agreed outcomes, a high degree of patience is recognized to be a concomitant requirement of the process. Patience is significant therefore both as an attribute of the mediator and as a function of the process. A renowned labour mediator expresses this vividly:

> The final demand is still for patience and endurance. Be patient, be patient and evermore be patient. Be not too patient! Never tire but watch for the gathering signs of fatigue in others. Then push over the pins that are already trembling. How? I cannot tell you. A sudden change in attitude, a deepening of the voice, a strident unexpected urgency … but no two cases are alike and even if they were, no two mediators would attack them on parallel lines.
> (A.S. Meyer as quoted in Douglas, 1962, p. 108)

It is contended that where empirical studies of mediation show favourable results, including high levels of party satisfaction, these occur regardless of the individual style or philosophical or professional orientation of the mediator, or whatever practice skills or models are adopted. It is asserted that it is the 'presence' of the mediator that has a major impact on the process, rather than what he or she does (Bowling and Hoffman, 2000). Preliminary findings in a recent study (confirming several prior studies) also suggest that mediator competence may be less a matter of mediator style and professional orientation and more a function of shared core characteristics, such as the mediator's energy, warmth, optimism, a non-judgmental stance, and a willingness to be flexible and adapt to the needs of the parties (Kressel *et al.*, 2012).

One of the most essential attributes of a mediator is the ability to maintain an intermediate position between the disputants, a position of 'non-partisanship', when the mediator either 'stands above contrasting interests and opinions and is actually not concerned with them, or if he is equally concerned with both … (Simmel, 1908b, p. 149). *Impartiality* constitutes not only a fundamental principle of mediation practice, a duty and a skill but also an essential attribute of the mediator.

KEY TEXTS
- Blacklock, R. and Roberts, M. (1994) 'Professional Standards in the Selection of Family Mediators', *Family Law*, 24: p. 206
- Bowling, D. and Hoffman, D. (2000) 'In Theory: Bringing Peace into the Room: The Personal Qualities of the Mediator and Their Impact on the Mediation', *Negotiation Journal* 5: pp. 5–27.
- Gale, J. *et al.* (2002) 'Considering Effective Divorce Mediation: Three Potential Factors', *Conflict Resolution Quarterly*, 19: pp. 389–420.
- Goethe von, J.W. (1809; trans., 1971) *Elective Affinities* (Harmonsworth: Penguin)
- Roberts, M. (2007) *Developing the Craft of Mediation: Reflections on Theory and Practice* (London: Jessica Kingsley Publishers)
- Simmel, G. (1908a) *Soziologie* translated in *The Sociology of Georg Simmel* (trans. K.H. Wolff (1955)) (New York: Free Press)

authority

SEE ALSO **decision-making; party control; power; principles of mediation**

The defining principle of *mediation* is respect for the authority of the parties to make their own decisions. This principle distinguishes mediation and is one of its primary benefits. It is integral to a range of *principles* and values which sustain and reinforce one another and which inform practice across fields of mediation practice. These principles are regarded as essential for safeguarding a safe and fair process and outcome and for protecting the parties.

They include the following:

- The principle of *voluntary participation* incorporates not only the right of the parties to make their own informed decision as to whether or not to participate in the process in the first place but also whether or not to continue with the process if they so choose.
- The demonstration of the fundamental ethic of *respect* for the autonomy of the parties and for their decision-making authority.
- The presumption of the competence of the parties to make their own decisions.
- The principle of *impartiality* and the demonstration of even-handedness.

Consideration of the issue of *party control* over decision-making cannot be separated from questions about the authority and power of the mediator who is only present at the invitation and with the consent of the parties. First, how can the authority of the mediator be exercised in ways that serve the essential objectives of the process, in particular the objective of party control? Second, when can the exercise of that authority exceed its limits and become an abuse of power with the exertion of unacceptable pressures on the parties who might then act (or fail to act) in ways they would not otherwise have done?

However unobtrusive the stance of the mediator and however non-coercive the process deployed, it must be recognized that subtle forms of power can be exerted by the mediator. This will reflect the style and model of practice adopted as well as the skill and integrity of the mediator. The difficult circumstances of dispute, the complex and unpredictable dynamics of the mediation process, and inherent tensions in the mediator role (the tension, for example, between the need to settle and the lack of power to do so) – all these impose therefore a heavy responsibility on mediators to bear constantly in mind and address in their practice the vital questions raised about their authority and power.

KEY TEXTS

- Fuller, L.L. (1971) 'Mediation – Its Forms and Functions', *Southern California Law Review*, 44: pp. 305–339
- Sennett, R. (2003) *Respect: The Formation of Character in an Age of Inequality* (London: Penguin/Allen Lane)
- Weber, Max (1917, 1978) *Economy and Society*, in G. Roth and C. Wittich (eds), E. Fischoff *et al.* (trans.) (New York: Bedminster Press)

b

bargaining

SEE ALSO decision-making; negotiation; the mediation process

There are two concepts that are fundamental to any understanding of *mediation* and the role of the *mediator*. First mediation serves a *negotiation* process, and second, the role of the mediator can be understood only within an understanding of that process

Gulliver (1979) has delineated the interlocking developmental and cyclical processes that together inform the negotiation process that the mediator orchestrates. The six overlapping developmental phases of the negotiation process identified by Gulliver include a late bargaining phase.

Bargaining refers to the series of offers and counter offers, demands and counter demands, the trading of concessions, the splitting of differences and the pooling of losses, a phase which, as Douglas's research shows, does not begin until the parties have reached agreement on the crucial negotiating issues (Douglas, 1962). This is when sometimes an outcome can be reached with unexpected suddenness – when 'agreement *per se* has become more important than the particular point of agreement' (Gulliver, 1979, p. 168).

In this context misunderstanding can arise where the two terms, 'negotiation' and 'bargaining', are used interchangeably. Bargaining and negotiation are not synonymous. Bargaining is associated with the cut and thrust of the marketplace. Negotiation, on the other hand, is much broader in scope, encompassing the processes of communication, exchanges of information and learning that can lead to improved understanding, the lessening of competition and hostility and therefore the willingness to make the necessary adjustments and modifications that can lead to agreement. The brief final bargaining phase occurs, therefore, once all the groundwork of communication has been accomplished.

The literature has long recognized the fact that all negotiations – private ordering, bilateral party negotiations, lawyer negotiations and mediation – do not take place in any vacuum. Mnookin and Kornhauser's famously coined phrase, 'bargaining in the shadow of the law', highlights the significance of those public norms, values and legal rulings that constitute the 'defining context' within which all negotiations occur (Mnooking and Kornhauser, 1979, p. 950; Hamnett, 1977, p. 5). Empirical research into the realities of bi-lateral lawyer negotiations in the Anglo Saxon world reveals, in fact, that lawyers' interests do not necessarily coincide with those of the parties and that many cases settle for reasons that have nothing to do with legal principles or moral standards.

KEY TEXTS

- Genn, H. (1987) *Hard Bargaining: Out of Court Settlement in Personal Injury Actions* (Oxford: Clarendon Press)
- Gulliver, P.H. (1979) *Disputes and Negotiations: A Cross-Cultural Perspective* (New York: Academic Press)
- Menkel-Meadow, C. (1993) 'Lawyer Negotiations: Theories and Realities – What We Learn from Mediation' in 'Special Issues – Dispute Resolution: Civil Justice and its Alternatives', *Modern Law Review,* 56 (3): pp. 361–379

bargaining power

SEE ALSO **domestic abuse; fairness; justice; party control; power**

It is well recognized that for *mediation* to be fair and effective there needs to be relative equality of bargaining power between the parties. However there is no precise definition of bargaining power nor is there any simple construction of the issue of power inequality. A consideration of what factors make up any assessment of bargaining power must include the following:

- Financial and material circumstances;
- Legal 'endowments' such as access to legal advice; legal rulings in relation to the subject matter in dispute, etc.;
- Emotional and social vulnerability;
- Readiness and ability to negotiate;
- De facto care and control of the children (in family disputes);
- Family history;

- Personal attributes;
- Gender and cultural differences etc.

Bargaining power involves therefore a complex interplay of forces, objective and subjective (for example, *perceptions* of vulnerability, whatever the objective circumstances, may be significant). It should not be assumed though that where one party has superior 'endowments' in mediation that power will necessarily be used or exploited. However, in order to be able to establish whether or not the differences of power between the parties are substantial, careful screening prior to mediation is essential for determining whether or not mediation is suitable (as in *family mediation*).

When there is a situation of manifest inequality, resorting to mediation could be not only inappropriate and unethical but also, in extreme situations, dangerous – for example, in cases where there has been abusive behaviour. The mediator has a fundamental ethical responsibility to end a mediation session where it appears that unfairness would result because of the exercise of duress over another or where cultural or other considerations deny a party the capacity to negotiate in their own right at all.

Disparity of bargaining power is not, of itself, a ground for the court to set aside a private agreement if there has been no unfair exploitation of superior bargaining strength and both parties have had the benefit of professional advice (*Edgar v. Edgar,* 1980).

No dispute resolution process, whether bi-lateral lawyer negotiations or adjudication, avoids the problem of power differentials. In fact new inequalities may be created – for example, unequal resources, disparities of professional competence of lawyers, or idiosyncratic court judgments.

KEY TEXTS

- Auerbach, J.S. (1983) *Justice without Law?* (New York: Oxford University Press)
- Gilligan, C. (1982) *In a Different Voice* (Cambridge, MA: Harvard University Press)
- Grillo. T. (1991) 'The Mediation Alternative: Process Dangers for Women', *Yale Law Journal,* 100 (6): pp. 1545–1640
- Mather, L., Maiman, R.J. and McEwen, C.A. (1995) 'The Passenger Decides on the Destination and I Decide on the Route: Are Divorce

Lawyers Expensive Cab Drivers?' *International Journal of Law and the Family,* 9: pp. 286–310

- Mnookin, R.H. (1984) 'Divorce Bargaining: The Limits on Private Ordering' in J. Eekelaar and S.N. Katz (eds), *The Resolution of Family Conflict: Comparative Legal Perspectives* (Toronto: Butterworths)

the Bromley Model of family mediation (includes the Coogler Model of Structured Mediation)

SEE ALSO the caucus; fairness; the mediation process; the mediator; models of mediation; party control; strategies

This is a *model* of mediation based on the *Coogler Model of Structured Mediation*, pioneered by O.J. Coogler, a North American lawyer and psychotherapist, and one of the founding fathers of family mediation in the USA. It was first introduced in the UK by Mr Fred Gibbons who established the SE London Family Mediation Bureau, which is situated in Bromley, hence the epithet, and constitutes the foundation of its practice approach to mediation.

The significance of the Coogler Model is two-fold:

- First, central issues of *party autonomy, mediator authority* and *power*, and the protection of a fair process, are explicitly addressed by means of structure. Coogler's emphasis is on the importance of a clear structure composed of the integration of three structural components – the Procedural, Value and Psychological Structures – designed to protect the parties procedurally (to secure an orderly process), ethically (to secure a fair process and ethical standards of exchange) and emotionally (to secure psychological and physical safety);
- Second, is the way in which these issues are addressed in practice, namely the focus on the 'modest' profile of the *mediator* as well as on the deployment of structure. The issues, whatever they are, are limited to those for which decisions are needed for settlement to be reached. The role of the mediator is to ensure that the parties are the decision-makers. There is advance agreement on the 'rules' of procedure and the guidelines to be followed.

There are a variety of structural arrangements that can frame the *mediation process* and no one model is best for all purposes. Examples include *co-mediation, shuttle mediation,* the anchor mediator, the use of *the caucus*, etc. Whatever model is adopted, the framework should serve two main purposes: first, to enable the parties to negotiate together in a way that would not have been possible on their own; and second, to secure fairness and equal participation of the parties in the negotiation process.

One of the distinctive features of the Coogler Model is that the framework builds in separate time with each party at an early stage in every session. This application of separate time is different from 'caucusing' which is almost always used in the mediation of international and labour relations disputes.

This feature is considered to be a vital structural safeguard for full and free expression and to avoid such dangers as *'negative positioning'* (see Cobb and Rifkin, 1990). Another feature is the encouragement towards direct communication/ *negotiation* between the parties themselves. Both these features may be contrasted with the model of another distinguished North American founding father of family mediation, Dr John Haynes, one whose central tenets of approach is, in contrast, that the mediator meets the parties jointly only never separately. Nor does Dr Haynes encourage direct communication between the parties, rather the mediator acts as the primary conduit of communication between them.

The Bromley Model exemplifies, therefore, an explicit, theoretically-based approach to achieving procedural *fairness* and meeting the needs of the parties, ethically and emotionally. It is an approach that is designed to make optimal uses of session time, in ensuring both purposive structuring and that the session length is sufficient for the negotiation process to be constructively realized (see Gulliver, 1979). The session is unlikely to end therefore at that stage in the process when conflict is at its most expressed.

KEY TEXTS
- Coogler, O.J. (1978) *Structured Mediation in Divorce* (Lexington, MA: Lexington Books/DC Heath)
- Haynes, J.M. (1993) *The Fundamentals of Family Mediation* (London: Old Bailey Press)
- Roberts, M. (2005) 'Hearing Both Sides: Structural Safeguards for Protecting Fairness in Family Mediation', *Mediation in Practice*, May, 23–32

c

the caucus (includes private meetings)

SEE ALSO the Bromley Model of family mediation; civil and commercial mediation; confidentiality; industrial relations mediation; models of mediation

The caucus, a term imported from North America but in the UK usually referred to as a 'private meeting', can be deployed as a powerful technique in mediation practice. This involves the mediator meeting individually with one side or a subset of a participant group (for example, lawyers only or clients only).

The primary purpose of the caucus is to enable the mediator to gain access to information and insights that cannot be obtained in the joint meeting. Other purposes include educating a party in their negotiating style, exploring possibilities of compromise, and addressing difficulties creating impasse in negotiations. Many commercial mediators regard confidential private meetings as essential for exploring the issues and the options for settlement. In *family mediation* the use of the caucus as the usual model of practice is rare. However the caucus can, on occasion, be deployed specifically to allow a party to reveal confidential information to the mediator that they do not wish to disclose to the other party, to explore personal feelings about the issues, or to raise matters too uncomfortable or risky for joint disclosure (Folberg and Milne, 1988). Resorting to the use of the caucus in family mediation does need to be distinguished from the application of separate time as a structural component of the joint session (for further detailed differentiation, see Roberts, 2005).

The *confidentiality* of exchanges, while one of the main advantages of the caucus, can create dilemmas for the mediator as it requires considerable skill to keep track of what is known, how that knowledge was obtained and from whom, and any constraints that attach to it. Disputants, for example, may have no means of knowing whether confidentiality has been breached if the topic crops up spontaneously.

Depending on the philosophy of the mediator, three dominant approaches to the caucus have been identified in practice: never caucus; the selective use of the caucus; and always/mostly use of the caucus such as in *civil and commercial, international* and *industrial relations* disputes (Menkel-Meadow *et al.*, 2005). This use of the caucus can lead to *'shuttle' mediation* where the mediator acts simply as a conduit between the parties (valuable in situations of extreme *conflict*) or, more actively, negotiating on behalf of the parties.

KEY TEXTS

- Folberg, J. and Milne, A. (eds) (1988) *Divorce Mediation: Theory and Practice* (New York: Guilford Press)
- Mackie, K. *et al.* (2002) *The ADR Practice Guide: Commercial Dispute Resolution* (London: Butterworths)
- Menkel-Meadow *et al.* (2005) *Dispute Resolution: Beyond the Adversarial Model* (New York: Aspen Publishers)
- Stulberg, J. (1987) *Taking Charge/Managing Conflict* (Lexington, MA: Lexington Books)

children and mediation

SEE ALSO **family mediation; international child abduction mediation; international family mediation; Specialist Child Care Mediation; third persons in mediation**

The focus on children in *family mediation* brings to the fore general themes that emerge in *mediation* in all fields of practice, for example:

- the role of *third persons* – those not involved directly in the negotiations but who are directly affected by the mediation process and its outcome;
- the ways in which mediation differs from other professional interventions and the importance of maintaining clarity of boundaries with those interventions – for example, the distinctive mediation-specific role of children in mediation needs to be differentiated from their involvement in such interventions as counselling, therapy, guidance, advice-giving and advocacy;

- the tension between the pursuit of individual rights and the ethics of collaboration and consensual forms of decision-making that distinguish mediation.

While there is general consensus that mediation, in promoting collaboration and communication between disputing parents, can enhance children's interests (in contrast to the competitive, oppositional stances of litigation and *adjudication*), much debate has been generated over the vexed question of the direct participation of children in the process. Associated with a fresh climate of thinking about the 'voice of the child' in decision-making generally (for example, the UN Convention on the Rights of the Child, 1989, the Children Act, 1989 and the Human Rights Act, 1998; see also research into how children are listened to in legal, administrative and mediatory processes), there is now a clear appreciation of the distinctive and precise role of children in mediation.

The policy question to be resolved was this: How can children's perspectives best inform a process in which the parents are the ultimate decision-makers? The answer lay in the concept of *consultation* which clarified both language (a variety of imprecise terms such as 'involving', 'working with', 'seeing', 'including' children had been in use) and resolved the substantive question – children can be *consulted* as part of their parent's decision-making within mediation and this could take place in two ways:

- indirect consultation by means of parents themselves bringing their children's views into the process – the preferred form of consultation because it encourages parents themselves to consider and give worth to their children's views, feelings and interests;
- direct consultation with children by the mediator within the process. Whether direct consultation is appropriate is a matter to be agreed jointly by the mediator, both parents with their child/ren's consent (for a full explanation of the policy and practice guidelines governing practice in the UK on the role of children and young persons in family mediation see UK College of Family Mediators, 2002, now the College of Mediators).[1]

'Child Inclusive Mediation' refers to a specific practice approach, piloted in Australia, that aims to embrace children's concerns and interests in all aspects of overall practice, whether counselling or mediation. It envisages supporting both the parenting role and the needs of the children throughout each process in a variety of ways, direct consultation of children being one critical option among others, including indirect approaches (such as group programmes, family therapy, etc). Concerns were raised that 'child inclusive mediation' might be understood to mean that *all* children would be seen in *all* cases, an assumption explicitly refuted by the consultants to the pilot (Commonwealth Department of Family and Community Services Report, 2002). Findings highlight the considerable resource, infrastructure, expertise and training implications of this model as well as its benefits for children.

The 'child inclusive mediation' approach (recommended as 'good practice' rather than 'best practice') is entirely consonant with that embodied in the policy and guidelines on children and young persons of the College of Mediators (formerly the UK College of Family Mediators) – in terms of objectives, definitions, terminology, principles and guidelines.

There are expanding applications of practice with respect to children and mediation including *international child abduction* and mediation; mediation in public law child protection cases (*Specialist Child Care Mediation (SCCM)*); adoption and mediation; and young people involved in mediation in the context of homelessness.

KEY TEXTS

- Fortin, J., Hunt, J. and Scanlan, L. (2013) 'Taking a Longer View of Contact: Perspectives of Young Adults Who Experienced Parental Separation'. Sussex Law School, University of Sussex, Brighton, UK. www.sussex.ac.uk/law/research/centreforresponsibilities/ takingalongerviewofcontact.
- King, M. and Trowell, J. (1992) *Children's Welfare and the Law: The Limits of Legal Intervention* (London: Sage Publications)
- McIntosh, J. (2000) 'Child Inclusive Mediation: Report on a qualitative research study', *Mediation Quarterly*, 18 (1): pp. 55–69
- Parkinson, L. (2011) *Family Mediation: Appropriate Dispute Resolution in a New Family Justice System* (Bristol: Jordans/Family Law)
- Roberts, M. (forthcoming 2014) *Mediation in Family Disputes: Principles of Practice*. 4th edn (Aldershot, Hants: Ashgate Publishing Ltd)

church mediation

SEE ALSO conflict; dispute resolution; disputes; grievance resolution; power

The current climate in the Church of England, the Methodist and the Roman Catholic Churches is one strongly supportive of the use of *mediation* to resolve *disputes* within the church. [The Quakers, it must be mentioned in this context, have had a long and distinguished record of involvement in the provision of secular mediation services, to individuals, to the community, in schools, and notably in their unobtrusive mediatory contribution in working for peace and conflict transformation in the international arena (see *International Mediation* entry)].

Those promoting fresh ways of thinking about the ways that *conflict* is addressed within the church cite the historic biblical and theological teachings that inform the scriptural foundations of informal dispute resolution and peace-building approaches, in both the Old Testament (for example, Genesis 13:8–9; Joab: Samuel 14:1–23; Moses: Exodus 2:14) and the New Testament, in particular, the teachings of Jesus (for example, Matthew 5 v. 9 – 'Blessed *are* the peacemakers; for they shall be called the children of God'; v. 23–48; Matthew 18 v. 15–35; see Behrens, 2003 for a full list of scriptural references). This Christian perspective sees the church as a family sustained by the values of open communication, *respect* and forgiveness with mediation (particularly in encouraging direct communication between those in dispute) perceived as a form of gospel activity, assisting the church in carrying out God's work of reconciliation and peace-making. Mediation has been used by Bishops and judges of the Church courts to reconcile disputing parties from the days of the early church (for example, in the Patristic period) to the present day (Behrens, 2003).

Mediation is expressly provided for as part of the dispute resolution processes of the Roman Catholic Church, the largest Christian denomination in the world. Although rarely used in practice, the recommendation of mediation, as an alternative dispute resolution approach for Bishops, has been embodied in the legal structure of the Roman Catholic Church since 1917.

When a person believes that he or she has been injured by a decree, it is greatly to be desired that contention between that

person and the author of the decree be avoided, and that care
be taken to reach an equitable solution by mutual consultation,
possibly using the assistance of serious-minded persons to mediate
and study the matter. In this way, the controversy may by some
suitable method be avoided and brought to an end. (See Behrens,
2003, quoting the Code of Canon Law, 1917, Canon, 1733, € 1)

The purpose of mediation, as endorsed in the context of church practice, includes an important educative as well as a dispute resolution
function. Mediation is intended therefore not only to be a practical
tool for handling church disputes more expeditiously (saving time
and money by avoiding expensive disciplinary proceedings and
tribunal hearings) but also, more ambitiously, to lead to 'a pathway
to the healing of the relationship involving apology, forgiveness and
reconciliation' (Patterson and McKay, 2012, 5.9, 10).

The kinds of cases that are considered to be particularly suitable
for church mediation (in all the Christian denominations) are those
where conflict has been caused by a breakdown in relationships
or communication. But most types of dispute are considered to be
potentially suitable for mediation and the earlier they are referred
the better, before the intractable entrenchment of positions has
occurred. The kinds of disputes most suitable for mediation include
therefore, personality conflicts, employment and work disputes;
pastoral decisions (deemed injurious or arbitrary, for example);
conflicts within parish communities; governance issues between
the church and diocesan authorities or the Bishop; financial (non-
criminal) and property disputes (including alterations to church
buildings); property ownership and commercial contract issues;
defamation; personal injury, etc (see also Roman Catholic Code
of Canon Law 1446 (Western Church) and Canon 1103 (Eastern
Church)). There is consensus too as to those cases that are considered to be less suitable for mediation – for example, gay and gender
issues and issues relating to doctrinal interpretation and forms of
worship – and cases that are unsuitable, such as those involving
alleged criminal activity (such as sexual abuse allegations, serious
sexual or ethical misconduct and other alleged criminal offences).

The Methodist Church has replaced its former formal adversarial
approach to dealing with disciplinary and complaint matters with
one that favours mediation and conciliation. These matters are not

generally mediated under the mediation schemes of the Church of England, which has specific disciplinary and complaints measures in place. However, a mediatory approach (in the form of conciliation) is used as a part of the Clergy Disciplinary Measure where the Bishop is of the view that a potential disciplinary matter referred to him could be dealt with more appropriately in this way.

Mediation is relatively new and untried method for solving church disputes in the British Isles compared to a greater experience of mediation in some countries in the wider Anglican Communion (for example, Australia, Canada, Hong Kong, New Zealand, South Africa and the USA). However, systematic efforts have been taken by the Church of England (strongly endorsed by its Conference of 2009) in developing structures for institutionalizing mediation as a routine part of church procedure for dealing with conflict and dispute. These include the development of guidelines of good practice designed to embody the principles of mediation (for example, voluntary participation, neutrality of forum, impartiality and confidentiality) and structured, customized models of practice appropriate to the circumstances of the case. These involve pre-mediation meetings with the parties, face-to-face dialogue wherever possible, and the option of adopting practice model adaptations whenever appropriate, such as shuttle mediation, multi-party mediation, group work, etc. (see for example, the Rochester Diocesan Mediation Guidelines, 2004). In addition, checks and balances have been introduced specifically to ensure that the deployment of mediation in any particular case has the support and authority of all constituencies within the church community, at senior level of leadership (Bishops and Archdeacons), at national and diocesan level, and at the local level of the parish (clergy and lay). Under the Rochester Scheme, for example, in order to ensure that the diocesan mediator does not act alone, referrals are channelled through the Archdeacon or Bishop with the Incumbent's agreement. While an Incumbent (vicar or rector) may self-refer directly to the diocesan mediator, the Archdeacon's consent is nonetheless necessary before the mediator is able to proceed with mediation (Rochester Diocesan Mediation Guidelines, 2004, p. 3).

While there is not yet in place any formal accreditation procedure for those practising as mediators in the church context in the UK, all mediators are required to have undergone mediation training (usually in community mediation) and are expected to have direct knowledge of church matters, as parishioner, as wife of a vicar, or as Incumbent from a different parish (in order to maintain impartiality).

In the Anglican Church abroad, surveys show that practice varies. Those acting as mediators come from the dioceses' own clergy, either from the diocesan list of mediators or using one of the diocesan clergy's personally recommended mediators. Only in New Zealand was the use of professional mediators a preferred choice (Behrens, 2003).

Alternative dispute resolution processes other than that of formal mediation may also be operating within the church and need to be distinguished from mediation. These can include one or more of the following kinds of intervention:

- Assisted informal discussion (also known as conciliation): this involves an untrained third person aiming to assist in a dispute by acknowledging different perspectives and trying to find a way forward.
- Judgement: a third person imposes an outcome on the disputing parties.
- Group reconciliation: this features a larger number of disputants (for example, a whole Parish Church Council); the deployment of a wide range of approaches; a staged approach to working with the problem; and in most cases, addressing the substance of the issue requires addressing underlying, often historic, causes of conflict.

In order to be able to apply the most appropriate intervention to the issue, a spectrum of interventions has been devised that seeks to answer the question: 'To what extent should either the process or the outcome be taken out of the hands of the disputants?' Where, for example, there is irreversible entrenched conflict and full control over both the process and the outcome by a third person becomes necessary, then judgement is likely to be the most appropriate intervention. Mediation is located in the middle of the spectrum as an intervention that requires the mediator to be in charge of the process but not of the outcome of mediation (Patterson and McKay, 2012).

An exhortation to embrace a fundamental change of approach in understanding both the nature of conflict and how best it can be addressed constitutes one of the primary challenges facing the Church of England (Patterson and McKay, 2012). Instead of conflict being perceived as negative and a source of tension, difference and damage, to be denied and avoided, as it has in the past, a fresh culture of thinking considers conflict to be a normal part of life as well as a creative challenge. If mediation is considered to be a valuable tool that can assist in a positive engagement with conflict in the church, it will require greater understanding at all church levels, and the commitment to promote and resource it. Mediation can then provide a unique opportunity for differences within the church to be effectively negotiated and resolved in the spirit of its own teachings.

KEY TEXTS

- Behrens, J. (2003) *Church Disputes Mediation* (Gracewing: London)
- Craig, Y. (1999) *Peacemaking for Churches* (SPCK, London)
- *Mediation in the Rochester Diocese* (Leaflet) mediation@rochester. anglican.org.
- Patterson, C. and McKay, A. (2012) *Making Mediation Work in the Church of England* (Bridge Builders Ministries: London)

civil and commercial mediation (includes cross-border mediation)

SEE ALSO applications of mediation; the caucus; dispute resolution; Harvard negotiation project; lawyers in mediation; models of mediation

The 1990s in the UK saw a radical shift from unduly adversarial approaches to civil and commercial *disputes* towards a more co-operative approach and the explicit recognition that the sponsorship of settlement was now the primary objective of civil justice. A turning point was the issue of a Commercial Court Practice Statement (10 December 1993) followed by a general Practice Direction (24 January 1995) culminating in the Woolf Report *Access to Justice* (1995) and in the introduction of new Civil Procedure Rules. These embody two requirements:

- a primary requirement on the parties to try to negotiate at the pre-litigation stage of proceedings laid down in Pre-Action

Protocols and re-enforced through an evolving case law on cost sanctions – as evidenced in the decisions of the Court of Appeal in *Dunnnett v Railtrack* [2002] EWCA Civ 302; *Virani v Manuel Revert* [2003] EWCA Civ 1651; *Halsey v Milton Keynes NHS Trust* [2004] EWCA Civ 576; and *Reed Executive v Reed Business Information* [2004] EWCA Civ 887;

• the introduction of a strict regime of case management once litigation has begun.

This new regime of civil procedure therefore officially endorsed the courts' sponsorship of *ADR* for reaching settlement (Roberts and Palmer, 2005). Dyson, LJ's judgement in the Halsey case contained this unequivocal instruction:

All members of the legal profession who conduct litigation should now routinely consider with their clients whether their disputes are suitable for ADR.

These developments have resulted in the emergence of many mediation training bodies and an ever-growing number of trained mediators, mostly lawyers, but also accountants and other business professionals, offering third-party intervention in a range of civil and commercial disputes (in areas such as personal injury, insurance, construction, and contract). A body of trained '*mediation advocates*' has also emerged to provide lawyer representation of the parties in mediation.

The civil–commercial model of mediation frequently deploys the use of *caucus* and a 'fixed-time' (for example, one day) approach, appropriate for most (though not all) commercial disputes. Styles of practice vary along a spectrum of intervention – from the less obtrusive facilitative style to the more evaluative approach where the mediator may give a recommendation about the merits of the case or the issues in dispute. It is interesting to note that major differences in practice models of mediation are more likely to be found *within* the same context of practice rather than between different mediation fields (Roberts, 2007). In the case of commercial mediation, this could be because its subject matter, 'money-driven' in many cases, dictates a pragmatic approach to its practice model to a greater extent than in other mediation fields.

While the primary purpose of civil and commercial mediation has been directed towards dispute resolution, innovative developments in this field are focussing on extending this objective to that of complex *transaction construction and management* and the prevention of dispute. Here the mediator's role involves participating both in the original decision-making relating to commercial transactions and in their continuous monitoring. This *application of mediation* is designed to avoid disputes arising in the first place, thus pre-empting cost, delay and associated conflict (see for example, the Neutral Risk Monitoring project and Capital Projects Risk Mitigation of ResoLex, 2011).

KEY TEXTS

- Brown, H. and Marriott, A. (2011) *ADR Principles and Practice.* 3rd edn (London: Sweet and Maxwell)
- Genn, H. (1999) *Mediation in Action: Resolving Civil Disputes Without Trial* (London: Calouste Gulbenkian Foundation)
- Mackie, K. *et al.* (2007) *The ADR Practice Guide: Commercial Dispute Resolution.* 3rd edn (London: Bloomsbury Professional)
- 3rd Mediation Symposium (2010) *Creating Confidence in Mediators* (London: Chartered Institute of Arbitrators)
- Richbell, D. (2008) *The Mediation of Construction Disputes* (Oxford: Blackwell Publishing)
- Singer, J. (2004) *The EU Mediation Atlas: Practice and Regulation* (London: LexisNexis)

collaborative law

SEE ALSO **law; lawyers in mediation; negotiation; representative negotiations**

Radical changes in dispute resolution approaches have challenged lawyers to adapt new ways in order to keep pace with the official legal bias away from litigation and adjudication towards more settlement-seeking and alternative dispute-resolution approaches (see, for example, the Pre-Action Protocol, Civil Procedure Rules 1998, Pre-Application Protocol, Mediation Information and Assessment Meetings (MIAMs) and the Family Procedure Rules, 2010). One recent new approach to lawyers negotiating disputes has its origin in the initiative of a North American family lawyer, Stuart Webb, who was dissatisfied with the adverse effects in family law cases of traditional litigation approaches to family disputes. In 2004 he devised a problem-solving negotiation approach called 'collaborative law' as an option for those clients wanting more specialized, customized solutions than those available in court and obtained by means of a collaborative rather than a costly and competitive process.

Collaborative law, created primarily for use in family disputes, involves lawyers, their clients (couples in the main) and other professionals (such as divorce counsellors and consultants) working together in four-way, round-table meetings to seek to negotiate financial and other agreements outside the litigation and the court process. A unique feature of this approach is that the 'collaborative' lawyers agree not to be involved in any subsequent litigation that might ensue in the same case should their 'collaborative lawyering' fail to resolve the issues. Collaborative law is characterized by the following features:

- A Participation Agreement establishes the principles of participation in the collaborative process and the objectives, expectations and values of each party.
- All the participants (the parties and their lawyers) commit themselves to making every effort to achieve a settlement.
- The object is to achieve a settlement more suitable and amicable than it is possible to achieve in the traditional litigation process.
- The Participation Agreement includes a commitment not to go to court, nor threaten to do so while participating in the process.
- Full, open disclosure and confidentiality are expressly agreed.
- The lawyers advise and represent their clients throughout the whole process negotiating within an interest-based rather than a positional bargaining framework.
- Face-to-face meetings enable the parties to contribute to the negotiations in a 'controlled, safe and respectful setting' (London Collaborative Lawyers).
- A multidisciplinary team of professionals can be involved with the parties' lawyers operating as additional 'neutral experts'. For example, a divorce counsellor, or a child or financial consultant can be brought into the process for the benefit of both parties. This is one way that the voice of the child can be brought into the discussion, concerns relating to the child addressed, and

specialist tax or financial input provided.
- The focus is on the future and the long-term resolution of the parties' issues according to their own wishes and objectives
- The Disqualification Agreement (DA) is a fundamental feature of the collaborative law approach. It provides that the parties' 'collaborative' lawyers may not represent them in any future litigation or in court proceedings in the same case if the collaborative process breaks down or is terminated. Nor may the lawyers act as witnesses in court proceedings.

The purpose of the Disqualification Agreement is to focus on the goals of problem solving and settlement-seeking. It is also intended to motivate the parties to avoid impasse, fully aware of the heavy price of failure to reach a settlement (in terms of additional costs, delay and uncertainty) and of having to resort afresh to litigation with new lawyers. The Disqualification Agreement also motivates the collaborative lawyers themselves to strive to succeed in their negotiations. A controversial aspect of the Disqualification Agreement is that the parties' fear of terminating the process can result in their feeling trapped within it, having already expended much time, effort, emotional energy and money. This puts heavy pressure on the parties to stay within the collaborative process even when it is faltering or failing.

The first British collaborative family law group trained in this approach was established in 2004. Many family lawyers, solicitors in particular, have since trained to become 'collaborative' lawyers. At present developments of collaborative law are confined to the family law field (for example, the collaborative law model provides an efficient, quick and sensitive forum for the making of nuptial agreements). It is not clear to what extent it has been deployed to resolve civil disputes. As yet there is no empirical research that establishes whether or not collaborative law offers benefits or is cheaper than either mediation (with or without lawyer representatives present) or conciliatory bilateral lawyer negotiations. However, even where there are multiple meetings and additional preparatory sessions where the lawyers meet to plan and strategize, collaborative law will be less costly than a full blown court case with counsel on both sides. Notwithstanding the large numbers of collaboratively trained lawyers in England, at present the practice appears to be more promoted than practised.

While collaborative law has been described as a 'close cousin' of mediation, there are significant differences between the two interventions (Tesler, 2008). There is a minimum of two professional interveners in the collaborative process, the two collaborative lawyers, whose roles are predominantly representative and advisory. There is a view that collaborative law is merely a disguise for 'a new tactic to lure the public away from mediation and back into 'the lawyer's den, only this time a den with chairs for mental health professionals' (Zaidel, 2008).

KEY TEXTS

- Ellis, J. (2012) 'Collaborative Law, a Waste of Time Or the Way Forward? A Critical Appraisal of the Use of Collaborative Lawyering in Family Law Disputes and Beyond', *Mediation in Ireland* CPD Seminars, 11th February 2012.
- McFarlane, J. (2005) 'The Emerging Phenomenon of Collaborative Family Law (CFL): A Qualitative Study of CFL Cases', Departments of Justice, Canada
- Tesler, P. (2003) 'Collaborative Family Law', 4 *Pepperdine Dispute Resolution Law Journal*, 4 (3): p. 317
- Tesler, P. (2008) 'Collaborative Family Law, the New Lawyer and Deep Resolution of Divorce-Related Conflict', *Journal of Dispute Resolution*, 1: p. 83.
- Zaidel, S. (2008) 'How Collaborative Is Collaborative Divorce?', *Family Mediation News*, 4

community mediation (includes neighbourhood mediation)

SEE ALSO **elder mediation; models of mediation; party control; principles of mediation; workplace mediation; youth mediation**

The growth in community mediation in the voluntary sector in the UK over the past two decades replicates its flourishing in the USA in the 1970s and 1980s where it was pioneered as an expression of popular justice with origins in community organizing and the legal reform movement of that period. Its early famous exponent, Albie Davis, saw community mediation as the 'soul' of the ADR movement, exemplifying the value, above all, of *respect* – for the parties' dignity and perspectives, whatever their background, race, class or gender and for their competence and creativity to design solutions to their own problems (Davis, A. in Kolb *et al.*1994).

At the heart of the movement lay the hope that in handling its own local problems through community-run schemes, the local community would be strengthened and enriched in its own governance and self-reliance, and local people empowered by retaining control over their own conflicts. However community mediation does not escape the critique of *informal justice* that challenges these ideals, questioning as mythic a 'construction of harmonious society in which local groups settled their problems without the intrusion of state law' (Merry and Milner, 1993, pp.10–15).

Community mediation covers many different kinds of disputes, some of which have become specialist mediation practice areas – *neighbourhood* disputes; homelessness; problems of *gangs*; *school conflicts*; youth misconduct; *elder mediation*; *special educational needs*; and some family quarrels.

KEY TEXTS

- De Sousa Santos, B. (1982) 'Law and Community: The Changing Nature of State Power in Late Capitalism' in Abel, R. (ed), *The Politics of Informal Justice* (New York: Academic Press)
- Ellickson, R.C. (1994) *Order without Law: How Neighbours Settle Disputes* (London: Harvard University Press)
- Liebmann, M. (2000) *Mediation in Context* (London: Jessica Kingsley Publishers)
- Mediation UK (1995) *Training Manual in Community Mediation* (Bristol: Mediation UK)
- Merry, S.E. and Milner, N. (eds) (1993) *The Possibility of Popular Justice: A Case Study of Community Mediation in the United States* (Ann Arbor: University of Michigan Press)

conciliation

SEE ALSO **Advisory, Conciliation and Arbitration Service (ACAS); alternative dispute resolution (ADR); decision-making; dispute resolution; mediation; privilege**

The term 'conciliation' has been loosely used historically to cover a general array of different conflict intervention approaches and styles in the UK and in North America at a time of renewed interest in alternatives to the formal processes of litigation and adjudication. Its rhetoric emphasized the values of harmony and honourable compromise as alternatives to those of *conflict* and competition encouraged by litigation (Auerbach, 1983)

The modern conciliation movement began in the UK with The Conciliation Act 1896 which provided the recognizably modern statutory framework for state-sponsored conciliation and *arbitration* of collective labour disputes, although such forms of intervention existed for several decades prior to the Act 1896. *Industrial relations* has therefore the longest practice history of an official conciliatory process in Britain. In the US the modern conciliation movement began in 1913 in Cleveland where a conciliation branch of the municipal court was authorized to assist litigants unable to obtain lawyers to settle their small claims (Auerbach, 1983).

In the context of the early development of alternative approaches to settling *family* disputes, the term 'conciliation' was first used to embrace a general approach to mitigating the harmful effects of family conflict (Finer, 1974). Usage grew to cover practices that were part of court procedure as well as voluntary and statutory services operating independently of the court. These included conciliatory methods adopted by court personnel in the course of their preparation of welfare reports; constructive bilateral approaches by some lawyers negotiating on behalf of their clients; as well as a document-based scheme of arbitration called a Conciliation Board, set up by the Family Law Bar Association to settle disputes over property and finance. The terms 'conciliation' and '*mediation*' were often used interchangeably too, by the early family mediators, a conflation which compounded misunderstanding for the public because of the frequent confusion of conciliation with reconciliation, the reuniting of estranged couples. In the late 1980s, for purposes of clarity and accuracy, the term 'mediation' was adopted because of its precise reference to the specific form of third-party intervention now being practised in the settling of disputes in the family arena. Today these terms do still have different definitions in a *labour-relations* context where mediation is associated with the making of formal recommendations (*ACAS* publication, para 29). In certain parts of Europe and Asia, judges themselves – called 'judge conciliators' – have the duty to try to settle cases where possible as part of standard litigation procedure (Mackie *et al.*, 2000).

KEY TEXTS

- ACAS (Advisory, Conciliation and Arbitration Service)(nd) The ACAS Role in Conciliation, Arbitration and Mediation (ACAS Reports and Publications)
- Auerbach, J.S. (1983) *Justice without Law?* (New York: Oxford University Press)
- European Directive on Civil and Commercial Mediation 2008
- Finer Report (1974) *Report of the Committee on One Parent Families*. Cm. 5629 (London: HMSO)
- Mackie, K. *et al.* (2000) *The ADR Practice Guide: Commercial Dispute Resolution* (London: Butterworths)

confidentiality

SEE ALSO **ethics of mediation; fairness; the mediator; principles of mediation; privilege; values**

Confidentiality is recognized to be one of the fundamental four characteristics which, with the *voluntary participation* of the parties, the *impartiality* of the mediator and the procedural flexibility of the process, underpin mediation (McCrory, 1981). It is these characteristics that make mediation, as a method of dispute resolution, of value to the disputants. Confidentiality is the cornerstone of the relationship of trust that must exist between the mediator and the parties and of the free and frank disclosure that is necessary if obstacles to settlement are to be overcome. The parties must not fear that they may be disadvantaged by any disclosure that may be used in subsequent legal proceedings or in any other way. So without the promise of confidentiality, the substance of discussions in mediation cannot be protected against the risk of subsequent revelation nor can the independence of the mediation process be secured.

Mediation codes of practice across fields of practice and European legal instruments on mediation are all rigorous in their embodiment of the principle of confidentiality and of its relationship, as legal *privilege*, to legal proceedings (see for example, European Directive on Civil and Commercial Mediation

2008, article 7; European Code of Practice for Mediators 2004, 4; Council of Europe Recommendation No R (98) 1 on Family Mediation 1998, III vi).

Confidentiality cannot be absolute as it is always subject to the requirement that the law of the land shall be complied with (*Parry-Jones v. Law Society*, 1968). The limits are those pertaining to all confidential or professional communications. Therefore the promise of confidentiality does not prevent the mediator from disclosing information in the exceptional circumstances where there is risk to life, health or safety of the parties or any other third person. The second exception to the promise of confidentiality relates to the disclosure to appropriate government authorities in respect of transactions involving criminal property, for example, money laundering (Proceeds of Crime Act, 2002). In addition to the exceptions already mentioned, a different order exception relates to legally aided mediation where there is an audit of files by the Legal Services Commission. The exception to the promise of confidentiality applies too to factual disclosures on financial or property matters made in mediation. Such factual data may be disclosed in any subsequent legal proceedings (see for example, CEDR Code of Conduct for Mediators, sections 6–8, in respect of commercial mediation; Code of Practice of the UK College of Family Mediators (now the College of Mediators), section 4.6.2).

While confidentiality can be promised by the mediator, confidentiality belongs to the parties. What information they may choose to pass on to their legal advisors or other third persons is a matter of their discretion. However a court will be reluctant to allow confidential exchanges between the parties to be used as evidence in any subsequent proceedings as public policy has always favoured the settlement of disputes and the policy of the law has also been in favour of enlarging the cloak under which negotiations many be conducted without prejudice (Cross and Tapper, 2007).

KEY TEXTS
- Allen, H. (2013) 'Confidentiality – a guide for mediators: How significant is mediation confidentiality in practice?' *ADR Times/* published by CEDR 31st January 2013

- Brown, H. and Marriott, A. (2011) *ADR Principles and Practice.* 3rd edn (London: Sweet & Maxwell)
- Mackie, K. *et al.* (2000) *The ADR Practice Guide: Commercial Dispute Resolution* (London: Butterworths)
- Roberts, M. (forthcoming, 2014) *Mediation in Family Disputes: Principles of Practice.* 4th edn (Aldershot, Hants: Ashgate), Chapter 9
- Walsh, E. (2006) *Working in the Family Justice System: The Official Handbook of the Family Justice Council.* 2nd edn (Bristol: Family Law)

conflict

SEE ALSO **alternative dispute resolution (ADR); dispute resolution; disputes; the mediation process; the mediator; stress**

Conflict – clashes arising from opposition – can be of many kinds, dimensions and levels; it can take many forms and can derive from a number of sources. These include intrapersonal, interpersonal, intragroup, intergroup, local and national clashes. Scholars across fields have developed a range of taxonomies for defining conflict (constructive and destructive) in its multiple manifestations in order to better understand and address it. (See for example, Moore, 1996 for his characterization of spheres of conflict, causes and interventions in the context of mediation; Menkel-Meadow *et al.* (2005) summarize some of the theoretical underpinnings of conflict and dispute resolution).

A Marxist view highlights structural inequalities as the fundamental origin of conflict, for example, in the clash of groups over scarce resources in a stratified society. This corresponds broadly with the pathological view of conflict underpinning Durkheim's social theory (Durkheim, 1893). In contrast, the German sociologist, Georg Simmel, portrays a non-pathological view of conflict in his famous essay on the subject:

> Just so, there probably exists no social unit in which convergent and divergent currents amongst its members are not inseparably interwoven. An absolutely centripetal and harmonious group, a pure 'unification' ('vereinigung') not only is empirically unreal, it could show no real life process. ... [conflict] is 'after all one of the most vivid interactions which furthermore, cannot possibly be carried on by one individual alone ... conflict is thus designed

to resolve divergent dualisms; it is a way of achieving some kind
of unity, even if it be through the annihilation of one of the
conflicting parties. (1908a, trans., 1971, chapter 4, pp. 72; 70)

In the context of *mediation*, it can be helpful to distinguish the concept
of conflict from that of *dispute* – the specific, identifiable issue that
divides the parties and the resolution or settlement of which is the
purpose of mediation. The settlement of a *dispute* is achieved when the
parties reach a mutually acceptable basis for disposing of the issue(s)
over which they disagree. This can occur even against the background
of continuing conflict (Cormick, 1982). This may be compared with
the resolution of *conflict* which is achieved when the basic differences
of value or fact or inequalities of power that divide the parties are
removed. The dispute that is brought to mediation may be the tip of
the iceberg so far as conflict between the parties is concerned.

In the international context, usage of the terms 'conflict resolution' and 'conflict prevention' meet with criticism because of their
implied emphasis on avoiding or ending conflict. The term 'conflict
transformation' is preferred because it reflects the importance of
the need to address underlying structural and cultural violence and
to recognize the inevitability of conflict in the process of change
(Francis, 2002). 'Conflict transformation', it is argued, denotes,
more accurately, a whole collection of processes at work and their
results – processes aimed at making relationships more just,
equal and respectful and including processes for developing a new
'constructive conflict culture' in the interests of contributing to the
well-being of society (Francis, 2002, p. 7).

KEY TEXTS

- Cormick, G.W. (1982) 'Intervention and Self-Determination in Environmental
  Disputes: A Mediators' Perspective', *Resolve*, Winter: pp. 260–265
- Durkheim, E. (1893, published in English 1947) *The Division of Labour
  in Society* (New York)
- Francis, D. (2002) *People, Peace and Power: Conflict Transformation in
  Action* (London: Pluto Press)
- Francis, D. (2010) *From Pacification to Peacebuilding: A Call to
  GlobalTransformation* London: Pluto Press.
- Lederach, J.P. (2003) *The Little Book of Conflict Transformation*
  (Intercourse, PA: Good Books)

- Moore, C. (1996) *The Mediation Process: Practical Strategies for Resolving Conflict*. 2nd edn (San Francisco: Jossey-Bass)
- Menkel-Meadow, C.J. *et al.* (2005) *Dispute Resolution: Beyond the Adversarial Model* (New York: Aspen Publishers)
- Simmel, G. (1908b) *On Individuality and Social Forms*, in D.N. Levine (ed) (Chicago: University of Chicago Press. 1971)

Confucianism and mediation

SEE ALSO **authority; craftsmanship; ethics of mediation; knowledge; mediation**

Mediation was the primary mode of dispute resolution for thousands of years in a traditional China, ruled by successive imperial dynasties until 1911. Confucianism, informed by the teachings of Confucius (551–478 BC), was the dominant humanist and political philosophy which, in the context of *dispute*, emphasized the virtues of non-litigiousness, of moral leadership and of harmony. This approach co-existed for centuries in China with the equally dominant ideology of legal formalism which advocated, in contrast, a strong centralized state, comprehensive law codes and a hierarchical court system. This dichotomy, embodied in the 'Legalist' and the 'Confucian' schools, has persisted in various forms through to the present day.

The Confucian approach has been to maintain that a formal 'law-based' approach encourages parties to be adversarial and to pursue their rights at the expense of substantive justice. It is far better for the social polity that a disputant 'yields' rather than stands on his/her rights and so avoids state administered lawsuits.

Chinese communism has also extolled the virtues of mediation over *adjudication* and its coercive context. However, while there are resonances between Confucian and communist approaches to dispute resolution, the values of Confucian mediation, as well as the identity and role of *the mediator*, have been redefined and politicized under communist influence. The political function of mediation has overshadowed its traditional settlement function with a more absolute approach to right and wrong (embodying communist ideology in the mediator) replacing the traditional search for compromise within a local network – family, clan, village, and guild – of personal and social relationships.

44

KEY TEXTS

- Lubman, S. (1967) 'Mao and Mediation: Policy and Dispute Resolution in Communist China', *California Law Review,* 55
- Palmer, M. and Roberts, S. (forthcoming 2014) *Dispute Processes: ADR and the Primary Forms of Decision-Making.* 3rd edn (Cambridge: Cambridge University Press)

court linked mediation (includes in-court mediation)

SEE ALSO **confidentiality; dispute resolution; judicial mediation; justice; principles of mediation**

Many different organizational arrangements characterize the practice of *mediation.* Broadly speaking a distinction can be drawn between services directly linked to the court and those that are independent of the court, based in the community. In fact, the picture is more complex and the influence of the court more pervasive – for example, court referrals to out-of-court *family mediation* and *civil mediation* services are common and court procedures, such as the Pre-action and Pre-Application Protocols (in civil and family proceedings respectively) which have a direct impact on out-of-court settlement processes including mediation. The Civil Procedure Rules (1999), which state (Rule 1) that the *primary* responsibility of the court is not to deliver judgment but to sponsor settlement, exemplify the courts' transformed role in dispute resolution. The degree of involvement in the judicial process is therefore a useful index for determining fundamental differences in mediation provision.

A variety of court-based settlement practices, variously termed for example, 'in-court conciliation', 'dispute resolution', 'settlement-seeking' and 'mediation', have characterized the Family Justice System in Britain. These practices, conducted either at the direction of the court, on court premises, or in the course of the preparation of a welfare report by officers of the court, have been part of early stage contested private law proceedings. Their purpose has been to assist the parties to reach a settlement without further legal intervention.

In a number of other jurisdictions, the American common law world in particular, mediation has been incorporated into the judicial process, either directly or indirectly. The range of practices extend from judges themselves acting as mediators in judicial settlement conferences, to court-appointed mediators presiding over compulsory mediation prior to any trial taking place as in court-annexed mediation in matrimonial cases (such as in California).

Research over decades shows that mediation is most effective when it is located well away from the coercive and pressurized context of the court – in fact, the lower the degree of judicial control, the better the outcome (Davis and Bader, 1985; Home Office, 1994; Trinder *et al.*, 2006). Genn *et al.* (2007), evaluating two civil mediation programmes, both court linked but one compulsory and the other voluntary, found that in respect of both schemes, what was critical to the success of mediation was the motivation and willingness of the parties to negotiate and to compromise. This finding sits uncomfortably with those promoting compulsory mediation (Genn *et al.*, 2007).

If the boundaries between different forms of interventions are to be understood and respected, attempts at promoting settlement as part of court proceedings need to be distinguished from the offer of mediation (Kirby, 2006). Mediation is a *voluntary, confidential* and *privileged* process of dispute resolution. The dangers of court-linked mediation, where these processes are combined, are two-fold: coercion in the mediation process *and* impairment of judicial authority.

KEY TEXTS

- Davis, G. and Bader, K. (1985) 'In-Court Mediation: The Consumer View', Parts I and II *Family Law*, March and April 15 (3): pp. 42–49, 82–86
- Genn, H. *et al.* (2007) 'Twisting Arms: Court Referred and Curt Linked Mediation Under Judicial Pressure', *Ministry of Justice Research Series* 1/07 May.
- Ingleby, R. (1993) 'Court Sponsored Mediation: The Case against Mandatory Participation', *Modern Law Review*, 56: pp. 441–451
- Kirby, B. (2006) 'CAFCASS: Productive Conflict Management Research and the Impetus for Change', *Family Law*, November, 36: pp. 970–974
- Trinder, L. *et al.* (2006) *Making Contact Happen or Making Contact Work? The Process and Outcomes of In-Court Conciliation*, DCA Research Series 3/06 (March. London: DCA)

craftmanship

SEE ALSO artistry; attributes of the mediator; knowledge; the mediator; quality assurance; styles of mediation;

Defining the nature of their task has long preoccupied *mediators* who, seeking to understand what constitutes effective practice in *mediation*, have queried whether this is *artistry*, a science, a craft, the skilled exercise of a technique, or a combination of all these. There is consensus that effective practice reflects the skilled integration of a range of components – theoretical knowledge, attention to process, skills and practice experience, commitment and the realization in action of certain essential if elusive personal attributes. These attributes include extraordinary patience; word sensitivity and power; attentive listening capacity; curiosity; imaginative thinking; and the ability to respond tactfully and readily with people who are engaged in the hard pursuit of co-operation in difficult circumstances (Sennett, 2012).

Mediation practice, in its essential common elements and in its rich diversity, has long been conceived as a form of craftsmanship (Davis, in Kolb, 1994). Craftsmanship requires the investment of self, of time, of care, of accumulated experience over time, and of quality in the task. Practitioners consider mediation to be a craft because of its distinguishing features, briefly summarized below (see Roberts, 2007 for a fuller discussion):

- Thinking like a craftsman represents the way in which the task of the mediator is perceived by mediators themselves – as persons curious, dedicated and fascinated, even obsessed about their work; and as practitioners committed, self-disciplined and self-critical in the pursuit of quality;
- A focus on getting something right for its own sake and an intolerance of incompetence;
- An apprenticeship model for acquiring skills and experience and continuing professional development in the guildhall mode (engaging with peers for consultancy and learning, for example);

* In using this term there is no intention to privilege either gender: the alternatives, craftswoman or craftsperson, would seem contrived.

- Learning how to get things right through trial and error;
- A value base in placing the parties first and respecting their decision-making authority;
- The role of the self as the main tool of the mediator's practice whether through individual charisma or quiet unobtrusiveness;
- An experiential knowledge base that requires extensive practice skill refined over time;
- Unique responses in every situation of practice;
- Autonomy of practice, notwithstanding institutional and funding constraints;
- Understanding the consequences of 'doing something well for its own sake' (Sennett, 2006, p. 104).

These characteristics cohere in what Sennett (2006, p. 104) describes as 'an embracing definition of craftsmanship' – doing something useful well and contributing something that matters to other people.

KEY TEXTS

- Bowling, D. and Hoffman, D. (2000) 'In Theory: Bringing Peace into the Room: The Personal Qualities of the Mediator and Their Impact on the Mediation', *Negotiation Journal*, 16: pp. 5, 5–27
- Coletta, C. and DiDomenico, A. (2000) 'Thoughts on Mediators as Craftspeople', *Alternative Dispute Resolution Reporter* 4: pp. 17
- Davis, A. in Kolb, D.M. *et al.* (1994) *When Talk Works: Profiles of Mediators* (San Francisco: Jossey-Bass)
- Roberts, M. (2007) *Developing the Craft of Mediation: Reflections on Theory and Practice* (London: Jessica Kingsley Publishers)
- Sennett, R. (2008) *The Craftsman* (London: Allen Lane)

critiques of ADR and mediation

SEE ALSO **alternative dispute resolution (ADR); ethics of mediation; fairness; informal justice; knowledge; power**

Enthusiasm for *ADR* has not been diminished by criticisms of the movement, also first expressed in the 1980s (for example, Abel, 1982; Auerbach, 1983; Fiss, 1984; Freeman, 1984; Matthews, 1988). These critiques, examining the political implications of *'informal justice'* identified a range of serious concerns – about *power, neutrality* and coercion – associated with the growth of private ordering. Fiss (1984, p. 2), for example, worried about the impact of power disparities on settlement processes, asserted the social value of the courts as public institutions devoted primarily, not to resolving *disputes*, but to giving meaning and 'operational content' to the values of society (such as liberty, equality, due process and freedom of speech): '*Adjudication* is the process by which judges give meaning to our public values'.

Alternative dispute resolution could be seen as an attempt to privatise the courts, trivializing their role and avoiding public accountability. Abel's findings, focusing on public mediation programmes in the USA, suggested that in some cases, alternative dispute agencies such as Small Claims Courts and Landlord and Tenants Courts, served to divert the legitimate claims of the more vulnerable groups in society (the poor, black people and women) away from legal channels into forms of second class justice that lacked the safeguards of due process and increased the risk of covert state regulation. While 'informal justice', it was claimed, processed the small claims and minor disputes of the poor, *justice* according to the law was reserved for the rich (Abel, 1982). Ironically concerns were also directed at private fee-for-service family mediation in the USA, only available to the rich.

In the early 21st century, the widespread proliferation throughout the world (for example, in Europe, South America, Eastern Europe, the Middle East and India) of procedures, directives and legislation relating to ADR, has re-ignited the 1980s debates and critiques of informal justice. (for example, Nader, 2002)

KEY TEXTS
- Abel, R.L. (1982) 'The Contradictions of Informal Justice' in R.L. Abel (ed), *The Politics of Informal Justice*. Vol. 1 (New York: Academic Press)
- Auerbach, J.S. (1983) *Justice without Law?* (New York: Oxford University Press)
- Bottomley, A. (1984) 'Resolving Family Disputes: a Critical View', in M.D.A. Freeman (ed), *State, Law and the Family* (London: Tavistock)
- Fiss, O.M (1984) 'Against Settlement', *Yale Law Journal*, 93: pp. 1073–1090
- Freeman, M.D.A. (1984) 'Questioning the Delegalisation Movement in Family Law: Do We Really Want a Family Court?' in J.M. Eekelaar and S.N. Katz (eds), *The Resolution of Family Conflict: Comparative Legal Perspectives*. (Toronto: Butterworths)
- Matthews, R. (ed) (1988) *Informal Justice?* (London: Sage)

cross cultural aspects of mediation

SEE ALSO international child abduction mediation; international family mediation; international mediation; the mediation process; United Nations mediation

Cross-cultural studies of *mediation* show that mediation, as a tried and tested mode of *dispute resolution*, has a long, empirically established heritage in many cultures, societies, and historical situations. Studies also show that despite marked differences in interests, ideas, values, rules, subject matter and assumptions, patterns of *negotiations* within mediation are essentially similar (Gulliver, 1979). The modern emergence of mediation in the latter half of the twentieth century represented a new and evolving application of this ancient and universal method of settling *disputes* (Roberts and Palmer, 2005). Diversity of style and models of practice are considered to be among the main strengths of mediation, welcomed for the benefits of flexibility, cultural sensitivity, creativity and consumer choice (see for example, Whatling and Kesavjee, 2005 on Ismaili models of mediation)

The presence of more than one culture in mediation is one dimension of this topic – for example, where one of the parties is of a different culture, ethnicity or nationality to the other party, and/or the mediator is of a different culture to either or both of the parties. Another complicating dimension arises with the impact of different jurisdictions on mediation and its outcome – for example, in respect of the enforceability of agreements resulting from mediation. In *international family mediation*, for example, the parties and their *children* may be living in different countries. This has significant structural, procedural, logistic as well as jurisdictional implications for the mediation of any dispute as well as for the kind of decisions to be made relating to practical arrangements, especially regarding contact with children.

European legal instruments govern the principles and practice guidelines (including ethics, training and quality assurance) for mediation in respect of cross-border commercial disputes (The European Mediation Directive, 2008) and family disputes (Recommendation R (98)1 1998, see section 74 on international family mediation in particular).

There are two core reasons why good professional practice of mediation necessitates that in every case consideration takes place of the impact of culture on the mediation process – first, it would be unethical to ignore characteristics of a disputant that would put them at a disadvantage; and second, understanding of culture could enhance the effectiveness and efficiency of the process.

KEY TEXTS

- Augsburger, D.W. (1992) *Conflict Mediation across Cultures-Pathways and Patterns* (Kentucky: Westminster/John Knox Press)
- Avruch, K. (1998) *Culture and Conflict Resolution* (Washington, DC: Institute of Peace Press)
- LeBaron, M. and Pillay, V. (2006) *Conflict across Cultures – A Unique Experience of Bridging Differences* (Boston, MA: Intercultural Press)
- Lederach, J.P. (1995) *Preparing for Peace: Conflict Transformation across Cultures* (*New York*: Syracuse University Press)
- Sen, A. (2007) *Identity and Violence: The Illusion of Destiny* (London: Penguin)
- Shah-Kazemi, S.N. (2000) 'Cross-Cultural Mediation: A Critical View of the Dynamics of Culture in Family Disputes', *International Journal of Law, Policy and the Family*, 14: pp. 302–325

d

decision-making (includes umpiring)

SEE ALSO adjudication; arbitration; authority; dispute resolution; mediation; negotiation; power

A valuable analytic model (see Roberts and Palmer, 2005, chapter 4) distinguishes, by means of a range of variables, the variety of forms of communication directed toward decision-making. These include the presence or absence of third-party intervention; the form of that intervention where it occurs; and the location of *power* in decision-making. On the basis of these variables three basic modes of settlement-seeking communication leading to decision-making can be identified:

- **Bilateral *negotiation*** – the 'dyad' recognized as the elementary and ubiquitous mode by means of which decisions are reached by those directly engaged in the process of communication (Simmel [1908a]; trans., 1950, 122).
- **Facilitated *negotiations*** – the presence of a third party, such as that which occurs in *mediation*, numerically transforms the dyad into the triad. This has additional radical and complex effects as the presence of the third party qualitatively transforms the interaction in a number of ways. For example, in one important respect, the third party in mediation, as in any *dispute resolution* process, transforms the interaction by embodying the principle of objectivity and reasonableness in decision-making (Simmel [1908a] trans., 1950). While the nature and extent of facilitated negotiation may vary across a spectrum of interventions, the primary role of the mediator is to facilitate communication exchanges between the parties to enable them to become the architects of their own decisions.
- *Umpiring* **processes** – the essential transformation here is that power over the outcome is transferred from the parties themselves to a third party decision-maker. Again, the nature

and characteristics of umpiring may vary widely, from that of the state-sponsored judge to the privately selected arbitrator. The fundamental attribute that distinguishes this mode of imposed decision-making is that the location of authority for decision-making lies with the third party, an authority derived either by invitation (as in *arbitration*) or by virtue of the office held (as in *adjudication*).

Mediation is therefore a form of intervention in which a third party, the mediator, assists the parties to the dispute to negotiate over the issues that divide them. The mediator has no power to impose a settlement on the parties who retain authority for making their own decisions.

In practice, given the recognized tensions and limits inherent in the mediator role, mediators need always to bear in mind vital questions about the exercise of their own authority and of their power in relation to the protection of *party control* of decision-making. These questions are part of a larger question of how the distinctive *principles of mediation* (such as *voluntary participation*), as well as its independence from other forms of intervention (including attempts to refurbish court procedures and adjudication) can best be secured in order to safeguard the essential objectives of the process, namely a safe, fair process and party control over decision-making.

KEY TEXTS

- Gulliver, P.H. (1979) *Disputes and Negotiations: A Cross-Cultural Perspective* (New York: Academic Press)
- Palmer, M. and Roberts, S. (forthcoming 2014) *Dispute Processes: ADR and the Primary Forms of Decision-Making.* 3rd edn (Cambridge: Cambridge University Press)
- Roberts, M. (2007) *Developing the Craft of Mediation: Reflections on Theory and Practice* (London; Jessica Kingsley Publishers)
- Roberts, S. (2013) *Order and Dispute: An Introduction to Legal Anthropology* in the Classics of Law and Society Series. 2nd edn (New Orleans, Louisiana: Quid Pro Books)

dispute resolution

SEE ALSO adjudication, alternative dispute resolution (ADR); arbitration; decision-making; mediation; representative negotiations

The term 'dispute resolution' covers a range of typologies of dispute processes. An extensive literature of the mid-twentieth century, based on ethnographic evidence (for example, Gulliver, 1979), delineates several core oppositions and distinctions – between fighting and talking ('war' and 'law'); between agreed and imposed *decision-making* (*'negotiation'* and *'adjudication'*); between different kinds of third-party interveners (for example, 'partisan' or *'impartial'*); and between different modes of intervention (for example, 'advice', 'representation' or 'decision') (Roberts and Palmer, 2005).

KEY TEXTS

- Gulliver, P.H. (1979) *Disputes and Negotiations: A Cross-Cultural Perspective* (New York: Academic Press)
- Menkel-Meadow, C. (ed) (2012) *Complex Dispute Resolution (vols. 1–3)*. Aldershot (Hants: Ashgate)
- Palmer, M. and Roberts, S. (forthcoming 2014) *Dispute Processes: ADR and the Primary Forms of Decision-Making.* 3nd edn (Cambridge: Cambridge University Press)
- Roberts, S. (2013) *Order and Dispute: An Introduction to Legal Anthropology* in the Classics of Law and Society Series. New Orleans, Louisiana: Quid Pro Books.

disputes

SEE ALSO **conflict; dispute resolution; mediation; negotiation**

A dispute may be defined as a sense of grievance over a specific issue which is communicated as a contested claim to the person regarded as responsible or blameworthy (Roberts, 1983b, p. 7). A complex evolutionary process is involved through which experiences of injustice and *conflict* become grievances, and grievances become disputes – the 'naming', 'blaming' and 'claiming' stages that characterize the emergence and transformation of disputes. (see Felstiner *et al.*, 1980–1981). Gulliver too charts the way in which a disagreement (large or small), when unable or unwilling to be resolved within a dyadic relationship in the private sphere, can be put in the public domain ('a different frame of reference and action') in order to ensure that, by appealing to others, 'something must be done' (1979, pp. 75–76). In this way a *disagreement* becomes a *dispute*.

Disputes can be about a range of issues – material goods (such as rights to land and property); social and personal relations; the right to make *decisions*; ways of grouping people together, short or long term; the need to highlight important differences; and the need to work out 'existential predicaments' such as the meaning of love, beneath the ostensible reasons, for example, land and sexual jealousy (Caplan, 1995, p. 2).

Anthropologists have identified too the importance of the dimension of time for understanding disputes. That certain structural relationships give rise to 'chronic eruptions' of dispute, even if each episode is settled temporarily, reflects the longer history of which each episode can be part (Falk Moore, 1995, p. 32).

The primary focus of *mediators* is on disputes, the specific identifiable issues that divide the parties and which are capable of being negotiated. Disputes need to be distinguished from the wider or underlying conflict that may also be present. The settlement of a dispute is achieved when the parties find a mutually acceptable basis for disposing of the issues over which they disagree even against a background of continuing conflict. (Cormick, 1982). This may be compared with the resolution of conflict that is achieved when the basic differences of fact of value or inequalities of power are removed (see entry on *CONFLICT*).

Typical of the *commercial disputes* brought to mediation are those between customers and suppliers of goods and services and bankers; insurance claims; personal injury claims (including *medical negligence*); and disputes between major corporations. In the *family* arena, typical of the disputes following separation and divorce are those over arrangements relating to the residence and contact of children, and the division of property and finance. Family disputes are recognized to generate strong emotional reactions although disputes of all kinds, particularly between individuals, can have a high emotional content as well. *Neighbourhood* quarrels such as those over noise form the stuff of *community mediation*.

International mediation involves a more complex characterization of issues. It does not address, on the whole, disputes between individuals, but rather conflicts involving the larger social dynamics of organized violence, even acts of political terror. Attempts have been made to classify international conflict according to various criteria such as severity, protraction and intractability but definitions and their applications are, in this context, recognized to be vague or inconsistent. This is a realm of multilayered dispute resolution, one of the most difficult, where the work of intermediaries is acknowledged to be extremely complex, slow and painstaking (Princen, 1992).

In this arena as well as that of *environmental mediation*, the ethical and practical repercussions of some of the kinds of disputes addressed are immense when considering their impact not only on those who are not direct participants in the process (for example, the mediation of peace agreements in the Balkans or Sierra Leone) but also on future generations who will be affected by the outcome (as in the mediation of nuclear waste storage or undersea carbon sequestration).

KEY TEXTS

- Caplan, P. (1995) 'Anthropology and the Study of Disputes' in P. Caplan (ed), *Understanding Disputes: The Politics of Argument* (Oxford: Berg Publishers)
- Felstiner *et al.* (1980–1981) 'The Emergence and Transformation of Disputes: Naming, Blaming and Claiming...' *Law and Society Review*, 15 (3): pp. 631–654
- Gulliver, P.H. (1979) *Disputes and Negotiations: A Cross-Cultural Perspective* (New York: Academic Press)
- Roberts, S. (2013) *Order and Dispute: An Introduction to Legal Anthropology* in the Classics of Law and Society Series. 2nd edn (New Orleans, Louisiana: Quid Pro Books)
- Roberts, S. (1983) 'The Study of Dispute: Anthropological Perspectives' in J.A. Bossy (ed), *Disputes and Settlements: Law and Human Relations in the West* (Cambridge: CUP)

domestic abuse (includes domestic violence)

SEE ALSO **bargaining power; fairness; mandation; power; principles of mediation**

The term' domestic abuse' is preferred to that of 'domestic violence' because it reflects the range of behaviours that can make up intimidatory, oppressive or coercive behaviour, not just physical violence (which is more commonly understood by the usage of 'domestic violence').

The problem of domestic abuse highlights, perhaps in its starkest form, central concerns about *fairness* and *power*, whatever *dispute resolution* process is involved – whether bilateral lawyer *negotiation*, *adjudication* or *mediation*. Fairness in mediation requires that there be relative equality of *bargaining power* between the parties. Where there is a situation of manifest inequality, especially one associated with domestic abuse, resort to mediation could be inappropriate, if not dangerous in certain circumstances, both to the abused party and/or their children.

Domestic abuse imposes therefore special demands on family mediators in particular, to be clear about the limits and boundaries of the process. This means ensuring that all the necessary safeguards are in place – both in determining, *prior* to mediation, suitability to engage in the process (in respect of the parties, the dispute and all the circumstances), *and* in protecting, during the process, a more vulnerable party – safeguards, for example, of *principle* (such as *voluntariness*); of structure (such as separate time with each party); of procedure (such as pre-mediation screening for suitability); of external review (such as legal advice) and of premises (such as separate waiting rooms).

Current policy on domestic abuse in the UK is distinguished both by the approach it adopts and by the wide definition of domestic abuse upon which it rests. First, pre-eminence is attached to the perspectives, meanings and experiences of the individuals concerned. It is the impact of domestic abuse *as experienced* by each/any person involved that is significant. Second, domestic abuse is defined broadly as *any* behaviour that seeks to secure power and control for the abuser over the abused including the use of any or all of physical, sexual, psychological, emotional, verbal or economic intimidation, oppression or coercion. (UK College of Family Mediators' policy and practice guidelines, 2000). This approach may be contrasted with that which is largely adopted in North America and involves the professional making a diagnostic assessment based on a typology of domestic violence profiles relating to the kind and intensity of the behaviour (for example, Johnston, 1993).

The practical implications of the UK policy require that there be effective screening for domestic abuse, both prior to and throughout mediation. The parties must be able to make a fully informed, unpressured and voluntary decision as to whether or not to mediate and to continue in the process. In addition safety considerations must include not only the participants in mediation but any other significant member of the family of either party.

KEY TEXTS

- Hester, M. *et al.* (2007) *Making an Impact: Children and Domestic Violence* (London and Philadelphia: Jessica Kingsley Publishers)
- Johnston, J. (1993) 'Gender, Violent Conflict and Mediation', *Family Mediation*, 3 (2).
- Keys Young (August 1996) *Research/Evaluation of Family Mediation Practice and the Issue of Violence* (NSW: Attorney General's Department).
- Lombard, N. and McMillan, L. (eds) (2012) *Violence against Women: Current Theory and Practice in Domestic Abuse, Sexual Violence and Exploitation* (London: Jessica Kingsley Publishers)
- UK College of Family Mediators (2000) *Domestic Abuse Screening Policy* (London: UKCFM)

e

Early Neutral Evaluation (ENE) (includes the mini-trial)

SEE ALSO alternative dispute resolution (ADR); applications of mediation; negotiation; Med-Arb

Early Neutral Evaluation (ENE) is one innovative forecasting device (another is *the mini-trial*) developed as a third-party aid to settlement in the course of lawyer negotiations. Rather than involving a third party, such as a *mediator*, directly in the *negotiation process*, the parties, through their respective legal teams, seek, at an early stage, some form of neutral and independent evaluation or review of the case (or of one of the issues) in the form of a preliminary assessment of its facts, evidence or legal merits. The purpose of obtaining a forecast of the likely judicial outcome is to assist the parties by providing them with information and advice not necessarily available at an early phase of the dispute given a traditional culture of late settlement; by dampening down their unrealistic expectations (perhaps stoked early on by legal teams themselves); by avoiding further unnecessary stages of litigation; and by encouraging them towards settlement on the basis of fuller, more realistic and better informed negotiations.

While ENE was developed initially by *ADR* specialists in support of negotiations by the parties' legal teams, it has also been adopted as part of innovative court practice as a specialized ADR technique for forecasting outcomes and sponsoring settlement (originating in the United States District Court for the Northern District of California). ENE in this context (for example in the English Commercial Court and Technology and Construction Court) takes the form of an early stage authoritative case appraisal by a judge, expert or senior lawyer. This is designed to generate and advance settlement discussion and may be combined with attempts at mediation, arbitration or continued litigation case management.

KEY TEXTS

- Brazil, W. (1990) 'Special Master in Complex Case: Extending the Judiciary or Reshaping Adjudication?' *University of Chicago Law Review* 53: p. 394
- Hay, C., McKenna, K. and Buck, T. (2010) *Evaluation of Early Neutral Evaluation: Alternative Dispute Resolution in the Social Security and Child Support Tribunal.* Ministry of Justice Research Series 2/10, January 2010 (London: Ministry of Justice)
- Mackie, K. *et al.* (2000) *The ADR Practice Guide: Commercial Dispute Resolution* (London, Dublin, Edinburgh: Butterworths)

elder mediation

SEE ALSO **bargaining power; community mediation; fairness; models of mediation; restorative justice**

The use of *mediation* in the context of *disputes* relating to older people raises a number of complex and delicate questions and concerns. It is estimated that one-fourth of the caseload of *community mediation* services involves older people. With the growing number of older people in the community, there is also a serious problem that affects a significant number of people (4%) – that of 'elder abuse'. Elder abuse can take many forms – institutional, structural, verbal, emotional, physical and financial. Elder abuse may be a deliberate, even criminal, act or it may be unintentionally inflicted, the result of inadvertent or neglectful behaviour.

One of the explicit aims of mediation in this arena of practice is to assist older people to prevent and resist abuse. Abuse itself, in any mediation context, is non-negotiable and mediation would be inappropriate where abuse is current. A related aim reflects the *restorative justice* strand of mediation practice, that of restoring peaceful and just relations between people (Roberts quoting Craig, 2007). Any mediated agreement must therefore be just if it is to be acceptable. The first vexed question that arises, therefore, is whether or not mediation is suitable in any circumstances of elder abuse or whether another intervention, advocacy, for example, might be more appropriate.

While abuse constitutes a peculiarly problematic and distressing feature of situations of *conflict* that can affect the elderly, there are other disabling aspects that complicate this context of mediation practice. These can have an impact both on considerations relating to the suitability of mediation, and on the expectations potential parties might attach to its purpose and outcome. For example, the institutional framework within which people live (such as sheltered housing or residential care) can have an impact on every aspect of a person's life especially in relation to the causes and the consequences of conflict (for example, in a dispute between a resident and the warden of a care home).

Furthermore other circumstances can circumscribe the chances of older people reaching even a limited mediated solution. These include the following: mental health illness (such as depression or obsessive disorders); decrepitude; physical frailty and illness, stress arising from separation, divorce or loss of partners through bereavement; geographic isolation from family and friends, material hardship and housing conditions (living in restricted residential accommodation rather in their own home); feelings of marginalization, social exclusion, cultural deprivation and loss of employment status and independence.

These substantial and circumstantial difficulties, not exclusive of course to the older community, and compounded in combination, can affect a person's capacity to participate effectively, or at all, in mediation – for example, where power imbalances may be gross (as in disputes with authority figures) or where there are concerns about a person's capacity to give informed consent to participate, to maintain *confidentiality* and understand its limits, to engage constructively, to make informed decisions and to keep to an agreement. In addition, strong feelings of bitterness and anger not only can exacerbate conflict (for example between two residents in a care home) but also have an energizing, if destructive effect, offsetting depression perhaps, but also creating conflict.

Those working in this field highlight the greater likelihood of mediation being effective when integrated with other forms of intervention and support and with close interdisciplinary professional collaboration (medical, legal, therapeutic and social).

Three aspects of mediation have been identified in this field of practice (Craig, 2003). With early mediation lies the hope of preventing disputes from developing – thereby *'halting'* disputes and preventing elder abuse from arising by addressing situations which expose a vulnerable person to the risk of abuse and/ or discrimination. Mediation can play a role too, at a later, more critical stage in *'holding'* disputes that already exist, by encouraging constructive exchanges and improving communication. Where there is entrenched conflict or where conflict may be too deep-rooted or intractable to be resolved by negotiation, mediation can also be a means of *'healing'* disputes with parties benefiting from a greater or restored sense of personal identity, self-worth and control.

A North American body of literature covers both the policy, quality assurance and training issues that govern the practice of elder mediation there, as well as highlighting the wide range of substantive subjects to which elder mediation has been applied (McCrearey, 2008). These include the following:

- Guardianship and care-giving
- Healthcare
- Consumer disputes
- Probate and financial planning
- Long term care
- Housing
- Family matters (grand-parenting issues, family support, etc)
- Driving, living and household, etc arrangements

The requirements of elder mediation impose heavy responsibilities on those who work in this arena of practice. Specialist knowledge is necessary and some older people with that knowledge and direct experience can make excellent mediators themselves. Mediators need to have huge reserves of patience and to be able to listen attentively and with care and compassion. In practice co-mediators can usefully 'model' real rather than ideal portrayals of behaviour. In post-mediation debriefing, for example, valuable lessons can be learned in the way co-working pairs of mediators themselves 'mirror' the circumstances of elder mediation – by frankly and openly admitting to human frailty and fallibility, legitimizing misperception, memory failure and confusion, and recognizing the necessity for a forgiving approach (Craig, 2003).

Vigilance is necessary to ensure that in cases where there are real deficits of competence, capacity or understanding, mediation does not proceed. The rhetoric and ideology of 'empowerment', or 'pseudo empowerment' as Craig puts it, in this particular context, can be at odds with ensuring that the parties' interests, as well as the *principles of mediation*, are protected (Craig, 2003; Roberts, 2007, p. 107).

KEY TEXTS

- Craig, Y. (2000) 'The Multicultural Elder Mediation Project (EMP: Empowerment for Older, Disabled and Mentally Frail Persons' in M. Liebman (ed) *Mediation in Context* (London: Jessica Kingsley Publishers)
- Craig, Y. (April 2003) 'The Complex Problem of Elder Abuse', *Mediation in Practice* (Bristol: UK College of Family Mediators/ Mediation UK), pp. 18–21
- Larsen, R. and Thorpe, C. (Spring 2006) 'Elder Mediation: Optimizing Major Family Transitions', *Marquette Elders Adviser*, 7 (2)
- McCrearey, B. (2008) *Elder Mediation Annotated Resource Library.* (Ann Arbor, Michigan: Centre for Social Gerontology, Inc)

environmental mediation

SEE ALSO **dispute resolution; international mediation; models of mediation**

Mediation can be a valuable form of environmental *dispute resolution* for conservationists, environmental pressure groups, local and national government bodies and industrial and commercial organizations with competing interests especially with respect to the use of land and resources (for example, between environmental protection and economic development). If the focus of *commercial mediation* is mostly on the substantive issues at stake, and that of *community* and *family mediation* on the individuals of those in dispute, environmental mediation (like that of mediation in *industrial* and organizational matters) often contains a mixture of both (Acland, 1990).

Environmental disputes suitable for mediation often fall into two main categories –

- those involving broad policy decisions that affect society as a whole but which affect individuals only indirectly, and perhaps not for years, such as resource allocation;
- and those, for example, over land use, between identifiable parties such as developers and communities.

Other environmental disputes suitable for mediation involve the allocation of finite resources, setting quality assurance standards and determining public policy priorities (Hoban, 1984).

The mediation of environmental issues is highly complex and time-consuming, involving a multi-issue and multi-party process sometimes involving large groups made up of participants, each with their own constituencies. The capacity to broaden the categories of potential parties (who would not otherwise have been incorporated in the *decision-making*) and so expand the discourse is one major advantage of mediation in this field. However, the difficulty of identifying the parties (which groups and how many participants) does also constitute only one of the heavy demands on the environmental mediator who must, in addition, ensure *party control* in designing the process, in defining the agenda of negotiable issues and in decision-making. Another essential requirement is to address not only the often huge imbalances of power (of expertise, resources and political experience) that may complicate the process but also problems of monitoring and compliance with agreements.

Environmental mediators adopt, therefore, pragmatic and flexible approaches to their work, necessary for devising appropriate models, structures and procedures to fit the specific circumstances and concerns to be addressed. In most cases these are of paramount political, economic and ecological importance (for example, the disposal of toxic waste, nuclear waste storage and undersea carbon sequestration) often with profound consequences for future generations. The fulfilment of these tasks requires a high level of transparency and of trust in the mediator.

KEY TEXTS

- Acland, A.F. (2007) in Roberts, M. *Developing the Craft of Mediation: Reflections on Theory and Practice* (London: Jessica Kingsley Publishers), Chapters 5, 8 and 9
- Cormick, G.W. (1982) 'Intervention and Self-Determination in Environmental Disputes: A Mediator's Perspective', *Resolve*, Winter: pp. 260–265
- Harrington, C.B. (1994) 'Howard Bellman: Using "Bundles of Input" to Negotiate an Environmental Dispute' in D. Kolb and Associates (ed), *When Talk Works: Profiles of Mediator* (San Francisco: Jossey-Bass)
- Hoban, T.M. (1984) 'Alternative Dispute Resolution and Hazardous Waste Site Cleanup Cost Allocation', *A Study of Barriers to the Use of*

Alternative Methods of Dispute Resolution. (South Royalton VT: Vermont Law School Dispute Resolution Project)

- McCrory, J.P. (1981) 'Environmental Mediation – Another Piece for the Puzzle', *Vermont Law Review,* 6 (1): pp. 49–84

ethics of mediation (includes respect and values)

SEE ALSO authority; fairness; principles of mediation

Many influences have created the heterogeneity and eclecticism that characterize the development of *mediation* in its various spheres. The ethical perspective represents one significant dimension of understanding about the foundations of mediation associated with its re-emergence in the West in the latter half of the twentieth century. That embodied, certainly for its early pioneers, the hope for a more humane *dispute resolution* process compared to that of the formal, institutionalized, professionalized and adversarial legal system. Two explicit and distinguishing features characterized this aspiration: first, the objective of mediation, of retaining *decision-making* authority with the parties themselves, was founded on core values held, by the disputants as well as by those who chose to become mediators, to justify its use. These values derive from a humanist tradition informed by the ideals of autonomy and *respect* (Lukes, 1973). This is a tradition of ideas about equality and liberty which accord respect for the inherent dignity, privacy and autonomy of the individual person. Second, in pursuit of that objective, the intervention of *the mediator*, however varied and powerful its impact, was different from that of the usual role of the professional intervener, namely, that of the dominant expert.

The values of mediation exemplify a fundamental ethic of respect – for the parties' perceptions, meanings and values, for their autonomy, and for their capacity to make choices through the exercise of critical reflection and the awareness of alternatives. These values are seen to be essential if the mediator is to have proper regard for the right of the parties, whatever the difficulties, to be the architects of their own agreements and if *party control* is to have meaning.

An attitude of genuine respectfulness by the mediator can draw a positive response from the parties encouraging their creativity and natural problem-solving skills including the difficult skills of 'hard co-operation' – skills of listening well, understanding, and responding to one another in order to act together (Davis, 1994, Sennett, 2012, p. 6). In addition, a third party qualitatively transforms their interaction, not merely by being there, but by embodying the principles of objectivity and reasonableness in exchanges that can lead to adult decision-making (Simmel, 1908a). Norms of fairness, mutual respect and equity of exchange are able to inform these expectations of adult behaviour that translate into expectations of reasonable exchange (Davis, 1984; Fuller, 1971; Rubin and Brown, 1975). The standard of respect that lies at the core of the *principles of mediation* practice interlocks not only with other principles of mediation such as *impartiality*, but also with other central aspects of practice such as the quality of the outcome, its *fairness* or *justice*.

The professional skill of the mediator lies, correspondingly, in acting in a manner that reflects an understanding of what has been described as 'the subtleties of respect' (Sennett, 2003, p. 149). Expectations such as these are seen to be of most value precisely because of the recognition that the circumstances of dispute and conflict – stress, hostility, strong emotions and insecurity –may bring out the 'worst' in people. The vulnerability of parties, the complexity of situations, and the difficulties of disputes, plus the unpredictable dynamics of mediation itself, complicate the realization of these principles in practice, thereby imposing an onerous responsibility on the mediator. Notwithstanding, experienced practitioners in all fields, from grass roots *community mediation* to high value *commercial mediation*, attest to how paramount in practice are these essential ethical principles of mediation (Roberts, 2007).

KEY TEXTS
- Cormick, G.W. (October 1977) 'The Ethics of Mediation: Some Unexplored Territory', unpublished paper presented to The Society of Professionals in Dispute Resolution, Fifth Annual Meeting (Washington, DC)
- Davis, A.M. (1984) 'Comment' in *A Study of Barriers to the Use of Alternative Methods of Dispute Resolution* (Vermont Law School Dispute Resolution Project. South Royalton, VT: VLSDRP)
- Fuller, L.L. (1971) 'Mediation – Its Forms and Functions', *Southern California Law Review*, 44: pp. 305–339
- Lukes, S. (1973) *Individualism* (Oxford: Basil Blackwell)

- Menkel-Meadow, C. (2001) 'Ethics in ADR: The Many C's of Professional Responsibility and Dispute Resolution', *Fordham Urban Law Journal*, 28 (4): pp. 979–990
- Sennett, R. (2003) *Respect: The Formation of Character in an Age of Inequality* (London: Penguin/Allen Lane)

evaluative mediation

SEE ALSO **arbitration; ethics of mediation; lawyers in mediation; party control; principles of mediation; quality assurance**

'Evaluative' mediation refers to a hybrid practice that combines features of both *mediation* and *arbitration*. It is often distinguished from what is termed 'facilitative' mediation where *the mediator*, in adopting a non-directive approach to facilitating the parties' own efforts to negotiate an agreement, refrains from giving any opinions or making any judgements. In evaluative mediation the mediator goes further either by making recommendations for settlement or by providing an assessment of the merits of the case or of the particular issues at stake. This approach can be requested informally by the parties or formally built into the process from the outset, as is common in some jurisdictions where this practice often occurs in close proximity to a court or tribunal.

The nature of the intervention is defined by the purpose for which the intervener activates the flow of information (Roberts and Palmer, 2005). Eliciting information for the purpose of facilitating *negotiation* and *decision-making by the parties* is considered to be quite different from a situation where information is elicited for the purpose of enabling *the intervener* to evaluate this information in order reach a diagnosis of the problem, issue a prescription on the basis of expert knowledge, and then attempt to persuade the parties to accept this solution.

In such a process three analytically distinct and contradictory roles are conflated – that of mediator, adviser and arbitrator. While the lines between the mediator, arbitrator and adviser role and function can be clearly drawn in analytic terms, in real-life processes these different roles may merge into one another, and styles and models of practice do vary across a spectrum.

There is much debate as to whether evaluative mediation can be conceptualized as mediation. Some argue that it is not mediation at all (Roberts and Palmer, 2005). Others argue that as long as the final outcome rests with the parties, evaluative mediation may be an approach of choice. A recent qualitative analysis of different mediator styles, confirming several prior studies, shows that facilitative mediators not only perform more skilfully than their evaluative (and transformative) counterparts, but also that disputants are found to be more satisfied with the facilitative approach than with a more evaluative one (Kressel *et al.*, 2012)

The move from facilitation to determination represents, in any event, a shift of power – from the parties to the intervener. That is why there must be no ambiguity, for the intervener and especially the parties, about the nature of the role and purpose of the intervention.

KEY TEXTS

- Della Noce, D.J. (2009) 'Evaluative Mediation: In Search of Practice Competencies', *Conflict Resolution Quarterly*, 27 (2): pp. 193–214
- Kressel, *et al.* (Winter 2012) 'Multidimensional Analysis of Conflict Mediator Style', *Conflict Resolution Quarterly*, 30 (2)
- Mackie, K. (ed) (2002) *A Handbook of Dispute Resolution: ADR in Action*. 2nd edn (London and New York: Routledge and Sweet and Maxwell)
- Palmer, M. and Roberts, S. (forthcoming 2014) *Dispute Processes: ADR and the Primary Forms of Decision-Making*. 3rd edn (Cambridge: Cambridge University Press), Chapter 8

f

fairness

SEE ALSO authority; impartiality; justice; the mediator; principles of
mediation; quality assurance

There is always a danger that more powerful interests can prevail
over weaker ones, whatever the *dispute resolution* process. This
concern, lying at the heart of the political and feminist critiques of
mediation in the 1980s, took form in a major debate about *justice*
and fairness in mediation – for example, it was argued that *informal
justice* meant 'cheap' or 'second class' justice and that mediation
damaged women's interests (assertions unsubstantiated by empirical research – see Kelly, 2004; Bordow and Gibson, 1994; Emery
et al., 2001; Bondy, Mulcahy *et al.*, 2009; etc).

This debate had complicated implications too in its application
to *international mediation* where understandings about *power*, its
distribution and dynamic, take complex and contradictory forms.

Fairness is regarded as a matter of central importance in mediation precisely because its advantages – that it is a private, confidential, flexible and informal process – also create potential risks – a
process without the safeguards of due process or, in most cases,
the presence of legal representatives (except in the field of civil and
commercial mediation).

Mediators draw a distinction between justice and fairness. In
Western culture, justice is understood to be impartial, rule determined, consistent and official state-sanctioned third-party decision-
making. Justice involves, therefore, a judgment, strictly speaking.
Access to justice has traditionally meant equal, adequate and ready
access to legal services and the courts. With the advent of ADR processes, access to justice also incorporates access to *choice* in relation
to the dispute resolution processes most appropriate to the type of
case (European Mediation Directive, 2008).

In mediation, fairness is determined by the parties themselves and involves personal norms (ethical and psychological) as well as legal norms. Fairness in mediation also embraces the necessity for there to be a fair process, fair procedures, structural fairness as well as fair outcomes. One principle of mediation, and an important advantage, is its procedural flexibility which provides the opportunity for the parties to discuss whatever matters to them including their often powerful concerns about fault and the historical context of the dispute, neither of which may be legally relevant. Fairness, when it is equated with formal equality, excludes this context by discounting concerns about the past or disallowing their expression. For fairness to operate in mediation, this context may well be relevant. Fairness in relation to outcomes refers to the principles that underlie the negotiated agreement, principles of equity, of equality and of need – as well as the extent to which the parties consider the outcome (its allocation of benefits and burdens) to be fair at the time and in the future.

KEY TEXTS

- Cobb, S. and Rifkin, J. (1991) 'Practice and Paradox: Deconstructing Neutrality in Mediation', *Law and Social Inquiry* 16 (1): pp. 35–62
- Menkel-Meadow *et al.* (2007) *On the Requirements for Structural Fairness*, Chapter 7
- Roberts, M. (forthcoming 2014) *Mediation in Family Disputes: Principles of Practice*. 4th edn (Aldershot, Hants: Ashgate)

family mediation (includes divorce and matrimonial mediation)

SEE ALSO children and mediation; domestic abuse; international child abduction mediation; international family mediation; Specialist Child Care Mediation

The focus of family mediation used to be primarily upon issues over *children* following separation and divorce – over which parent was to have day-to-day care of the child ('residence') and how, when and for how long the non-resident parent could have time with the child ('contact'). (The Children Act, 1989 replaced the legal concepts of 'custody' and 'access' with orders for 'residence' and 'contact' because of the conflict between parents generated by the former. The new orders were designed to resolve practical, concrete arrangements relating to children, rather than confer rights. However the recommendation of the Family Justice Review 2011 (supported by government) is that residence and contact orders should be repealed because of the conflict these labels cause. It is now recommended that these be replaced by a 'child arrangements order' which will set out arrangements for the upbringing of the child in case of dispute.

Financial, property as well as children issues are now routinely mediated as well as issues over whether or not the relationship is over, occasionally the first matter to be decided. Disputes can also occur over the divorce itself – whether there should be a divorce, who should petition, on what 'grounds', etc. A wider range of issues are also currently addressed in family mediation, some involving grandparents, step-parents, adult family members, local authorities in *public law* (child protection) cases, adoption and *young homeless* people. *Mediation* is increasingly adopted in cases of *child abduction* and other *international family* disputes (such as relocation) where two inter-related dimensions become significant – a cross-cultural component and an international element. These cases can give rise to unique problems – linguistic, geographic, cultural, jurisdictional and logistic.

Though disputes of any kind involving individuals can evoke high emotional responses, family disputes do frequently generate intense emotional reactions (Simmel, 1908a). These kinds of dispute frequently reflect the difficulties of disengaging the parenting from the spousal role following family breakdown. The opportunity provided in mediation for the expression of strong feelings can therefore be an important advantage over other forms of dispute resolution.

There has long been consensus that family mediation can offer a number of additional advantages particularly where children are concerned – such as providing a forum for the voice of the child to be heard (directly or indirectly); reducing *conflict* and *stress*; fashioning voluntary agreements that are more likely to be adhered to because they are consensual; and improving communication, including an improved capacity to be able to negotiate together in the future as co-operating co-parents (Davis and Roberts, 1988).

It is recognized that family mediation is not suitable in all cases and good practice requires that there be arrangements in place to screen out, prior to mediation, unsuitable cases such as some situations of *domestic abuse*; where there is a child protection concern; or where there are serious imbalances of *power* between the parties (UK College of Family Mediators Policy on Domestic Abuse, 2000).

Government policy and legal instruments in the UK and Europe endorse support for an expanding and central role for voluntary mediation in family disputes in suitable cases (Family Justice Review, 2011 and Government Response, 2012).

KEY TEXTS

- Conneely, S. (2002) *Family Mediation in Ireland* (Aldershot, Hants. Ashgate Publishing Ltd)
- Coogler, O.J. (1978) *Structured Mediation in Divorce Settlement* (Lexington, MA: Lexington Books/D.C. Heath)
- Haynes, J. (1993) *The Fundamentals of Family Mediation* (London: Old Bailey Press)
- Parkinson, L. (2011) *Family Mediation: Appropriate Dispute Resolution in a New Family Justice* System. 2nd edn (Bristol: Jordans Publishing)
- Roberts, M. (forthcoming, 2014) *Mediation in Family Disputes: Principles of Practice*. 4th edn (Aldershot, Hants: Ashgate Publishing Ltd)
- Roberts, S. (1983) 'Mediation in Family Disputes', *Modern Law Review*, 46: pp. 337–357

g

grievance resolution

SEE ALSO **adjudication; arbitration; dispute resolution; the Ombudsman**

At the adjudicative end of the spectrum of decision-making processes lie various grievance resolution schemes including that of *the Ombudsman*. These schemes are designed to provide cost-effective and prompt redress, for example, to consumers of goods and services or those working in government and other public bodies and in industry. The avenue through which parties may pursue their complaints combine the features of several processes including neutral fact-finding, *mediation* and *adjudication*. The law imposes obligations on employers and employees in relation to *workplace* grievances – for example, contract law covering contracts of employment and the statutory grievance procedure contained in Schedule 2 to the Employment Act 2002.

Grievances must be seen to be dealt with effectively, fairly and transparently. Their resolution involves procedures that need to be accessible, speedy and cheap, independent and well-resourced, and fair and just. These procedures are designed to fulfil a larger purpose that involves accountability and responsiveness in the exercise of *power*.

KEY TEXTS
- Cane, P. and Conaghan, J. (2008) *The New Oxford Companion to Law* (Oxford: Oxford University Press)
- Mackie, K. (2002) *A Handbook of Dispute Resolution: ADR in Action.* 2nd edn (London and New York: Routledge and Sweet and Maxwell)
- Mackie, K. *et al.* (2000) *The ADR Practice Guide: Commercial Dispute Resolution* (London: Butterworths)

h

Harvard Negotiation Project (includes principled negotiation)

SEE ALSO mediation; models of mediation; negotiation; research; theory

The Harvard Negotiation Project is a research project based at Harvard University in the USA. Its work focuses on understanding negotiation problems and on developing and disseminating improved methods of *negotiation* and *mediation*. Its activities include the following:

- **Theory building:** The Project works on developing negotiation theory in conjunction with scholars from other distinguished North American academic institutions. The method of *principled negotiation* expounded in the renowned text, *Getting to Yes: Negotiating Agreement Without Giving In* (Fisher and Ury, 1981), is one famous product. Other ideas include the 'one-text' mediation procedure used by President Carter as mediator in the Camp David Middle East peace negotiations in 1978. This tool, effective in the management of complex negotiations, involves the mediator devising a working draft text which both parties amend and improve, without commitment, until each is satisfied it meets their respective objectives, interests and needs. The aim is to avoid parties becoming locked into rigid positions which can lead to stalemate. More recently, the Harvard International Negotiation Initiative, affiliated to the psychiatry department of Harvard Medical School, is exploring the emotional dimensions of *conflict* and negotiation.
- **Education and training:** The Project develops training courses for professionals (diplomats, military officers, lawyers, journalists, business people, government officials and union

leaders) as well as academic courses for students at university and high school.

- **Publications:** Practical materials (case studies, check lists, pro forma documents, etc.) are prepared for practitioners such as negotiators and mediators, such as *International Mediation: A Working Guide.*
- **Conflict Clinic:** This provides participants in conflict situations (domestic and international) with the opportunity to join Project members in learning more about negotiation processes.

KEY TEXTS
- Fisher, R. and Ury, W. (1991) *Getting to YES: Negotiating Agreement Without Giving In.* 2nd edn (London: Business Books)

impartiality

SEE ALSO confidentiality; ethics of mediation; fairness; neutrality; principles of mediation

Impartiality is recognized to be one of the four fundamental and universal characteristics of *mediation* (McCrory, 1981). Maintaining an intermediate position between the disputants is one of the most essential attributes of the mediator, who has to be even-handed in respect of the parties and to be above suspicion that s/he is biased for or against one or the other party. This depends on knowledge and skill as well as personal integrity and commitment. Impartiality is therefore essential to the achievement of the trust that the parties must have in the mediator if that intervention is to be effective. The credibility of the mediator depends not only on being impartial but on being perceived to be so. The 'non-partisanship' required of the mediator can manifest itself when the mediator either stands above contrasting interests and opinions or is equally concerned with both. This is not uncomplicated:

> It is the fusion of personal distance from the objective significance of the quarrel with personal interest in its subjective significance which characterises the non-partisan position. This position is the more perfect, the more distinctly each of these two elements is developed and the more harmoniously, in its very differentiation, each co-operates with the other. (Simmel, 1908a, p. 149)

Impartiality vis-à-vis the parties has to be distinguished from the separate matter of *neutrality*. Confusion of these can create misunderstanding and problems as mediators are not neutral, each having their own values, views and prejudices. The claim to neutrality overstates what is possible, laying mediators open to legitimate challenge. Nor would it be appropriate, or even safe, to assert neutrality in situations of inequality. That is why the mediator needs to be vigilant in protecting impartiality in practice – for example, by making an explicit commitment to impartiality; giving due weight to each parties' views and objectives; avoiding any pronouncement of the merits of each parties' position or imposing views; avoiding structural or procedural arrangements which might create '*negative positioning*' or other unfairness (Cobb and Rifkin, 1991), and ensuring sensitivity to cultural norms.

KEY TEXTS
- Cobb, S. and Rifkin, J. (1991) 'Practice and Paradox: Deconstructing Neutrality in Mediation', *Law and Social Inquiry*, 16 (1): pp. 35–62
- Deutsch, M. (1973)*The Resolution of Conflict: Constructive and Destructive Processes* (New Haven, CT: Yale University Press)
- McCrory, J.P. (1981) 'Environmental Mediation – Another Piece for the Puzzle', *Vermont Law Review*, 6 (1): pp. 49–84
- McCrory, J.P. (1985) 'The Mediation Process', paper delivered at the Bromley Conference, April 1985. Bromley, Kent: SE London Family Mediation Bureau.
- Simmel, G. (1908a) *The Sociology of Georg Simmel*, trans. K.H. Wolff (1955) (New York: Free Press)
- Whatling, T. (2012) *Mediation Skills and Strategies: A Practical Guide* (London: Jessica Kingsley Publishers)

industrial relations mediation

SEE ALSO **Advisory, Conciliation and Arbitration Service (ACAS); arbitration; the caucus; workplace mediation**

Industrial relations has the longest practice history of an official conciliatory process in Britain. The Conciliation Act 1896 provided the basis of the modern statutory framework for state-sponsored conciliation, mediation and arbitration of collective labour disputes, although such forms of intervention existed for several decades prior to the Act of 1896. The Industrial Courts Act 1919 made early provision for the appropriate minister of the day to take steps, one of which was conciliation, to bring about the settlement of trade disputes. The current legal framework is contained in section 212 of the Trade Union and Labour Relations (Consolidation) Act 1992. Within this legal framework, the independent public body, the *Advisory Conciliation and Arbitration*

Service (ACAS), which was established under the Employment Protection Act 1975, is charged with the duty of promoting the improvement of industrial relations. ACAS has no powers of compulsion, seeking to discharge this responsibility through the voluntary co-operation of employers, employees and their representatives, and providing its various services without charge. These include advisory and information services, conciliation (in trade disputes and individual cases of complaint), mediation and arbitration.

ACAS distinguishes between *arbitration, conciliation* and *mediation* in specific ways in this labour-relations context. Conciliation is conducted by an official directly employed by ACAS, who follows the dispute carefully and, if appropriate, seeks to intervene to promote a settlement – a process termed 'running alongside a dispute'. For its mediation and arbitration work on the other hand, ACAS has a Panel of Independent Persons, former academics mostly, but also ex-consultants and lawyers, who are appointed to act as arbitrators and mediators. Mediation, in contrast to conciliation, is associated with a more directive role for the intervener which includes the making of recommendations. Functions can be combined, for example mediation and consultancy or mediation and arbitration, as long as this is what the parties want. It all depends on the terms of reference which have to be explicit about the nature of the process being deployed. What is important is that there is consistency with the terms of reference and therefore any change of intervener role has to be made clear in the brief from the outset.

The model of mediation adopted for industrial relations is usually the use of *caucus*, keeping the parties separate in 'side rooms' with the mediator shuttling between. This is seen, in this context, to be the best approach for managing *conflict* most effectively where emotions run high, as is common in cases of individual employment disputes as well as collective disputes. This has significant implications for protecting both *impartiality* and the *confidentiality* of exchanges.

KEY TEXTS
- ACAS (n.d.) *The ACAS Role in Conciliation, Arbitration and Mediation* (London: Advisory, Conciliation and Arbitration Service)

- Lewis, R. and Clark, J. (eds) (1993) *Employment Rights, Industrial Tribunals and Arbitration: The Case of Alternative Dispute Resolution*, (Liverpool: Institute of Employment Rights)

informal justice

SEE ALSO **alternative dispute resolution (ADR); bargaining power; critiques of ADR and mediation; mediation; negotiation; power**

The early trajectory of the growth of the *alternative dispute resolution* movement and its associated radical and general transformations – of language (from 'cases' to 'disputes'); of focus of discussion (away from court-centred dispute resolution processes towards the possibilities of private spheres of *negotiation*); and of practice and policy developments – have been well documented (Menkel-Meadow *et al.*, 2005; Nader, 2002; Roberts and Palmer, 2005). Early initiatives, manifest in the growth of community justice, especially *neighbourhood mediation*, were motivated by the ideals of both restoring a sense of identity between the individual and their local community or neighbourhood, and of achieving the 'empowerment' of local people. Roberts and Palmer (2005) set out the distinguishing features of informal justice that reflect these ideals: for example, non-bureaucratic, informal structures, lay participation, avoidance of expensive professionals such as lawyers, local accessibility, understanding of underlying causes of problems, and the promotion of flexible, common sense and mutually acceptable solutions rather than the application of legal rules imposed by a court.

What the literature of informal justice highlights, however, are its criticisms. Its aspirations and ideals have been the subject of extensive and serious challenge, expressed first in the 1980s (for example, Abel, 1982; Auerbach, 1983; Fiss, 1984; Freeman, 1984; Matthews, 1988). These critiques, examining, in particular, the political implications of 'informal justice', identified a range of concerns – about *power, neutrality* and coercion – associated with the growth of private ordering. These critiques sought to argue that informal justice, rather than removing disadvantage and restoring harmony and community solidarity, in fact entrenched inequality and extended the scope for state manipulation and coercion. The findings reported in Abel's book highlighted the impact of *power*

disparities on settlement processes by focusing on public mediation programmes in the USA. These findings suggested that, in
some cases, alternative dispute agencies such as Small Claims
Courts and Landlord and Tenants Courts served to divert the legitimate claims of the more vulnerable groups in society (the poor,
black people and women) away from legal channels into forms
of second class justice that lacked the safeguards of due process
and increased the risk of covert state regulation. While 'informal
justice', it was claimed, processed the small claims and minor
disputes of the poor, justice according to the law was reserved
for the rich (Abel, 1982). Ironically concerns were also directed at
private fee-for-service family mediation in the USA, only available
to the rich.

Other arguments against informal justice include those raised by
Fiss (1984). His famed assertion was to uphold the social value of
the courts as public institutions whose primary purpose was to be
devoted, not to resolving disputes, but to giving meaning and 'operational content' to the values of society (such as liberty, equality, due
process and freedom of speech): '*Adjudication* is the social process
by which judges give meaning to our public values' (Fiss, 1984, p. 2).
Informal justice could be seen as an attempt to privatize the courts,
trivializing their role and avoiding public accountability. There were
those who argued too that, because of the close connections between
informal justice and the formal justice system, the ideals and ambi-
tions of informal justice could only be sustained with difficulty and
were therefore unlikely to be realized (Fitzpatrick, 1993).

Recent empirical research on the use of *mediation* in public law
judicial review cases shows that mediation, while not necessarily
cheaper or quicker than judicial review, can be useful, particularly
where *negotiations* have been impossible, difficult or have broken
down. Furthermore, in this context, mediation can be the Rolls
Royce option in its capacity to provide innovative and long-lasting
benefits. It cannot be described therefore as either cheap or second
class justice (Bondy, Mulcahy *et al.*, 2009).

KEY TEXTS

- Bondy, V. and Mulcahy, L. *et al.* (2009) *Mediation and Judicial Review:
  An empirical Research Study* (London: The Public Law Project)
- Fiss, O. (1984) 'Against Settlement', *Yale Law Journal*, 93: pp. 1073–1090

- Fitzpatrick, P. (1993) 'The Impossibility of Popular Justice' in S. Engle Merry and N. Milner (eds), *The Possibility of Popular Justice: A Case Study of Community Mediation in the United States* (Ann Arbor: University of Michigan Press)
- Harrington, C.B. (1985) *Shadow Justice: The Ideology and Institutionalization of Alternatives to Court* (Westport. Conn.: Greenwood Press)
- Harrington, C.B. (1992) 'Delegalisation Reform Movements: A Historical Analysis' in Richard Abel (ed), *The Politics of Informal Justice, Volume 1: The American Experience* (New York: Academic Press)
- King, M.S. *et al.* (2009) *Non-Adversarial Justice* (Annandale, NSW, Australia: The Federation Press)

international child abduction mediation (includes child abduction mediation)

SEE ALSO **children and mediation; cross cultural mediation; family mediation and international family mediation**

As family relationships increase in their internationalism and family ties become more fragile on separation and divorce, there is an increased risk of extreme *conflict*, exemplified in the resort to international child abduction.

Child abduction may not appear, at first sight, to be suitable for *mediation* given the high levels of conflict and the cultural, language, practical and jurisdictional complexities entailed. Notwithstanding such unfavourable circumstances, research and practice experience show that mediation can play a valuable role at different stages in the developing dispute that escalates into an abduction (Child Find of America, 1990: *reunite* Report, 2006).

The potential for mediation has been increased more recently in the context of the kind of abductions now taking place – 60–70 per cent of Hague Convention cases involve abduction by the child's primary carer, usually their mother. In these cases, although a speedy return would be inevitable, often there are other relevant issues that have to be considered. In many cases, for example, the left-behind parent may want to secure contact arrangements rather than primary care or the permanent return of the child. Yet an application under the Hague Convention for the pre-emptory return of the child may appear to be the only option available and the only way to secure contact with the child. There exist, therefore, strong incentives for mutually agreed outcomes that could limit damage, delay and expense; avoid disruptive physical relocations; and reduce conflict and trauma especially for children. For the abducting parent too, their unilateral, non-consensual act of abduction could be re-characterized as an agreed relocation (*reunite* Report, 2006).

The integration of mediation with child abduction proceedings of the court under the Hague Convention 1980 is considered to be essential. Research findings show too that it is crucial that the mediators undertaking this work have expertise in the field of international child abduction and the 1980 Hague Convention, although it is not necessary to have a specialist family law background. This is a model of practice that requires that there be co-working mediator pairs with complementary mediation expertise and specialist knowledge. While mixed gender co-mediation is ideally to be preferred, from the parents' perspectives it is the expertise of the mediators that matters, rather than their gender. The key requirements for effective practice are found, therefore, to be the quality and professional skill of the mediators. It is also recognized that separate pre-mediation screening for suitability for mediation is crucial (*reunite* Report, 2006).

A European network of trained mediators from 21 European countries has been established to advance the provision of bi-national pairs of mediators equipped to co-work together at short notice (Mikke, 2011).

KEY TEXTS

- Buck, T. (2012) *An Evaluation of the Long-Term Effectiveness of Mediation in Cases of International Parental Child Abduction* (Leicester: Reunite International Child Abduction Centre)
- Paul, C. and Kiesewetter, S. (2011) *Cross –Border Family Mediation: International Parental Child Abduction, Custody and Access Cases.* Frankfurt (Germany, Wolfgang Metzner Verlag)

international family mediation (includes cross border mediation)

SEE ALSO **children and mediation; cross cultural aspects of mediation; family mediation; international child abduction mediation**

International family mediation encompasses two inter-related dimensions – a cross-cultural component where either of the parties and/or *the mediator* may come from different cultures; and an international element where the parties and significant others with a stake in the *dispute* are resident in different states.

This combination of cultural complexity and transfrontier relocation gives rise to complicating factors – linguistic, geographic, cultural, legal and logistic. Therefore international family mediation, where *child abduction* is *not* involved, goes further than cross-cultural mediation in requiring distinctive considerations to be taken into account both in relation to the context and operational content of *family mediation* knowledge and practice (to take account of geographic, cultural, language and cost implications), and in relation to the legal procedural and jurisdiction implications (particularly in respect of *confidentiality* and enforcement).

International family mediation, as a relatively new area of practice, incorporates novel technical applications and practice *models* for meeting its distinctive challenges such as *online mediation* and *co-working* bi-national pairs of mediators.

The Network of International Family Mediators, launched in April 2012 and consisting of over 70 mediators from over 27 countries, has benefited from a European Commission funded, 60-hour training in a bi-national, bi-cultural, bi-lingual and bi-professional mediation model. This is intended to equip these mediators to be able to co-work effectively and creatively in high *conflict* situations, across different cultures and languages, to achieve realistic outcomes often bridging large distances (www.crossbordermediator.eu).

KEY TEXTS

- Hodson, D. (2008) 'The EU Mediation Directive: The European Encouragement to Family Law ADR', *International Family Law*, December: pp. 209–216
- Paul, C. and Walker, J. (2008) 'Family Mediation in International Child Custody Conflicts: the Role of Consulting Attorneys', *American Journal of Family Law*, 22 (1), Spring: pp. 42–45
- Roberts, M. (2008) 'International Family Mediation and Recommendation No R (98) 1: A Chronicle of Expansion Foretold', *International Family Law*, December: pp. 217–220

international mediation

SEE ALSO **the caucus; cross cultural mediation; justice; United Nations mediation**

Mediation is resorted to where the parties involved in an international *dispute* (for example, disputing states) cannot themselves resolve their differences by bi-lateral negotiation. Intermediary third-party intervention may take several forms, three of which have been identified by Merrills (2005):

- **'Good offices'**: a minimal form of intervention which refers to the simple encouragement towards the resumption of *negotiations* contributed by a third party.
- *Conciliation:* This process involves the third-party intervener being assigned the investigation of the dispute followed by the presentation to the parties of formal proposals for its resolution.
- *Mediation:* The parties retain control over decision-making in a confidential process where the third party intervener, the mediator, can offer informal proposals made on the basis of information provided by the parties rather than as a consequence of an independent investigation (which distinguishes mediation from conciliation).

Princen (1992) identifies two different ideal types of mediatory interventions in international disputes, each with specific characteristics and distinct advantages:

- **'Principal'** mediators who have clout and their own interests in the dispute (whether national, regional, religious or prestige). Examples include USA's Jimmy Carter mediating between Egypt and Israel (1997), the Papal involvement in 1978 in the war between the two Catholic countries of Chile and Argentina, and Algeria's mediation between Iran and Iraq in 1975 which greatly enhanced its influence and prestige in the Moslem world;
- **'Neutral'** mediators whose very lack of power affords opportunities for demonstrating their non-alignment and for building trust by creating 'realistic empathy' through direct interaction – such as individual mediators influenced by Quaker, Buddhist or Christian pacifist values and the moral ideals of justice and reconciliation, and non-governmental organizations motivated by humanitarian and peace and security concerns such as the International Committee of the Red Cross (ICRC) (Princen, 1992, p. 27; Roberts, 2007).

Analytic clarity (however useful) cannot reflect accurately the complexity, difficulty and frequent confusion arising in situations of political tension, long standing *conflict* and violence. This is highlighted not only in the literature but by international mediators themselves, who, whilst appreciating the value of 'groupings of convenience', recognize that in practice distinctions frequently become blurred and that the 'almost dichotomous ideal types ... probably break down in actual practice' (Francis and Hoffman in Roberts, 2007, pp. 222, 106). Aspects of mediation, unique to its international context and which distinguish it significantly from mediation in other fields, include the multi-layered dynamics of *power*; the significance of culture and ethnicity; the impact of conflict; and the devastating effects of violence – personal, social and historical – which itself begets further crimes of violence irrespective of its origin.

Multi-level practice approaches reflect these conditions of international mediation, highlighting major differences from other fields of mediation practice. As international mediation involves the facilitation of groups rather than the conflict of individuals, international mediators need to be able to address the dynamics of group conflict, including the larger social dynamics of organized violence and acts of political terror. Understandings about these complex and contradictory dynamics and the distribution of power, require therefore, the application of appropriate theories of practice and appropriate models, methods and skills of practice as well as far more complex time management arrangements. For example, mediatory intervention can include support for local actors (such as mixed groups and organizations or people from different countries); training in the concepts and skills of conflict transformation; and facilitating dialogue and strategy workshops. 'Second-track' negotiation is a term of art in the literature that describes the informal negotiation and facilitative processes that occur in parallel with, and complementary to, the formal negotiation process where decision-making authority lies. 'Second track' negotiation, as well as encouraging informal exchanges and explorations, has the advantage of enabling linkages to be made across political levels, from the elite decision-making level, to the mid-level political actors and structures, to the grassroots and civil society level of the nongovernmental organization.

In the light of the conditions that characterize international disputes, the limitations of mediation become clear. First, it is regarded as a core principle of international mediation that a mediator must never get involved or drawn into a situation other than by the invitation to participate of those involved in the conflict themselves. Mediation may be sought out by the parties or be offered by outsiders but it cannot be forced on the parties. They must consent both to the process and to the mediator, whether a 'neutral mediator' whose personal reputation and relevant attributes inspire trust with those on both sides involved in the conflict, or a 'principal mediator', such as a state, with a possible vested interest but which is also acceptable in respect of the particular circumstances, place and timing of the dispute – such as Algeria, a non-aligned Moslem state mediating between Iran and Iraq in 1975. Even where a state has a special relationship with one party, this can be an advantage rather than a disqualification to mediate as that very closeness may well create the expectation in the other party that this will induce both a positive influence, generating greater co-operation, and a greater prospect of delivering a desired outcome (Merrills, 2005).

Mediation will not take place where a government (such as the South African Nationalist government during the apartheid era), by accepting mediation, has then to acknowledge that its dispute is a legitimate matter of international concern and international accountability (Merrills, 2005). Few mediators would be able or willing to act in those cases where it is clear that it would be a futile endeavour – such as in the Falklands war of 1982 where it is suggested that, despite offers of mediation from the USA and the United Nations, and the wish to appear politically reasonable, the cultural imperatives of 'machismo' and 'dignidad' of the Argentine military leadership made defeat in battle preferable to dishonour (Merrills, 2005).

Where international mediation does take place, it is a slow, painstaking, difficult and often dangerous activity, often taking years of patient effort. In some cases mediation can only be partially successful providing temporary respite from violence but only postponing resolution of the fundamental issues in dispute – such as Egypt's welcome mediatory intervention in 2012 following conflict in Gaza between Israel and the Palestinians.

Whatever the limits of mediation in international affairs, the core *principles of mediation – voluntary participation, confidentiality* of exchanges, *impartiality* and procedural flexibility – remain as central as in any other arena of mediation practice. However limited the prospect of a successful *outcome*, and however likely the probability of failure, the advantages of talking rather than fighting make the exhaustive efforts of mediators worthwhile. The *process* of mediation provides the opportunity for the effective facilitation of the kind of communication that can bring about the acknowledgement of suffering and grievance; an improvement in understanding; explanation and interpretation that can reduce anxiety and hostility; the exploration of a range of options for possible solutions; and the hope of a mutually acceptable agreement.

KEY TEXTS

- Bercovitch, D.J. (ed) (1996) *Resolving International Conflicts: The Theory and Practice of Mediation* (Boulder, CO: Lynne Rienner Publishers)
- Burton, J. (ed) (1990) *Conflict: Human Needs Theory* (London: Macmillan)
- Curle, A. (1971) *Making Peace* (London: Tavistock Publications)
- Francis, D. (2010) *From Pacification to Peacebuilding: A Call to Global Transformation* (London: Pluto Press)
- Merrills, J.G. (2005) *International Dispute Settlement*. 4th edn (Cambridge: CUP)
- Princen, T. (1992) *Intermediaries in International Conflict* (Princeton NJ: Princeton University Press)

j

judicial mediation (includes the case management conference)

SEE ALSO adjudication; court linked mediation; decision-making; mandation

Judicial mediation refers to the practice that takes place when, in certain circumstances, judges abandon their traditional, authoritative, third-party role and adopt the new and different role of *the mediator*. This transformation from authoritative judicial decision-maker to facilitator of the *decision-making* of others represents both a fundamental shift across diametrically opposed ends of the intervention spectrum, as well as the reversal of the location of decision-making authority. This is manifest most starkly in the contrast between the outcome of an imposed judicial order, backed by the threat of sanctions for contempt of court for its breach, and the outcome arising from the voluntary and consensual decisions freely negotiated by the parties themselves.

Judicial mediation can take a number of different and hybrid forms, all of which are officially encouraged forms of *ADR*. These various manifestations are found mostly in the United States and in Australia (Mackie *et al.*, 2000). They include the following:

- The judge as mediator where no settlement has been reached;
- Judge conciliators;
- Court appointed mediators;
- Court annexed mediation;
- Court directed mediation;
- *Special or Settlement Masters* (a peculiarly North American practice);
- Settlement conferences promoted by the judge such as the *case management conference;*
- The pre-trial review or directions appointment;
- *Early Neutral Evaluation;*

- Advisory Arbitration;
- Settlement weeks;
- Multi-door courthouse.

These institutional innovations have emerged in response to the gradual yet fundamental cultural transformation that has characterized the civil and family justice systems in the West. Galanter (1986: pp. 261–262) has charted this growing judicial endorsement of settlement from its early manifestation in the USA in the 1930s – officially ratified in 1983 in Rule 16 of the Federal Rules of Civil Procedure which allowed judges 'to consider *and take action* with respect to … the possibility of settlement or the use of extra judicial procedures to resolve the dispute' (emphasis added). Roberts and Palmer (2005) chart a similar trajectory with respect to England and Wales climaxing in the introduction of the Civil Procedure Rules which came into force in 1999 following the Woolf Report (1996). These developments reflect not only a drive towards the administrative convenience of the courts (in the face of heavy caseloads and resource restrictions) and the negative experience of the parties (facing the costs, delays, uncertainties, and inequalities of litigation as well as the risks associated with the black/white, win/lose outcomes of adjudication) but also a general view that has prevailed, particularly in the USA, namely, that settlement, freely negotiated, could produce a superior outcome, closer to the ideal of justice. This veteran judge proclaimed:

> [o]ne of the fundamental principles of judicial administration is that, in most cases, the absolute result of a trial is not as high a quality of justice as the freely negotiated, give a little, take a little settlement. (Quoted in Galanter, 1986, p. 257)

The active promotion of, and direct participation in, settlement by judges may now be common practice but it has not occurred without controversy (see Fiss, 1984). More research is needed to establish whether in situations where the judge assumes a direct managerial role in the settlement process, more settlements are produced. What research does establish so far, is that where *alternative dispute resolution* processes (and *mediation* in particular), are directly co-opted by the court, the closer their association with its coercive context, the less effective these processes become. Concerns relate to the following: whether participation is properly informed and voluntary; the risks of pressurization; the lack of choice in respect of the mediator; the non-neutral forum; the confusion of roles and functions; the lack of clarity in relation to intervention boundaries; inadequate facilities, problems of remuneration and court account-ability, and, above all, the loss of *party control* (see for example, Davies, 1985; Home Office, 1994, section 5.34; Trinder *et al.*, 2006; Genn *et al.*, 2007).

Where judges relinquish their traditional *umpiring* role in favour of a mediatory one, there is a risk that both *adjudication* and media-tion may be damaged – 'to link mediation to the world of the law will arguably sap the vitality of both' (Roberts, 1983, p. 537; see also Fuller, 1963, 1978).

KEY TEXTS

- Eckhoff, T. (1969) 'The Mediator and the Judge' in V. Aubert (ed), *Sociology of Law* (Harmondsworth: Penguin)
- Galanter, M. (1985) '"A Settlement Judge is not a Trial Judge": Judicial Mediation in the United States', *Journal of Law and Society*, 12 (1): pp. 1–18
- Galanter, M. (1986) 'The Emergence of the Judge as a Mediator in Civil Cases', *Judicature*, 69: pp. 257–262
- Genn, H. *et al.* (May 2007) 'Twisting Arms: Court Referred and Court Linked Mediation under Judicial Pressure', *Ministry of Justice Research Series*, 1/07: pp. 1–232
- Shapiro, M. (1981) *Courts: A Comparative and Political Analysis* (Chicago and London: The University of Chicago Press)
- Wall, J.A. and Rude, D.E. (Summer 1985) 'Judicial Mediation: Techniques, Strategies and Situational Effects', *Journal of Social Issues*, 41 (2): pp. 47–63

justice

SEE ALSO **adjudication; decision-making; fairness; informal justice**

Justice is a complex philosophical concept varied in its applications. It is associated in moral terms with human relationships (indi-vidual and social justice), with historical, economic and political events (putting past wrongs right including *restorative justice*), as well as with the operation of the law and its institutions (natural, procedural and substantive justice) (Campbell, 2008).

Justice in Western cultures is symbolized by a blind goddess holding the sword of state power in one hand, and in the other, balancing exactly, the scales of justice. Justice thus understood is impartial, rule-determined, consistent and state-sanctioned third party determination. Justice, in this context, involves therefore, a judgement and so is not applicable to *mediation* where the parties make their own decisions.

On the other hand, *fairness* is regarded as a matter of central importance in mediation – that the parties consider that they have been treated fairly and with 'parity of esteem', and that the outcome they reach is fair, or as fair as is practicable in the circumstances (Francis, 2002, p. 38). Unlike justice, fairness is determined by the parties themselves. They need to be content that there is a proper basis for their agreement which is one that fulfils personal, ethical, economic and legal norms. In *international mediation*, where understandings about *power*, its distribution and dynamic, take complex and often contradictory forms (including victim-hood), the inter-relationship between justice and peace is central. (Francis, 2002, 2010)

An important dimension of the political critique of mediation revolved around the debate about justice and fairness in mediation. Concerns about more powerful interests prevailing over weaker interests apply equally to all dispute resolution processes – private *negotiations*, bi-lateral or multi-lateral *lawyer negotiations*, door-of-the-court settlements and *adjudication*. Research reveals the fact that the ideal of equal justice of the law is, in fact, incompatible with the social and economic realities of unequal wealth, power and opportunity (Auerbach, 1983).

Traditionally, access to justice has meant equal, adequate and ready access to legal services and the courts. Since new lawyer settlement-seeking processes (for example, 'collaborative law' negotiations) and alternative dispute resolution processes have become increasingly available, access to justice now also includes access to *choice* in relation to the dispute resolution process most appropriate to the dispute, the parties and all the circumstances (European Mediation Directive, 2008 (2)).

KEY TEXTS
- Auerbach, J.S. (1983) *Justice without Law? Resolving Disputes without Lawyers* (Oxford: Oxford University Press)

- Campbell, T. (2001) *Justice* (London: Palgrave)
- Francis, D. (2002) *People, Peace and Power: Conflict Transformation in Action* (London: Pluto Press)
- Genn, H. (1999) *Paths to Justice: What People Do and Think about Going to Law* (Oxford: Hart)
- Sen, A. (2009) *The Idea of Justice* (London: Penguin/Allen Lane)

k

knowledge

SEE ALSO craftsmanship; dispute resolution; theory

The modern emergence of *mediation* represents the discovery of a mode of *dispute resolution* with its own long-established and autonomous historical and cross-cultural heritage (Roberts, 1979; Rwezaura, 1984; Acland, 1995). Mediation has always been informed by this large and distinguished body of knowledge from which *mediators* have been able to draw for an understanding of *theory* and practice (for example, Douglas, 1957; Stevens, 1963; Gulliver, 1979).

Until relatively recently, North American influences have tended to dominate the mediation literature across fields of practice (for example, Meyer, 1960; Coogler, 1978; Haynes, 1981; Folberg and Taylor, 1984; Burton, 1987; Princen, 1992; Bush and Folger, 1994; Kolb *et al.*, 1994; Lederach, 1995; Menkel-Meadow, 1995; Lang and Taylor, 2000; Riskin, 2003; LeBaron, 2005, etc.) This body of *negotiation* and mediation knowledge can be distinguished from the range of distinct disciplines that also contributes to a broader study of *conflict* and dispute resolution – the academic literature, for example, of sociology, anthropology, political science, peace studies, law and socio-legal studies, economics, international relations, social psychology, family systems thinking and neuro-linguistics.

The knowledge base recommended for the training of mediators covers both generic mediation knowledge applicable (for example, the nature and *process of mediation*; roles and responsibilities of mediators, negotiation theory and processes; *models* and structures, communication processes, conflict management, and *ethical principles* including codes of practice, policies and practice guidelines) as well as knowledge specific to the relevant subject matter of mediation (for example, for family mediation, knowledge about family transition and psychological and social processes of divorce and separation; child development; child protection procedures and domestic abuse; financial information and family legislation etc).

The existence of a distinct and recognized body of mediation knowledge constitutes the first of the three essential hallmarks – with mechanisms for its transmission, as well as mechanisms for self-regulation, evaluation and accountability – necessary for achieving the professional status of mediation practice.

KEY TEXTS

- ADR Bibliography (n.d.) London: Standing Conference of Mediation Advocates (SCMA). website@mediationadvocates.co.uk.
- Menkel-Meadow (ed) (2012) *Complex Dispute Resolution. Foundations of Dispute Resolution,* Vol. I; *Multi-Party Dispute Resolution, Democracy and Decision-Making,* Vol. II; *International Dispute Resolution,* Vol. III (London: Ashgate)
- Palmer, M. and Roberts, S. (forthcoming 2014), *Dispute Processes: ADR and the Primary Forms of Decision-Making.* 3rd edn (Cambridge: Cambridge University Press)

1

law

SEE ALSO adjudication; justice; representative negotiations

The identity of law, as represented in the West, has specific defining features:

- It constitutes a regulatory regime that controls everyone, even those in power including the government.
- It operates by means of formal rules and procedures.
- It is managed by specialist professional experts, namely, lawyers and judges.
- It implements a particular mode of third party decision-making, namely *adjudication*.
- It is enforced through centralized sanctions (Roberts, 2005).

The benefits of *mediation* are seen to lie precisely in the process being a true and viable alternative to such a system and this institutional independence has been officially affirmed by the Court of Appeal in its landmark decision on privilege in mediation, *Re D*, (1993). Their Lordships stated explicitly that mediation did not form part of the legal process.

Current concerns arise because alternative processes are increasingly becoming adjuncts of the court system, manifesting hybrid processes and co-opted to subserve diversionary, cost-saving procedures designed to encourage settlement rather than adjudication as the court's primary function, often without the protection of either due process or a lessening of court control. Because of the changing nature of the contemporary court, mediation has to struggle to remain a discrete and autonomous intervention, separate from and independent of the court.

Mediation cannot, however, be a substitute for legal advice (or for that matter, other interventions, such as therapy). Mediation presupposes that the parties will obtain the necessary independent advice so that they are properly appraised of relevant legal matters for the making of informed and fair decisions. In addition, *negotiation* processes including mediation do not take place in a vacuum and the law, its norms and institutions impose powerful constraints on the conduct of negotiations (such as transforming the discourse from one of negotiation to one of law; knowledge of the likely outcome in the event of the dispute being adjudicated, etc.) – encapsulated in Mnookin and Kornhauser's memorable description of lawyer negotiation as 'bargaining in the shadow of the law' (1979). While the law can provide protection from individual aggression and state intrusion, 'it also encourages the isolation that makes protection necessary' (Auerbach, 1983, p. 13). Furthermore,

> [a]lthough a lawyer can provide reassuring guidance, in loco parentis, the price of protection is still dependence. Even as a dangerous adversary is fended off, the judge looms as a menacing authority figure, empowered to divest a litigant of property or liberty. Autonomy vanishes as mysteriously as the smile of the Cheshire cat. (Auerbach, 1983, p. viii)

KEY TEXTS
- Auerbach, J.S. (1983) *Justice without Law?* (New York: Oxford University Press)
- Mnookin, R.H. and Kornhauser, L. (1979) 'Bargaining in the Shadow of the Law: The Case of Divorce', *Yale Law Journal*, 88: pp. 950–997
- Roberts, S. (2005) 'After Government?' Chorley Lecture published in the 68, *Modern Law Review*, 1

lawyers in mediation (includes mediation advocacy)

SEE ALSO **dispute resolution; representative negotiations and third persons in mediation**

Official enthusiasm for *mediation* has transformed the civil and family justice systems (Woolf, 1996; Norgrove, 2011). With such endorsement, it is not surprising that lawyers have been training as *mediators* in their hundreds, fearing the growing challenge to their traditional monopoly of control as specialists in *dispute resolution*. As in the United States which witnessed, a decade earlier, the dangers of lawyers seeking to dominate the development of alternatives, now too in the UK 'legal professionals tumble over each other in their enthusiasm for non-legal dispute resolution alternatives' (Auerbach, 1983, p. 139).

The Law Society has sought even to appropriate mediation as a specialism within the normal practice of a solicitor, an attempt that highlights the extent to which lawyers are willingly abandoning the exclusive partisan, advisory and representative role that they have traditionally monopolized in pursuit of a new and potentially lucrative area of professional practice (Auerbach, 1983; ACLEC Report, 1999; Roberts, 2002).

These developments can generate professional tension both in the mediation community (with lawyer mediators privileging their profession of origin over others in respect of training needs and status) and within the legal profession (as in Germany, where there has been hostility to those lawyers promoting alternative approaches to dispute resolution).

Lawyers can act in a multiplicity of roles within or adjacent to mediation:

- **As mediators:** This requires a transformation from a specialist advisory and championing role to one that is essentially different, namely, an impartial and facilitative role orchestrating other peoples' own negotiations rather than acting as negotiators themselves. Mediators' codes of practice also draw a clear line between the giving of legal information, provided as an impartial resource to both parties, which is appropriate in mediation, and the giving of legal advice which is inseparable from a partisan relationship of representation and which is, therefore, not appropriate in mediation. Informed consent as to the nature and objective of the professional relationship protects the parties and the lawyer, when acting as a mediator (Riskin, 1984). This is of particular relevance in the practice of *commercial mediation* where mediators are predominantly practising commercial lawyers whose legal and negotiation expertise equips them to act either as *mediation advocates* or representatives, mediators, or in *Med-Arb*, as arbitrators. Acknowledgment of the variety of roles that lawyers can and do occupy imposes reciprocal acknowledgement of the importance of distinguishing these different capacities unequivocally – given the recognized hazards of blurring, combining or confusing interventions.

- **As consultants in mediation:** Where external expertise (legal, welfare rights, financial, tax information, etc) is required to inform discussion in mediation, it may be introduced in two ways – either by the mediator or via a consultant outside the process providing the necessary data to the parties or to the mediator.

- **As lawyer representatives or advocates within mediation:** The presence of lawyers representing the parties within the mediation process is rare except in the fields of civil and commercial mediation where such presence is routine. *Mediation advocacy* has developed as a specific technique for representing the client in mediation – 'presenting and arguing a client's positions, needs and interests in a non-adversarial way' (Guidelines for Lawyers in Mediation, Standing Conference of Mediation Advocates (SCMA)). This requires specialist training to address the requirements of representation in the context of mediation – for example, the explicit recognition that the parties to a dispute should control its content and outcome, and the recognition that the objective of mediation advocacy is to assist the disputants to come to a mutually acceptable agreement that meets the needs and interests of *both* parties. This approach is premised on the view that a negotiated outcome is more likely to be satisfying, workable, flexible, effective and durable than a court imposed order (SCMA). Commercial mediators have the added task therefore of managing the *negotiations* not only of the parties, but also of their lawyer representatives, including the nature and extent of their participation. This can affect the choice of model of practice – for example, a preference for adopting more plenary meetings (compared to caucusing) better to limit lawyer dominance and enhance opportunities for party self-expression and inter-party dialogue.

- **As advisers outside the process:** Mediation is neither a substitute for legal advice nor an alternative to legal representation. Legal advice should be available when needed from the parties' independent legal advisers outside the process so that negotiations in mediation can be effective and decisions fully informed. Research on mediation in family property and financial disputes has shown that the thoroughness of discovery and disclosure of assets make it extremely unlikely that mediated agreements need to be unpicked by solicitors. These findings also showed that parties value the partisan support they receive from their solicitors during the process of mediation, especially the protection against unfavourable settlements (Walker *et al.*, 1994).

- **As negotiators outside the process:** It is not uncommon that negotiations between solicitors, and even litigation, over some areas in dispute (for example, family finance and property) occur in parallel with mediation over others (such as children issues). While many family lawyers seek to adopt conciliatory approaches in their bi-lateral negotiations, findings show too that a powerful (and understandable) financial disincentive is one significant reason for the reluctance of lawyers (in civil and family disputes) to refer suitable cases to mediation (Genn, 2006; NAO Report, 2007). The attitude of lawyers to mediation, the course of their prevailing negotiations, the imminence of hearing dates, etc. are legal influences that affect the environment within which mediation takes place.
- **Lawyers in negotiation-related practices:**
    a) The *'mini-trial'* (sometimes called the 'modified settlement conference' or 'executive tribunal') was first developed in North America to provide a predictive/forecasting approach in commercial disputes as a means of informing clients both about the strengths and weaknesses of their respective cases and the likely outcome of adjudication, in order to encourage settlement. This procedure has two main differences from traditional lawyer negotiations – first, the parties themselves are primarily and directly involved in having to hear and evaluate their options; and second, an independent third party, the neutral expert, is introduced to provide an advisory and forecasting function.
    b) A new approach (since 2004) to lawyers negotiating family disputes is one called *'collaborative family law'*. Also derived from North America, this involves lawyers and their clients (couples usually) and possibly other professionals (such as divorce counsellors) collaborating in round-table meetings to negotiate, outside the litigation and court process, financial or other settlements. A feature of this procedure

is that 'collaborative' lawyers agree not to be involved in any subsequent litigation that might ensue in the same case.

KEY TEXTS

- Genn, H. (2007) 'Twisting Arms: Court Referred and Court Linked Mediation under Judicial Pressure', *Ministry of Resolution,* Vol. 1, *Justice Research Series,* 1/07, May)
- *Guidelines for Lawyers* (nd) Standing Conference of Mediation Advocates. website@mediationadvocates.co.uk.
- Menkel-Meadow, C. (ed) (2012 Series) *Complex Dispute Resolution. Foundations of Dispute* (Aldershot, Hants: Ashgate Publishers Ltd)
- Menkel-Meadow, C. *et al.* (2005) *Dispute Resolution: Beyond the Adversarial Model* (New York: Aspen Publishers)
- Riskin, L.L. (1984) 'Towards New Standards for the Neutral Lawyer in Mediation', *Arizona Law Review,* 26: pp. 330–362

m

mandation (includes compulsory mediation)

SEE ALSO **bargaining power; domesic abuse; party control and principles of mediation**

Mandation in relation to *mediation* consists of direct compulsion to attend mediation before the parties are entitled to a court hearing. There is no mandatory mediation in the UK. Judges have no formal power to order mediation and judicial opinion on the whole supports encouragement for mediation rather than compulsion, regarding 'compulsory mediation' as both unworkable and a contradiction in terms (Lord Chancellors Department, 1995a; Lord Woolf Access to Justice Report, 1996; Court of Appeal judgment in *Halsey v. Milton Keynes NHS Trust* [2004] 1 WLR 3002; President of the Family Division Speech to Resolution members, 2012).

However, with courts actively pursuing settlement as a primary objective, there is a danger that this may become associated with a growing pressure toward introducing mandatory mediation in response to overloaded court lists and increasing numbers of litigants in person (given serious restrictions in legal aid as in the family justice system).

There is, in principle and in practice, a clear distinction to be drawn between the requirement to attend at a *pre-mediation* information and suitability assessment meeting to hear about and consider *the option* of mediation, and participation in mediation itself, which remains a voluntary matter. The Pre-Action Protocol in civil proceedings and the Pre-Application Protocol in family matters embody this critical distinction and even in respect of the latter, there is no compulsion, rather a strong expectation, for self-funding parties (compared to legally aided parties for whom there is already a requirement) to attend a pre-mediation information and assessment meeting (termed a 'Mediation and Information Assessment Meeting' or MIAMs) before making an application to court. However the current 'strong expectation' to attend a MIAMs will shortly become a requirement for all parties (legally aided and self-funding) once the Children and Families Bill is enacted. Recent legislation in Germany also affirms the importance of this distinction (Law on the Reform of Proceedings in Family Cases and in Matters of Voluntary Jurisdiction, June 2005, section 144).

All mediation codes of practice, whatever the field of practice, and European directives affirm the cardinal principle of voluntary participation in mediation.

For the reasons explaining why mandation is so problematic in mediation, see the entry on *principles of mediation* in particular.

KEY TEXTS
- Council of Europe (1998) Recommendation No. R (98) 1 of the Committee of Ministers to Member States on Family Mediation, Strasbourg
- European Mediation Directive (2008) of the European Parliament and of the Council of 21st May, 2008/52/EC
- Ingleby, R. (1993) 'Court Sponsored Mediation: The Case against Mandatory Participation', *Modern Law Review*, 56: pp. 441–451
- Practice Direction 3A-Pre-Application Protocol for Mediation Information and Assessment, April 2011 (London: Ministry of Justice)
- Roberts, M. (Summer 2005) 'Family Mediation: The Development of the Regulatory Framework in the UK', *Conflict Resolution Quarterly*, 22 (4): pp. 509–526

Med-Arb

SEE ALSO **Alternative Dispute Resolution (ADR); applications of mediation; arbitration and informal justice**

Med-Arb is one of several hybrid processes developed, largely in North America, as a modification of the primary processes of dispute management – *negotiation, mediation* and *umpiring*/third party *decision-making* (as identified by Roberts and Palmer, 2005). Med-Arb is a mediation-related innovation that seeks to reinforce mediation by linking it sequentially with *arbitration*. Parties adopting this procedure give permission, embodied in advance in the terms of reference, for *the mediator* to convert to an arbitrator role in the same case and make a binding award should a mediated settlement not be possible. Most practices give primacy to the mediation phase of the linkage, using the threat of arbitration in order to enhance the efficacy of mediated negotiations – 'mediating with a club' (Roberts and Palmer, 2005, p. 289). Whilst not in common use, Med-Arb is deployed in some labour disputes in the UK (see *ACAS* entry) and increasingly in the North American construction industry, with support growing too, internationally.

Med-Arb has attracted serious criticism, both of principle and, even where the parties have given their full consent, of practice. Fuller (1963), for example, has argued that mediation and arbitration are essentially different – in their purpose, their processes and in their morality. Mediation is a co-operative process based on the goal of optimum settlement realized through the building of mutual trust, understanding and a shared responsibility that enables the parties to work out their own rules of engagement and 'pay-offs' (giving what is less valuable to the giver but more valuable to the receiver and receiving what is more valuable to the receiver but which is less valuable to the giver). Arbitration, on the other hand, involves a third party making a decision in the light of the presentation of proofs and arguments in each party's favour in a competitive process based on a contractual agreement to enter into arbitration (Fuller, 1963). The confusion of roles entailed in Med-Arb in theory undermines both processes with the essential *confidentiality* of information exchanges in mediation, and the integrity of *adjudication*, through a breach of the rules of natural justice, equally compromised. Even the most skilled and experienced of practitioners would be unable to overcome the inherent limitations in these fused roles.

Notwithstanding these concerns, Med-Arb is seen to be effective in a variety of dispute contexts where procedural adjustments have been introduced to address some of the problems that have been raised. Those who argue in favour of Med-Arb cite, as well as savings of costs and time, its efficacy, for example, in contested child custody cases (as in the state of California where the fusion of the mediation and arbitration roles gives the mediator the authority to make a recommendation to the court should the parties not agree in mediation) and in the mediation of grievances under a collective bargaining contract by (see Folberg and Taylor, 1984; Goldberg, 1982).

KEY TEXTS

- Elliott, D.C. (1996) 'Med/arb: Fraught with Danger or Ripe with Opportunity', *Arbitration*, 62 (3): pp. 175–177
- Fuller, L.L. (1963) 'Collective Bargaining and the Arbitration', *Wisconsin Law Review*, (18) 3: pp. 39–42
- Goldberg, S.B. (1982) 'The Mediation of Grievances under a Collective Bargaining Contract: An Alternative to Arbitration', *Northwestern University Law Review*, 270 (77): pp. 281–284
- Newman, P. (1994) 'Mediation-Arbitration (MedArb): Can it Work Legally?' *Arbitration*, 60 (3): pp. 174–176
- Spencer, J.M. and Zammit, J.P. (1976) 'Mediation-Arbitration: A Proposal for Private Resolution of Disputes between Divorced or Separated Parents', *Duke Law Journal*, 911: pp. 932–938

mediation

SEE ALSO **Alternative Dispute Resolution (ADR); authority; decision-making; ethics of mediation; the mediation process; the mediator; negotiation and principles of mediation**

Mediation is a form of intervention in which a non-aligned third party, *the mediator*, assists parties in *dispute* to negotiate over the issues that divide them. The mediator may have no stake in the dispute (other than its resolution) and should not be identified with any of the competing interests involved. The mediator has no power to impose a settlement on the parties who retain authority for making their own consensual joint decisions.

Fundamental to an understanding of mediation is an understanding of how mediation serves a *negotiation* process (Douglas, 1962; Gulliver, 1979):

> The most important point to remember when discussing mediation is that it is nothing more or less than a device for facilitating the negotiation process. Negotiations can and do occur without a mediator but mediation can never occur in the absence of negotiation. (Cormick, 1981)

Gulliver (1977) has described the negotiation process realized through mediation as the gradual creation of order and of co-ordination between the parties. The mediator achieves this by orchestrating a process of communication, information exchange and learning in which the parties begin with a degree of assumed knowledge but also, both consciously and unconsciously, with a considerable degree of uncertainty and ignorance. That knowledge is tested, altered and refined in the interaction which proceeds, in overlapping phases, through progressive and orderly movement towards the possibility of settlement. By these means, a *dispute* is placed, gradually, in a context of increasing knowledge – about all the circumstances, pressures, feelings, attitudes, perceptions and needs that surround it – that leads to greater understanding, shifts of attitude, demands, preferences and expectations, and terminates in the mutually acceptable joint decision that ends the dispute. What propels the process is the basic contradiction between the parties' antagonism (the dispute itself) and their simultaneous need for joint action.

This delineation of *the mediation process* – its interconnected developmental and cyclical processes – follows the stages of the negotiation process:

> Thus, one might say, the wheels [of cyclical communication exchange] turn and the vehicle moves [through the developmental phases]. (Gulliver, 1979, p. 83; brackets and their contents added)

This process has not only a *negotiation* logic but a psychological and social coherence too, in moving the parties from hostility, insecurity and anxiety towards a lessening of intense emotion and stress. Real-life negotiations are inevitably more complex and unpredictable than the analytically distinct processes outlined by Gulliver. But without conceptual clarity as to the nature of the process and its regular pattern of expectations, adjustments and behaviour, negotiations may be prolonged, damaged or fail. This is a process that has to be experienced by the parties themselves, as negotiators, participating in a dynamic exploration – of the issues in dispute, all the circumstances and themselves.

KEY TEXTS

- Gulliver, P.H. (1979) *Disputes and Negotiations: A Cross-Cultural Perspective* (New York: Academic Press), Chapter 7
- Roberts, S. (2008) 'Mediation', *The New Oxford Companion to Law* (Oxford: Oxford University Press)
- Stenelo, L-G. (1972) *Mediation in International Negotiations* (Malmö, Sweden: Nordens Boktryckeri)

the mediation process (includes communication and process)

SEE ALSO the mediator; models of mediation; negotiation; principles of mediation; strategies and styles of mediation

Empirical analyses of the process of mediation, across a range of cross-cultural, interdisciplinary studies, and fields of *mediation* practice, confirm its universally identifiable components (Stevens, 1963; Douglas, 1962; Stenelo, 1972; Gulliver, 1977, 1979). Two concepts are found to be fundamental to an understanding of mediation and the role of the mediator:

- Mediation serves a *negotiation* process;
- The role of the mediator is understandable only within an understanding of that process.

Whatever the differences – in the society or the culture, the historical period, the kind or complexity of the dispute, the length of time needed to reach a settlement, the strands of practice or the framework – the process of mediation itself generates a recognizable internal structure of its own, a 'succession of stages' that are common to all negotiations, even though two instances are not the same (Stevens, 1963, p. 10).

The mediation process, in effecting the successful realization of the negotiation process, achieves the gradual creation of order and of co-ordination between the parties (Gulliver, 1977). Research data establishes the 'one conclusion' that exemplifies this process – that 'movement, orderly and progressive in nature, stands out as a staid property ... which terminates in agreement' (Douglas, 1957, p. 70).

When a disagreement in a relationship cannot or will not be tolerated further, it can be precipitated into a *dispute*. One or both parties may then seek to engage the involvement of others and the issue then enters the public, or semi-public, domain.

The parties begin with a degree of assumed knowledge but also, both consciously and unconsciously, with a considerable degree of uncertainty and ignorance. It is the task of the mediator to structure and orchestrate a process that will allow that knowledge to be tested, altered, enlarged and refined in exchanges between the parties. These exchanges proceed through a series of 'overlapping phases' by means of which progressive and orderly movement towards settlement becomes possible.

There are two interlocking processes at work at the same time – the cyclical process and developmental process – which together constitute the process of mediation:

> In negotiation there are two distinct though interconnected processes going on simultaneously: a repetitive cyclical one and a developmental one. A simple analogy is a moving automobile. There is the cyclical turning of the wheels....that enables the vehicle to move and there is the actual movement of the vehicle from one place to another. (Gulliver, 1979, p. 82)

While these two processes of negotiation are integrated simultaneously, there is a logic in discussing the cyclical process first – 'thus one might say the wheels turn and the vehicle moves' (Gulliver, 1979, p. 83). The information exchanges between the parties result in more than mere communication exchange, as cognition and learning follow. Shifts may be induced – of attitude, demands, preferences and expectations:

> Thus there is and has to be exchange of information or more accurately of messages. Strictly speaking, information is not exchanged but *shared* since the giver himself retains that which is given, in contrast with economic exchange of goods. A party must respond and wishes to respond to the receipt of message by giving his own in return. As in other kinds of social reciprocity, a party offers messages in order to obtain a response and to be able to claim a response, or at least some kind of reaction that carries a message. Refusal to exchange messages may, in the short run, draw further messages from the opponent and may be intended to do so. Continued refusal – or what is effectively the same thing, mere repetition of previous messages – leads to impasse and the possible breakdown of negotiations.
> (Gulliver, 1979, pp. 84–85, emphasis added)

This cyclical process of negotiation enables the parties to move through a staged process, the developmental process of negotiation. This follows closely the model of six overlapping phases identified by Gulliver (1979):

1. **Searching for an arena:** This stage incorporates the personal, geographic, cultural and social aspects of participation; a calm, safe, neutral forum free of stigma, coercion and confusion with other interventions; and the setting-in-place of the

requirements necessary to enable the parties to communicate with one another in a way not possible on their own (establishing ground rules, for example).

2. **Defining the agenda:** Issues capable of being negotiated need to be distinguished from those that, however significant and powerful (such as fault, facts, values and the past), cannot be negotiated over.

3. **Exploring the field:** This is the phase, characterized by 'vivid monologues', when typically the parties explore 'the dimensions of the field' and when extreme assertions and maximal demands are made. This is when conflict and animosity are most likely to be expressed and when the distance between the parties will be greatest – a distance necessary if movement towards its narrowing is to be perceived.

4. **Narrowing differences:** It is only once 'the outer limits of the range within which the parties must do business' are explored, when the possibilities of difference have been exhausted, that there will be no alternative but to move towards the consideration of common interests and the possibility of consensus (Douglas, 1957, p. 73). The progressive shift in orientation from difference and hostility towards co-ordination, even co-operation, may be accomplished by the mediator resorting to different strategies – by addressing issues separately, by dealing with the less difficult issues first, etc.

5. **Bargaining:** This is when the pooling of losses or the splitting of differences takes place as a 'mopping up' operation. Bargaining can take place on those items that have been the most difficult to resolve, though they may not be the most important objectively. Parties are not likely to begin to engage in bargaining until they have reached agreement on the crucial negotiation issues (Douglas, 1962).

6. **Ritualizing the outcome:** If all goes well and agreement is reached, there is usually a ritualization of that agreement. This means that the outcome is marked in some way, according to culture – the shaking of hands, the breaking of bread, the drawing up and signing of a document, etc.

The negotiations have been concluded and there may a good deal of amity. On the other hand, a persisting antagonism

and a number of disagreements may remain; the parties
may be bitter rivals still. For the moment, however, there is
agreement, whether limited or broad, and a mutuality in the
achievement of an outcome. (Gulliver, 1979, p. 169)

The stages of mediation necessarily follow the stages of the negotiation process. These phases have a psychological and social as well as
a logical coherence. For example, at an early stage, when the parties
are furthest apart in every sense, anxiety and antagonism will be
greatest. With the articulation of difference, the exchange of information and the improvement of understanding, stress diminishes.
Yet this difference is necessary if subsequent movement is to be
apparent.

The two most significant tasks of the mediator are:

1. to ensure the progress of successive stages through the process,
   in particular, managing the difficult transitions between stages,
   and;
2. to promote the effective facilitation of communication
   throughout, as the main engine of change.

Change is therefore intrinsic to this process which the parties must
experience themselves as negotiators, participating in the dynamic
process of exploration and learning – what has been called 'the
exploratory interaction' and 'the search process' (Gulliver, 1979;
Stenelo, 1972). What propels this whole process is the basic contradiction between the parties' antagonism (that is, the dispute itself)
and their simultaneous need for joint action.

This is a model of the process of mediation that is empirically
grounded and provides conceptual clarity, of particular value in
circumstances of conflict and dispute. When turmoil, uncertainty,
unpredictability and turbulence are normal and the dynamic reality
is one of complexity and variability, both of content and context, this
is a process that both reflects and offsets that 'messiness of reality'
(Gulliver, 1979, p. 118).

KEY TEXTS
- Douglas, A. (1962) *Industrial Peacemaking* (New York: Columbia
  University Press)

- Gulliver, P.H. (1977) 'On Mediators' in I. Hamnett (ed), *Social Anthropology and Law* (London: Academic Press)
- Gulliver, P.H. (1979) *Disputes and Negotiations: A Cross-Cultural Perspective* (New York: Academic Press), Chapter 7
- Stenelo, L-G. (1972) *Mediation in International Negotiations* (Malmö, Sweden: Nordens Boktryckeri)
- Stevens, C.M. (1963) *Strategy and Collective Bargaining Negotiation* (New York: McGraw Hill)

the mediator

SEE ALSO **aptitude; attributes; decision-making; ethics of mediation; the mediation process; negotiation; party control and principles of mediation**

Two core features distinguish the mediator's role across cultures – it is both a non-aligned and a non-determinative role in contrast both to the partisan role of the lawyer and the *decision-making* role of the judge or *arbitrator*.

It is well recognized that the presence of a third party qualitatively transforms an interaction and that, merely by being there, the relationship between the parties is altered. Yet this minimal numerical transformation of the dyad into the triad can also have radical, complex and paradoxical effects – intellectual, social and psychological. The 'third person' has always been present in the social world– as a family member, a neighbour, a member of the community or a religious leader – though not necessarily labelled as or acknowledged to be a mediator. In the context of *dispute resolution*, the third party acting as mediator transforms an interaction in another important respect, by embodying the principle of objectivity and reasonableness in party decision-making – 'the non-partisan tempers the passion of others' (Simmel, 1908b, p. 152).

The main functions of the mediator have been identified as catalyst and facilitator (Deutsch, 1973; Rubin and Brown, 1975; Gulliver, 1979; Pruitt, 1981; Stulberg, 1981). These represent the prototype of the disinterested intervener whose self-consciously limited role is confined to carrying responsibility for managing *process* in order that the parties are enabled to reach their own consensual decisions on the *substance* of the issues that divide them.

As catalyst, the mediator exerts influence in the following ways:

- by bringing about an interaction that would not have been possible otherwise;
- as a reminder that the issues in dispute are there to be confronted;
- by generating pressures towards co-ordination, even co-operation.

The mediator's main function as facilitator is to orchestrate the negotiation process between the parties and protect their right to be the architects of their own agreement. This incorporates the following functions:

- **as educator** – the mediator assists the parties to explain and inform by elucidating reasons, circumstances, meanings, constraints, etc. to enhance mutual understanding;
- **as translator** – the mediator conveys each party's proposals in a manner that ensures both maximum receptivity and vigilance to desired objectives;
- **as 'agent of reality'** – the mediator helps the parties to attend to the practicality and feasibility of proposals (Stulberg, 1981).

Catalogues of the *attributes* of the good mediator cite both personal qualities, including especially *aptitude* for mediation and patience, and qualifications, including knowledge of the substance of the issues in dispute (Stulberg, 1981; Raiffa, 1982; Roberts, 2008). What emerges is consensus about a combination of attributes – intellectual, moral and personal – that goes towards the making of a mediator.

One of the most essential attributes of a mediator is the ability to maintain an intermediate position of 'non-partisanship' between the disputants:

The mediator ... stands above contrasting interests and opinions and is actually not concerned with them, or if he is, equally concerned with both ... But the mediator must be subjectively interested in the persons or groups themselves who exemplify the contents of the quarrel ... It is the fusion of personal distance from the objective significance of the quarrel with personal interest in its subjective significance which characterizes the non-partisan position. This position is the more perfect, the more distinctly each of these two elements is developed and the more harmoniously, in its very differentiation, each cooperates with the other. (Simmel, 1908b, p. 149)

Impartiality may be protected in several ways – by explicit commitment; by giving due weight to each party's views and objectives; by not pronouncing on the merits of either party's position; by behaving, and being seen to behave, in an even-handed manner; and by adopting models of practice that protect against 'negative positioning' or other bias (Cobb and Rifkin, 1991).

Additional ethical responsibilities are carried by the mediator – to those not party to agreements but who are affected by them (such as children or grandparents in family disputes); to cultural needs and other requirements; and in practising with integrity and competence. This requires recognizing inherent tensions in the mediator role including its lofty and ambiguous demands and the objectively difficult circumstances in which negotiations typically occur (Kressel, 1985).

KEY TEXTS
- Gulliver, P.H. (1977) 'On Mediators' in I. Hamnett (ed), *Social Anthropology and Law* (London: Academic Press)
- Kolb, D.M. (ed) (1994) *When Talk Works: Profiles of Mediators* (San Francisco: Jossey Bass)
- Kolb, D.M. (1985) *The Mediators* (Cambridge, Massachusetts; London: The MIT Press)
- Simmel, G. (1908a) *The Sociology of Georg Simmel,* trans. K.H. Wolff (1955) (New York: Free Press)

medical mediation

SEE ALSO **conflict; decision-making; dispute resolution and mediation; disputes;**

Decision-making in the field of health care is a highly complex matter with decision-making authority shared among often multiple healthcare professionals and with multi-faceted implications for those involved – doctors, nurses and other medical staff, hospital employees, health authorities, not to mention the patient and their family. Every decision in health care, taken by those with responsibility, requires the integration of a volume of data – information, advice, perspectives and experience (Marcus and Roover, 2003). Decision-making in this context is correspondingly complex and has critical ramifications, including the risk of serious, even devastating, repercussions which may be life-threatening, disabling and painful and, at worst, involving loss of life.

Traditional approaches to resolving *conflict* in this arena of practice, relating to medical negligence claims in particular, have been those of litigation and *arbitration*. These aim to consider liability and award financial compensation following adversarial proceedings, with a focus on 'winning' rather than on the achievement of a workable, long-term solution acceptable to all the stakeholders. *Mediation*, emerging in this field as an alternative mode of resolving medical conflicts, has a different aim. Rather than blame, the objective is to engage in practical problem-solving by exploring options for the mutually acceptable resolution of *disputes* in respect of the patient–doctor relationship. It has been argued that the *principles of mediation*, founded on the core precepts of *voluntary participation, confidentiality,* a non-judgemental approach and an impartial third-party presence, accord with the values of contemporary medical ethics (Craig, 1996). The value of the mediation process in healthcare decision-making is affirmed as follows:

> The value of a communicative ethic is to find commonly agreed-upon ways of negotiating our differences when we fail to agree on binding principles or rules...in a shared discourse among persons who respect the position of others in the communication process itself. (Moody, 1988, 1992)

Concerns about both the way medical negligence claims have been managed traditionally as well as the increasing incidence of those claims have generated increasing support for mediation. Plaintiffs have experienced health authorities, trusts, solicitors and individual doctors involved, as being 'overly defensive' in their management of claims when what was wanted was more openness and the opportunity to understand what had happened, to have questions answered and to receive apologies (Mulcahy *et al.*, 2000, p. xiii). North American studies highlight too that where medical treatment results in an adverse outcome or where there has been error, patients and family members are primarily interested in:

- learning about what happened or what went wrong;
- receiving an acknowledgement or apology from those responsible, and
- seeking to ensure that lessons learned will prevent the recurrence of what has happened and improve patient safety for the future (Marcus and Roover, 2011).

The opportunity afforded by mediation for the confidential and direct exchanges that can lead to these kinds of remedies and outcomes, as well as financial settlement, are not available in adversarial modes of *dispute resolution* such as litigation and *adjudication*.

The subject matter of cases suitable for mediation cover disputes over a range of medical specialities. The findings of a mediation pilot in respect of medical negligence claims, reveal that half of the cases related to the speciality of obstetrics and gynaecology (Mulcahy *et al.*, 2000). Mediation can also be deployed to resolve disagreements, between patients and their families and health and social care professionals, over treatment approaches – for example, in the making of care decisions in neo-natal medicine. In these kinds of situations mediation can provide the opportunity for early stage discussion on rationales for medical and treatment decisions, and also for new treatment plans to be explained. Even in cases more suitable for formal dispute resolution (where a precedent is necessary on a matter of public interest, for example), mediation can assist in clarifying and narrowing the issues prior to adjudication.

Criteria have been identified for making the difficult and delicate decision as to whether mediation could be a suitable approach. In addition to the desire to set a precedent, there are cases that are clearly unsuitable for mediation – for example, where there is a lack of settlement potential, insufficient information on which to base negotiation or a high-value claim (Mulcahy *et al.*, 2000). Criteria of suitability include the following:

- where the costs (financial, personal, legal) of not resolving the dispute are high;

- where the consequences of the dispute becoming public would be negative for the health authority;
- where speedier resolution is necessary and/or desirable;
- where non-legal remedies such as explanations and apologies are being sought;
- where patients and their families want a greater involvement in case management and;
- where there is likely to be a long-term relationship with the healthcare providers (Mulcahy *et al.*, 2000; Marcus and Roover, 2003).

Two matters give rise to particular challenges in respect of the mediation of medical disputes. First, while the responsible doctor may not always be present, his/her direct participation in the mediation process can often be the critical turning point towards progress in the *negotiations*, enabling there to be personalized exchanges and explanations and for catharsis to be possible. Second, the power imbalances that characterize relationships in this context are profound and the sources of *power* complicated. These include formal institutional authority, medical expertise, professional and personal authority, control over information and resources, as well as procedural and financial sources of power. In addition, Health Authorities are not only 'repeat players' but are also almost always represented by lawyers in mediation. This can, paradoxically, be a cause for concern for the claimant rather than be viewed as a tactical advantage (Mulcahy *et al.*, 2000).

The legislative framework is strongly supportive of ADR initiatives in the arena of medical disputes. In 1998 a Pre-Action Protocol for the Resolution of Clinical Disputes was introduced under the Civil Procedure Rules 1998 promoting ADR initiatives. This endorsed the introduction of ADR schemes by the National Health Service. Judicial encouragement for mediation in this context is also strong as is exemplified, for example, in *Burne v. A* [2006 EWCA Civ 24] where Sedley LJ observed, in the first of three riders to the judgment allowing the appeal, that the case 'calls out for *alternative dispute resolution*. Both parties need to take stock of their position and to enter into mediation in the light of it. No further step should be taken in the remitted action until this has been done.'

As the vast majority of claims are abandoned or settled at relatively low cost early on in the litigation process, resort to mediation could be seen to have the potential to increase the costs of the settlement process (Mulcahy *et al.*, 2000). However, as Ward LJ observed in *Egan v. Motor Services (Bath) Limited* [2007 EWCA Civ 1002, para 52]: 'The cost of mediation would be paltry by comparison with the costs that would mount from the moment of the issue of the claim. In so many cases, and this is just another example of one, the best time to mediate is before the litigation begins. It is not a sign of weakness to suggest it. It is the hallmark of commonsense. Mediation is a perfectly proper adjunct to litigation'.

Research on the use of mediation in medical negligence disputes highlights that, notwithstanding the fact that the main parties come to mediation with different agendas, aims, values and motivations, 'there are considerable benefits to mediated settlements and plaintiffs in particular have much to gain'. Mediation is found, however, not to be suitable in all such cases and while mediation is certainly not a panacea for the problems of medical negligence litigation, '…it clearly has the potential to encourage more appropriate and effective resolution of disputes (Mulcahy *et al.*, 2000, p. xviii).

KEY TEXTS

- Marcus, L.J. with Dorn, B. and McNulty, E. (2011) *Renegotiating Health Care: Resolving Conflict to Build Collaboration*. 2nd edn (Sand Francisco: Jossey-Bass Publishers)
- Marcus, L.J. and Roover, J.E. (2003) 'Healing the Conflicts That Divide Us: Health Care and Mediation' in *AC Resolution*, Spring: pp. 17–19
- McVeagh, N. (2006) 'Mediation in Clinical Negligence Cases and NHS Complaints – A Way Forward?' www.restorativejustice.org.uk/Health_Sector/MediationJournalJune06
- Mulcahy, L. with Selwood, M., Summerfield, L. and Netten, A. (2000) *Mediating Medical Negligence Claims: An Option for the Future?* (University of London, London: The Stationery Office)
- Pre-Action Protocol for the Resolution of Clinical Disputes (1998) Department of Constitutional Affairs (London: Stationery Office) www.justice.gov.uk/civil/prorules.

models of mediation (includes shuttle mediation)

SEE ALSO the Bromley Model of family mediation; the mediation process; the mediator; principles of mediation and styles of mediation

It has been famously stated: 'For of mediation one is tempted to say that it is all process and no structure' (Fuller, 1972, p. 307). What this observation serves to highlight is the difference between the processes involved in *mediation* and those involved in *adjudication* – the latter characterized by formal procedures, institutional rules, and clearly demarcated roles and authority that make up the formalities of due process for dealing with *disputes*. No such institutional framework occurs in *negotiation* processes where the parties seek to sort their differences by voluntary exchanges. However certain structural changes are inevitable when a simple bilateral process is transformed by the arrival of a third party whose very presence imposes the rudiments of a structure on the encounter – who is to participate; where; for how long.

A model of mediation practice is identified by the structural features that frame the process. An effective model of mediation is one that best achieves the realization of a constructive and fair process and it can be argued that some structural features, rather than others, better promote the realization of good practice – for example, by ensuring that the order in which parties state their issues and concerns, and the ways in which they do so, do not mirror the adversarial mode and create the disadvantages of '*negative positioning*' (Cobb and Rifkin, 1991). This is avoided by structural safeguards, in the form of separate time with each party at each session, that are necessary too, for ensuring that continuing screening for *domestic abuse* in *family mediation* can take place.

There are a variety of structural arrangements or models that can be used in mediation to accommodate the specific requirements of a situation and no one model of practice fits all circumstances. Many variables, including the cultural, judicial and institutional context of practice, have a direct impact on determining possible structural arrangements. Nor does any single field of practice appear to be associated with a particular model of practice. In fact, it has been noted that major differences are more notable *within* the same context of practice (within the family and within the commercial contexts, for example) rather than *between* fields of practice (Roberts, 2007). It appears that working models of mediation tend to reflect the preferences of the individual mediator rather than any context-linked determinants (Roberts, 2007).

Examples of the variety of models of mediation in use are described below. The main distinction lies in whether all the parties are brought together at the mediation meeting or are located in separate rooms.

- **Pre-mediation/preparation or intake sessions:** Preferred practice is to devote separate time to each party in direct face-to-face meetings or by telephone, if this is not possible, prior to mediation. The purpose of pre-mediation intake is both to ensure suitability and safety for mediation and informed and voluntary engagement if it proceeds. It can have additional advantages, for example, generating a fresh attitude and positive thinking in respect of the dispute. Among commercial mediators, one main difference between them lies in the reliance which is placed on the need for advance comprehensive documentary preparation for mediation. If a separate intake session is not possible, time needs to be built in for these purposes at the beginning of mediation.
- **Plenary/joint meetings:** This involves the presence of all the disputants at the mediation meeting. Powerful arguments can be made in favour of mediation being conducted in the presence of all parties. Not only is direct communication, inter-party dialogue and an improved capacity for future *negotiation* more likely to be advanced, but the parties can experience directly for themselves, their own effort and achievement in reaching agreement – and so enjoy the fruits of the 'process' benefits that are unique to mediation.
- **Caucus/separate meetings/shuttle mediation:** These are variants of models of practice that involve the mediator meeting individually with one party or a subset of participants located in different rooms and acting as a conduit of negotiation between them – deployed routinely, for example, in international, commercial and labour mediation. [See caucus and models of mediation entries for more detail including advantages (for example, to limit expressed conflict); and disadvantages (for example, more difficult and time consuming) in this form of structural arrangement)].
- **Co-mediation:** This occurs when two mediators, ideally one male and one female, co-work together. This model has distinct

advantages where there are a number of parties, where there is high conflict or particularly difficult circumstances, or where complementary expertise may be needed, for example in *international child abduction* cases. Disadvantages also exist among which are the risks of gender bias (where the two mediators are of the same sex), where there are conflicting styles, approaches or assertions of authority, and where increased pressure could be exerted on the parties.

- **Eclectic models/combinations of any of the above:** Many mediators, whatever their field of practice, use a mix of models mostly involving a combination of plenary/joint with separate sessions or the caucus. In *international mediation* a plenary meeting can be held in parallel with workshops, study visits, fact-finding on the ground for 'reality' checking, bilateral exchanges with individual participants, and multi-layered discussions – all combined in a complex interplay of plenary, caucus and co-working models that best advance the often lengthy and complicated process of mediation. In environmental mediation unique models of practice can be constructed, in consultation with the parties, to take into account considerations of power, complexity and culture.

KEY TEXTS

- Cobb, S. and Rifkin, J. (1991) 'Practice and Paradox: Deconstructing Neutrality in Mediation', *Law and Social Inquiry*, 16 (1): pp. 35–62
- Menkel-Meadow, C. (ed) (1995) *Mediation Theory, Policy and Practice* (Dartmouth, Aldershot: Ashgate)
- Roberts, M. (2007) *Developing the Craft of Mediation: Reflections on Theory and Practice* (London: Jessica Kingsley Publishers), Chapter 8

n

negotiation

SEE ALSO Alternative Dispute Resolution (ADR); bargaining; conflict; decision-making; disputes; the mediation process and representative negotiations

Negotiation represents the primary, universal route to *decision-making* in the social world. The core features of negotiation are to be found in widely different contexts, ranging from the unself-conscious routines of everyday life to the formalized, set-piece exchanges of an international conference. These fundamental features remain constant whether the issue is non-contentious or a focus of extreme *conflict*. Thus negotiation, as a mode of decision-making, can span everyday interaction and the more complex, stressful exchanges encountered in the context of *dispute*, conflict or hostility.

The features of negotiation are revealed most clearly in simple, bilateral exchanges in which information flows in both directions, understanding is achieved and an outcome is reached. So negotiation involves communication, leading to consensual joint decision-making. It is a process over which the parties retain control; exchanges take place within a common universe of meaning; and these determine the outcome. This may be contrasted with both the *arbitration* and adjudicatory process in which *power* over the outcome lies with a third party. The absence of a third party decision-maker constitutes 'the fundamental characteristic of negotiation' (Gulliver, 1979, p. 3).

A number of identifiable conditions are necessary if negotiation is to take place. First, the parties must recognize that their conflict or disagreement is not readily resolvable. It may be that one party prefers the status quo to any other outcome in which case negotiations will not begin (Gulliver, 1979). However, where both parties consider that a negotiated outcome is preferable to the status quo, some medium of communication must be found that will allow messages to pass backwards and forwards between the parties; this may, but need not, involve finding a mutually acceptable forum. Second, the parties must formulate and successfully communicate to each other their goals, what they want to achieve in the exchange. Third, in the light of those mutually understood goals, the parties must identify and evaluate the options available to them. It will sometimes be the case that the greater understanding resulting from an exchange of information will reveal a convergence or compatibility of goals, resulting in an agreed outcome without any need for a shift of position. Otherwise, if an agreed outcome is to be achieved, this will involve an accommodation reached through further exchanges in which the respective bargaining endowments of each party may be brought to bear.

When two parties negotiate therefore, they engage in a problem-solving process in which they attempt to reach a joint decision on matters of common concern over which they may be in conflict, disagreement or dispute. The nature of the negotiation process is essentially a process of communication and learning through a series of exchanges of information. The process is not in itself either haphazard or chaotic. If it were, negotiations would be doomed to failure. Whatever the differences in the society, the kind or complexity of the dispute, the length of time needed to reach an accommodation, or the framework, the process itself generates an internal structure of its own, 'a succession of stages', that is common to all negotiations, even though no two instances are the same (Stevens, 1963, p. 10). This intrinsic structure emerges from and is shaped by the process of negotiation itself. It also manifests in the rules the parties themselves create, and the mutual understanding that is a product of the process. The process must be experienced by the parties themselves, as negotiators, participating in a dynamic process of exploration and learning, personally experiencing the 'search process' (Gulliver, 1979; Stenelo, 1972, p. 192).

An invaluable processual analysis of negotiation and its relationship to *mediation*, derived from empirical research in the sphere of labour relations in the USA and in dispute resolution processes in East Africa respectively, is described in the work of Stevens (1963) and of Gulliver (1977, 1979). Gulliver highlights two concepts that are fundamental to an understanding of mediation, its relationship to negotiation, and the role of the mediator:

- mediation serves a negotiation process;
- the role of the mediator is understandable only within an understanding of the negotiation process.

Gulliver (1977) has described the negotiation process realized through mediation as the gradual creation of order and of co-ordination between the parties.

KEY TEXTS
- Gulliver, P.H. (1979) *Disputes and Negotiations: A Cross-Cultural Perspective* (New York: Academic Press)
- Roberts, S. and Palmer, M. (2005) *Dispute Processes: ADR and the Primary Forms of Decision-Making* (Cambridge UK: CUP)
- Stevens, C.M. (1963) *Strategy and Collective Bargaining Negotiation* (New York: McGraw Hill)

neutrality

SEE ALSO **ethics of mediation; impartiality; principles of mediation and party control**

Neutrality has been used in the literature of *Alternative Dispute Resolution* (*ADR*) as an umbrella concept – for example, the terms 'third party neutral' or 'professional neutral' have been used to refer to the general non-aligned, non-partisan stance of the *mediator* or arbitrator. However more complex implications and applications of neutrality also emerge.

Maintaining an intermediate position between the disputants is considered to be one of the most essential attributes of the effective mediator. Yet this *impartiality* of the mediator has been distinguished from the separate concept of neutrality (McCrory, 1985). This is not just a terminological distinction. Assertions of neutrality by the mediator can bring their own problems for two main reasons – first accuracy (a mediator cannot claim neutrality as, inevitably, s/he has their own values, views and prejudices); and second, fairness and safety (claims to neutrality lay the mediator open to legitimate challenge and can even be dangerous in situations of serious inequality).

However there are some mediators who do assert that they are neutral in respect of the outcome of mediation, in comparison with others for whom that outcome must be fair and just. Cultural sensitivity notwithstanding, it would be unethical for a mediator to tolerate behaviour that is clearly unacceptable to one or both parties or that breaches their human rights or those of other third persons affected by the outcome. In such a case the mediator has a responsibility to end the mediation or seek expert guidance (see National Family Mediation (NFM) Cross Cultural Mediation Policy and Practice Guidelines, 1998, section 2).

In the context of *international mediation*, two different ideal types of mediatory intervention have been identified, each with specific characteristics and distinctive advantages (Princen, 1992). There are the 'principal' mediators who have clout and their own interests in the disputes such as Jimmy Carter mediating between Egypt and Israel at Camp David in 1977; and there are the 'neutral' mediators whose very lack of *power* and status affords opportunities for demonstrating their neutrality and building trust through direct interaction, such as those international mediators influenced by Quaker and Buddhist values or Christian pacifism. Princen (1992, p. 63) draws a distinction between impartiality, which refers to questions of *acceptability*, and neutrality, which applies to the *effect* of the intervention on the parties' interaction – 'this distinction appears more useful analytically than those that equate the two or that simply claim intermediaries *are* impartial and neutral or that the intermediaries are never impartial or neutral'.

The application of the concept of neutrality to the forum for mediation and its venue is not a complex matter. The location of mediation should be neutral – namely, free from any stigma, free from coercion (such as the coercive environment of the court) and free from confusion with other forms of intervention (such as legal or therapeutic interventions).

KEY TEXTS

- Cobb, S. and Rifkin, J. (1991) 'Practice and Paradox: Deconstructing Neutrality in Mediation', *Law and Social Enquiry*, 16 (1): pp. 35–62
- Princen, T. (1992) *Intermediaries in International Conflict* (Princeton, NJ: Princeton University Press)

O

the Ombudsman

SEE ALSO Alternative Dispute Resolution (ADR); arbitration; decision-making; dispute resolution and grievance resolution

The Ombudsman, Ombuds or Ombudsperson, are terms used to describe the role and function of an official, appointed by government, to resolve disputes arising from complaints made by citizens against public and private administration, in an informal and flexible manner. The Ombudsman fulfils an investigative and *umpiring* role that involves receiving, examining and deciding on complaints, largely of maladministration. The Ombudsman has a jurisdiction far broader than that of the courts (limited to addressing legal claims), which extends to such matters as incompetence, neglect, delay, inattention, mistakes and inequity.

The *dispute resolution* approach adopted by the Ombudsman is a hybrid one, incorporating several of the following processes – an inquisitorial approach to establishing facts; *negotiation*; *mediation*; *conciliation*; counselling; the making of recommendations; and the making of judgements. If the primary objective is to investigate complaints and make a judgment about maladministration, the secondary, but no less important objective is to enhance standards of governance and practice. The two main functions of the Ombudsman are therefore:

- the handling of individual grievances (once internal complaints procedures have been exhausted) as an alternative to going to court; and
- establishing benchmarks of good practice within the relevant sector of operation (Cranston, 2008).

The idea of the Ombudsman first originated in Scandinavia and New Zealand but the office has now evolved in different jurisdictions throughout the world. The first Parliamentary Ombudsman (now the Parliamentary and Health Service Ombudsman) in England, appointed by the Crown (on the recommendation of the Prime Minister) in 1967, has the remit of investigating matters of maladministration by public officials associated with central government. While complaints to the Parliamentary Ombudsman have to pass the 'MP filter' (i.e. referrals must come via a Member of Parliament), and the Parliamentary Ombudsman is accountable to both Houses of Parliament, the Parliamentary Ombudsman remains independent of both the government and the Civil Service. The Ombudsman office has now proliferated in the UK to encompass both the public sector, such as local government, the National Health Service, and the police and probation, and the private sector, including legal services, housing, the media, pensions, conveyancing, insurance, and banking.

As members of the public can bring complaints to the relevant Ombudsman, usually at no cost and without the strict letter of the law having to apply, the office fulfils the larger aim of enhancing access to justice – 'delivering rapid, unlegalistic justice without cutting too many legal corners' (the words of a judge quoted by Cranston, 2008). The high volume of cases dealt with by Ombudmen (rarely involving oral hearings), far greater than the number of trials and small claims hearings in the courts, testifies to this accessibility (Cranston, 2008).

The British and Irish Ombudsman Association has identified four key criteria which have to be met if the Ombudsman is to be granted formal recognition. They are independence, effectiveness, fairness (according the principles of natural justice) and public accountability. The Ombudsman's powers of investigation are wide and equivalent to that of the High Court. However, the Ombudsman has no power to compel adherence of a public authority to his/her findings although in practice, public authorities will comply. In the exceptional situation where there is noncompliance, there is the power to publicize that fact. The remedies of the Ombudsman can include an apology and financial compensation for hardship, loss or injustice suffered. The publication by the Ombudsman of annual reports, which include information about anonymous investigations, promotes not only 'bargaining in the shadow of the Ombudsman', but also the dissemination of good practice guidance and input to government which can lead to the introduction of new law.

The Ombudsman is an officially appointed decision-maker, with an investigative responsibility to establish the facts of a complaint and the authority to make a judgment. In these respects the purpose and process of this intervention stand in sharp contrast to those of mediation.

KEY TEXTS

- Cranston, R. (2008) 'Ombudsmen' in P. Cane and J. Conaghan (eds), *The New Oxford Companion to Law* (Oxford: Oxford University Press)
- Harlow, C. and Rawlings, R. (1997) *Law and Administration*. 2nd edn (London: Butterworths)
- Verkuil, P.R. (1975) 'The Ombudsman and the Limits of the Adversary System', *Columbia Law Review*, 75: pp. 845–856
- Wiegand, S.A. (1996) 'A Just and Lasting Peace: Supplanting Mediation with the Ombuds Model', *Ohio State Journal on Dispute Resolution*, 1 (12): pp. 95–144

online mediation

SEE ALSO confidentiality; dispute resolution; models of mediation and professional regulation

Online mediation, like other processes of Online Dispute Resolution (ODR) such as *negotiation* and *arbitration*, is defined by its use of technology as the main vehicle for interaction and communication (Abdel Whahab, Katsh and Rainey, 2012).

Online mediation first arose as a means of addressing *conflicts* that arose online in auction transactions or other e-commerce, which both parties wanted resolved, and for which there was no other dispute resolution option. It was of two types, both suitable for the kind of 'one-off', commercial relationships involved – that of the 'de-personalised', automatic settlement of money claims by means of a computer programme; and what was termed 'content-based' online mediation which involved the use of email, instant messaging and other systems of communication with the parties, jointly or separately (Doyle, 2001).

The benefits of online dispute resolution, and online mediation in particular, especially in more expanded forms, have been widely recognized (Summers Raines, 2004, 2006; Ebner, 2012). Those commonly cited include, amongst others, enhanced flexibility and convenience, expertise and accessibility (including to a wider range of parties), accommodation of physical disabilities, the avoidance of face-to-face meetings where these would be problematic, reduced cost, time-investment and travel. Less well recognized or promoted are the green benefits, the environmental advantages of online dispute resolution – such as the elimination of carbon emissions resulting from travel; the reduction or elimination of paper use; the elimination of the need for office space; and energy savings (Ebner and Getz, 2012).

One of the few ODR service providers to assess its own environmental impact is the *Distance Mediation Project* (also known as the *Technology Assisted Family Mediation Project*) piloted between 2009 and 2010 in the remote, non-urban areas of British Columbia.

Online mediation also has recognized disadvantages. In the context of e-commerce, it operates in a competitive rather than a co-operative environment increasing the risk of secrecy amongst providers (Doyle, 2001). It cannot provide important and subtle knowledge conveyed directly via the face-to-face mediation experience, for example by body language, tone of voice and other cues of emotional communication. *Confidentiality* cannot be secured, adequately protected or policed.

Another well-documented scheme in Australia, is the Online Family Dispute Resolution (OFDR) (Relationships Australia OFDR Final Report, 2011). Building on its established national telephone mediation service, the OFDR project now provides an innovative technical solution (internet web conferencing) to enable mediation in family disputes to take place as an alternative to traditional face-to-face mediation where circumstances (such as distance and the expense and difficulty of travel) make this impossible. While face-to-face mediation is acknowledged by parties to be the preferred approach, a web-based camera service has been found to appeal more to parties than the more impersonal telephone mediation service. As well as user accessibility and usability, online security to protect confidentiality has been a key consideration in the setting up of this scheme. Research shows that this method is flexible enough to deliver online sessions with or without video conferencing and for various models of practice to be adopted where necessary – such as preliminary intake and screening for *suitability* for mediation; separate and joint sessions; co-mediation; *shuttle mediation*; and the use of translators, including for sign language (OFDR, 2011). Findings in respect of the cross-cultural implementation of online mediation for Aboriginal and Torres Strait Islander clients have proved positive following careful consultation and engagement with those communities (OFDR Report, 2011).

KEY TEXTS

- Abdel Wahad, M.S., Katsh, E., and Rainey, D. (eds) (2012) *ODR: Theory and Practice* (The Hague: Eleven International Publishing)
- Ebner, N. and Getz, C. (2012) 'ODR: The Next Green Giant', *Conflict Resolution Quarterly,* 29 (3): pp. 283–307
- Getz, C. (2010) 'Evaluation of the Distance Mediation Project: Report on Phase II of the Technology-Assisted Family Mediation Project', http://www.mediatebc.com/PDFs1–2-Mediation-Services/Distance-Mediation-Project-Evaluation-Report. aspx (accessed 28 July 2011).
- Relationships Australia (2011) 'Development and Evaluation of Online Family Dispute Resolution Capabilities.' Final Report. *Commonwealth of Australia (Attorney General's Department) and Relationships Australia (QLD)*
- Rule, C. and Friedberg, T. (2006) 'The Appropriate Role of Dispute Resolution in Building Trust Online', *Artificial Intelligence and Law,* 13 (2): pp. 193–205
- Summers Raines, S. (2006) 'Mediating in Your Pajamas: The Benefits and Challenges for ODR Practitioners', *Conflict Resolution Quarterly,* 22 (4): pp. 437–451

p

party control (includes autonomy and decision-making authority)

SEE ALSO authority; decision-making; mediation; the mediator; power and principles of mediation

What distinguishes mediation as a dispute resolution process, as well as constituting its chief benefit, is the location of *decision-making* authority. This lies with the parties themselves. The term 'party control' encapsulates this defining principle. Party control in mediation reflects understandings about competence. All fields of mediation practice place central importance on party control although terminological usage may vary – for example, 'party autonomy', 'empowerment', 'self-determination', 'responsibility' and 'party authority'. 'Autonomy' is a concept fraught with complexity and variability across a range of disciplines such as philosophy, sociology, economics, political science and psychology. *Party control* is therefore the preferred usage in the context of mediation generally because of its greater precision.

'Self-determination' too has problematic implications when adopted in mediation. As an ideal of social work practice, it may appear superficially to resemble the party control of mediation. However the client in social work is subject to the controlling authority vested in the social worker. While the client may be encouraged to participate in the solution to problems, it is the social worker who retains ultimate decision-making authority about 'essentials' (McDermott, 1975).

Party control is inseparable from the fundamental purpose of *mediation. The mediator* is there only with the permission of the parties. The authority of the mediator is derived therefore from a tacit understanding between the parties and the mediator based on their consent. To the extent that they are aware of their right *not* to participate if they so choose, the parties retain ultimate control. It is the central task of the mediator to ensure that by engaging voluntarily in the mediation process, the parties' participation is equal and fair and that they retain control both over the *content* of their communication and over the decision-making *outcome*. It is the task of the mediator to ensure too that the vital but limited mediator role of orchestrating and managing the *process* of mediation is not exceeded.

In *family mediation* an incompatibility may appear to exist between the principle of party control and the principle that informs the legal and ethical framework for decision-making over *children*. This is the principle that guides the court, namely, that the best interests of the child must be the first and paramount consideration (Children Act, 1989, section 1). Research findings that show that the basis of what is best for the child lies in agreement between parents (or between parents and social workers) resolve in practice these tensions of principle.

Competence is a basic premise of mediation. However vulnerable or desperate their situation, parties are presumed to be competent to make their own decisions, other than in exceptional circumstances (where there should be effective pre-mediation screening for unsuitability such as gross imbalances of *power*, illness, *domestic abuse*, etc.). A calm, safe and neutral forum and the implicit expectations of mediation – reasonableness, mutual respect, reciprocity and adult behaviour – are of most value precisely because circumstances may bring out the worst in people. Mediation can therefore provide the means by which party control may be retained, restored or enhanced.

If party control defines the purpose of mediation, it also reflects its core ethic, that of *respect* – for the inherent dignity, equality and privacy of each party, for their autonomy, for their capacity to participate in the process (whatever the difficulties and pressures), for their own meanings, and for their right to be the architects of their own agreements. The connection between equality, autonomy and respect is distilled below in a way that is of singular relevance for mediation:

Rather than equality of understanding, autonomy means accepting in others what one does not understand about them. In so doing, the fact of their autonomy is treated as equal to your own. The grant of autonomy dignifies the weak or the outsider; to make this grant to others in turn strengthens one's own character. (Sennett, 2003, p. 262)

The ethic of respect that underpins party control, interlocks not only with other principles of mediation but also with central aspects of practice, the quality of the outcome, its *fairness* or justness, in particular.

KEY TEXTS

- Davis, A.M. (1984) 'Comment' in *A Study of Barriers to the Use of Alternative Methods of Dispute Resolution* (Vermont Law School Dispute Resolution Project, South Royalton, VT: VLSDRP)
- Gulliver, P.H. (1979) *Disputes and Negotiations: A Cross-Cultural Perspective* (New York: Academic Press), Chapter 7
- Kressel, K. and Pruitt, D.G. (1985) 'Themes in the Mediation of Social Conflict', *Journal of Social Issues*, 41 (2): pp. 179–198
- Lukes, S. (1973) *Individualism* (Oxford: Basil Blackwell)
- Lukes, S. (1974) *Power: A Radical View* (Basingstoke: Macmillan Education)
- Sennett, R. (2003) *Respect: The Formation of Character in an Age of Inequality* (London: Penguin/Allen Lane)

power

SEE ALSO **bargaining power; fairness; party control and principles of mediation**

Power, as a force for coercion and domination – in the simple (Weberian) sense of the capacity of one to make another do something they would not otherwise have done – is of relevance with respect to all *dispute resolution* processes. Neither bilateral lawyer negotiations nor *adjudication*, for example, avoids the problem of power differentials. Notwithstanding the ideal of equality of formal justice before the law, exploitation of the weaker party by the stronger party is recognized to be endemic in the civil justice system (Woolf, 1995). New inequalities may be created depending on the parties' resources of power (wealth, status, legal endowments, etc) or sources of relative weakness (lack of access to legal aid, unequal social and economic opportunity, etc.) (Auerbach, 1983; Ingleby, 1992; Mather *et al.*, 1995)

Power is an essential feature too of *negotiation*. Three factors are recognized to affect the processual dynamics of mediation (Gulliver, 1979):

1. the parties' use of the resources available to them and the type and scale of the disparities that result from the unequal distribution of those resources;
2. the mediator's potential to exceed their legitimate authority by influencing or manipulating the course of negotiations as well as the substantive issues in discussion, with the result that unacceptable pressures can be put upon one or both of the parties who then act, or fail to act, in ways they would not otherwise have done; and
3. the impact of the macro-social context – 'the impingement of the outside world' – on negotiations which do not occur in a social or cultural vacuum and are affected, however diversely and diffusely, by prevailing norms, rules and standards as well as by the external pressures on parties in mediation from those who are non-participants (Gulliver, 1979, p. 187).

Furthermore where mediation is mandated, compulsion officially privileges one party (the willing party) and creates new vulnerabilities (for the unwilling party) and therefore new imbalances in *power* (Ingleby, 1993).

It is recognized that there is no precise definition of *bargaining power* nor any simple construction of the issue of power inequality, just as there is no single truth about relationships, rather a 'repertory of truths' (Lukes, 1974; Seidenberg, 1973, 1997). Much more needs to be known too about the actual operation and significance of power in the negotiations that take place in mediation (Gulliver, 1979). Yet while its operational significance is undeniable, power is difficult to pin down in the way it affects the parties' negotiating behaviour.

Gulliver distinguishes between potential power and persuasive strength, highlighting the complexity and unpredictability inherent in the dynamics of the actual interaction, and the danger of assuming an inevitable conversion of potential power into effective persuasive strength:

Negotiations are the interplay of relative strengths as they
work, through both antagonism and co-ordination, toward an
outcome. (Gulliver, 1979, p. 206)

An early feminist critique, unsubstantiated by empirical findings, raised serious concerns that *family mediation* could damage women's interests. Women, it was asserted, inevitably faced their former male partners as unequals. Intrinsic gender power inequalities in the family, it was argued, would be concealed because family *disputes*, instead of emerging in the 'public sphere of formal justice', became 'privatized' in mediation (Bottomley, 1985, p. 180). Consensus could mask and therefore perpetuate the conflict that characterized the *power* inequalities of relationships within families. Prevailing findings confirm the view that this critique oversimplifies the complex, multi-faceted and inter-dependent nature of the circumstances, issues and disputes associated with family conflict. As a process, mediation is not inherently good or bad for women, or for men. What is decisive is the skill and competence of *the mediator* (Menkel-Meadow, 1985; Roberts, 1996; Kelly, 2004; Walker, 2012).

Good practice of mediation is based on the assumption that there must be relative equality of bargaining power between the parties. Where differences are so great that unfairness would result or where cultural or other considerations would deny a party the capacity to negotiate in their own right at all, mediation ceases to be suitable. The less equal the relative power of the parties, the greater the ethical responsibility of the mediator (Cormick, 1982). The central dilemma for the mediator – of how to settle without the power to do so – is an inherent tension characterizing the mediator role (Silbey and Merry, 1986). This requires constant vigilance on the part of the mediator in order to monitor the subtle forms of power actually at play influencing interventions and interactions.

KEY TEXTS

- Auerbach, J.S. (1983) *Justice without Law?* (New York: Oxford University Press)
- Lukes, S. (1974) *Power: A Radical View* (Basingstoke: Macmillan Education)
- Seidenberg, R. (1973) *Marriage between Equals: Studies from Life and Literature* (New York: Doubleday Anchor Press)
- Weber, M. ([1917] 1978) *Economy and Society,* in G. Roth and C. Wittich (eds), E. Fischoff *et al.* (trans) (New York: Bedminster Press)

principles of mediation (includes procedural flexibility and voluntary participation)

SEE ALSO confidentialty; ethics of mediation; fairness; impartiality and mediation

The task of *mediation* is itself defined in terms of its core principles. These principles of mediation – ethical and professional – go beyond the endeavour of acting properly and competently. These principles additionally inform the panoply of mediation safeguards – procedural, structural and professional – that are designed to ensure the realization of a safe and fair process and outcome.

The essential principles of mediation interconnect not only with one another but also with other central aspects of practice, such as the authority of the mediator and the quality of the outcome.

The fundamental principle of mediation is *respect* – for the parties, their issues and their expression, their universe of meanings, their feelings and perceptions, their time, and their capacity to make their own decisions (Davis, 1984). The patience of the mediator is a core attribute recognized, across fields of practice, to be essential for advancing the objective of realizing in practice, the principle of respect (Roberts, 2007). The German concept of 'Balanzierte Wertschatzung' (a 'balanced respect') unites several core principles of mediation – respect, *impartiality* and a balanced and fair outcome.

Impartiality is another defining principle of mediation requiring the demonstration of even-handedness in relation both to the management of *negotiations* and to the objectives of the parties. The realization of this principle in practice is essential to the achievement of the trust that the parties must have in the mediator and in the process if the intervention is to be effective.

Voluntary participation in mediation is the third core principle that characterizes mediation. Notwithstanding manifold threats to voluntary participation (for example, pressures arising from overloaded courts and even from a minority in the mediation field itself), this principle is affirmed in all mediation codes of practice, European legal instruments, statute (in the labour field), and case law.

Confidentiality is another of the fundamental principles of mediation (McCrory, 1981). Subject to explicit exceptions (such as risk of harm or criminal activities), it is integral to the relationship between the mediator and the parties and is the cornerstone of trust that must exist for there to be the free and frank disclosure that is necessary if obstacles to settlement are to be overcome.

Finally, what distinguishes mediation, and constitutes its primary benefit, is what is termed '*party control*', namely, respect for the parties' own *decision-making* authority. The mediator is there only with the permission of or by invitation from the parties. To the extent that they are aware of their right not to participate if they so choose, the parties retain ultimate control. The authority of the mediator is therefore derived directly from this understanding, tacit or explicit, between the parties and the mediator.

The principles of mediation are integral, sustaining and reinforcing of one another. However, the complexity of circumstances, the intensity of *conflict*, the difficulties of the *dispute*, and the vulnerability of the parties, plus the inherent unpredictability of the mediation process itself, compound and complicate the challenge of realizing these principles in practice, thereby imposing an onerous responsibility on the mediator.

KEY TEXTS

- Davis, A.M. (1984) 'Comment' in *A Study of Barriers to the Use of Alternative Dispute Resolution* (Vermont Law School Dispute Resolution Project. South Royalton, VT: VLSDRP)
- McCrory, J.P. (1981) 'Environmental Mediation – Another Piece for the Puzzle', *Vermont Law Review*, 6 (1): pp. 49–84
- Sennett, R. (2003) *Respect: The Formation of Character in an Age of Inequality* (London: Penguin/Allen Lane)

privilege

SEE ALSO **confidentiality; mediation and principles of mediation**

Privilege refers to the protected status of confidential exchanges in relation to legal proceedings. As public policy has always favoured the settlement of *disputes* and the reduction of litigation to the minimum, the privilege of 'without prejudice' negotiation – that is, without prejudice to the legal rights of the maker of the statement – has long been a principle of English law. Disclosures, statements, offers of compromise, etc. made by the parties and their legal advisers in the course of negotiating settlements cannot be used in subsequent legal proceeding without the consent of both parties. The policy of the law has been in favour of enlarging the cloak under which negotiations may be conducted without prejudice and over the years it has been extended to cover new categories of cases including mediation in matrimonial cases where the purpose was to effect a reconciliation between the parties (for example, *Mole v. Mole*, 1950).

Mediation, occurring within a legal framework, relies largely on this head of privilege. Agreements are encouraged by the court which would not want either party to be disadvantaged by prior attempts to settle. The court is unlikely, therefore, to allow either party to make use of evidence derived from failed negotiations in mediation. The 'without prejudice' privilege is, however, subject to three limitations when applied to mediation (Cross and Tapper, 2007):

- the privilege belongs to the parties jointly, not to the mediator or the process. It can be waived therefore and the mediator compelled to testify;
- the cloak of the privilege does not cover statements that are not sufficiently related to the dispute that is the subject matter of mediation;
- a binding agreement that results from privileged negotiations is not itself privileged. It is important therefore that the status of a mediated agreement be clear to all concerned.

In respect of *family mediation*, from as early as 1971, Practice Directions issued by the Family Division of the High Court, recognized that both reconciliation and conciliation negotiations conducted by a court welfare officer should be legally privileged. English case law further clarified the legal position in relation to family mediation, establishing the privilege of exchanges relating to the resolution of disputes over *children* as an independent head of privilege (*Re D Minors*, 1993). This was based on the public interest in encouraging the settlement of issues concerning children, and in reducing the burden of the cost and delay of litigation. This Court of Appeal decision is, however, confined to the circumstances of the case and the privilege is subject to the same limitation as the 'without prejudice' head of privilege, namely, that the parties can waive their privilege and the mediator can be compelled to testify.

McCrory (1988) has argued for the removal of this limitation by the extension of privilege to matrimonial mediation on the basis of public interest immunity. This is founded on the principle that mediation serves an important public interest in promoting co-operative decision-making and the reduction of *conflict*, and that the privilege should attach, therefore, to the *mediation process* itself, immunity from disclosure being essential to the effectiveness of the process.

In Scotland, the privilege of exchanges that occur in family mediation is protected by statute (the Civil Evidence (Family Mediation) (Scotland) Act, 1995).

The European Mediation Directive 2008 (article 7) approved by the European Parliament in respect of civil and commercial matters in cross-border disputes, introduced provisions confirming confidentiality and privilege in mediation, a privilege enacted in relation to mediation for the first time in this context.

KEY TEXTS

- Allen, H. (2013) 'Confidentiality – A Guide for Mediators', *ADR Times* (London: CEDR)
- Cross, R. and Tapper, C. (2007) *On Evidence*. 11th edn (Oxford: Oxford University Press)
- McCrory, J.P. (1988) 'Confidentiality in Mediation of Matrimonial Disputes', *Modern Law Review*, 51 (4): pp. 442–466

professional regulation of mediation (includes standards)

SEE ALSO **family mediation; quality assurance; supervision and UK College of Family Mediators**

Because *mediation* is conducted privately and informally, necessarily without the safeguards of due process, the imperatives of professional regulation demand that the intervention be subject to standards of quality and accountability.

Whilst approaches to the nature and scope of regulation range across a spectrum of views, there is majority consensus, across fields of practice, in favour of a limited form of basic regulation in order to ensure that the quality of service provided be monitored and improved in the public interest. These accepted basics of professional regulation are training and accreditation, adherence to a code of practice, peer mentoring and support, and continuing professional development. There is strong consensus too that any regulation should be self-regulation by mediators themselves rather than imposed regulation by any external body.

However, also associated with the subject of professional regulation of mediation are serious, complicated and unresolved dilemmas of principle and of practice. These relate to the following aspects:

- the distinctive nature of mediation as a discrete and autonomous practice;
- whether mediation should be considered a separate profession at all;
- what are the qualities of the good mediator;
- what constitutes competent practice;
- whether or not practice should be subject to standards of quality and accountability;
- who should regulate mediators and have 'ethical control' in this multi-disciplinary field (Menkel-Meadow, 2001, p. 980).

Notwithstanding continuing debate about these questions, European directives on mediation clarify two important issues: first, the importance of separating the functions of standard-setting and accreditation from those of selection, training and the supply of mediation services in order to avoid any risk of a conflict of interest; and second, the recommendation of self-regulation over mandatory public instruments of regulation (Recommendation No. R 98 (1) 1998 on Family Mediation; EU Green Paper on ADR, 2002).

The differences that epitomize regulatory developments in the various fields of practice reflect their history, ethos and context. *Family mediation* in England and Wales, for example, is the only field of mediation practice to have in place a comprehensive and rigorous regulatory regime. The primary purpose behind the introduction of regulatory standards for family mediators has been the need to protect the public, given the special vulnerability of the parties and their *children* undergoing family breakdown. In addition, the advent in 1996 of public funding, in the form of legal aid, for family mediation brought with it, for the first time, the imposition of external regulation by government – for example, stringent quality assurance standards in the form of statutory requirements in relation to compliance with a code of practice; procedures for the consultation of children and for screening for domestic abuse; and rigorous quality assurance standards relating both to the competence assessment of practitioners, and to audits of standards of training and service provision and delivery (Legal Services Commission, *Quality Mark Standards for Mediation,* 2002).

At the same time a single professional body, the *UK College of Family Mediators* was established with government support, with the primary objective of setting and monitoring standards of training and practice. The establishment of the UK College of Family Mediators marked the formal arrival in the UK of family mediation as a new profession as the three hallmarks characterizing the achievement of professional status were now officially in place – namely, a recognized and distinct body of knowledge; mechanisms for the transmission of that body of knowledge; and mechanisms for self-regulation, evaluation and accountability (for example, disciplinary and complaints procedures). In confining its functions only to standard setting and monitoring (for practitioners and training), leaving the provision of training and service delivery to other, provider, bodies, the UK College secured the vital separation of functions necessary to prevent the recognized risk of conflicts of function and interest (European Recommendation No R (98) 1 on Family Mediation). However, the powerful family mediation training and service provider bodies, reluctant to submit to independent audit by the UK College and fearful of financial loss in losing membership to the College, broke away from the UK College and established their own Family Mediation Council (FMC). This body removed itself from any independent regulation and, notwithstanding conflicts of interest, delegated the overseeing of standards of member bodies to those bodies themselves (FMC Constitution, 4.4, 2007). This state of affairs has now been recognized officially as insufficient to protect the public. The FMC is currently required to re-establish those very institutional safeguards that it chose to discard in leaving the UK College (Family Justice Review Final Report, 2011; McEldowney Report, 2012).

Government, mindful of the urgent need for the quality assured provision of family mediation in the light of its enhanced role in family dispute resolution, and impatient with divisiveness within the profession, has threatened the imposition of external regulation unless there is rapid progress (Family Justice Review Final Report, 2011).

The UK College of Family Mediators, renamed the College of Mediators to reflect its wider field of membership, remains, institutionally, the sole professional mediator membership body in the country with an exclusive regulatory function.

Tensions can be found too in the civil and commercial mediation field whose representative body, the Civil Mediation Council, is a forum for exchange, education and promotion of mediation, rather than a regulatory body. One central anxiety for commercial mediators (most of whom are qualified lawyers) about regulation is their focus on the danger of lawyer monopolization of the field as a consequence of the professionalization project – a curious paradox.

The problematic nature of external funding and regulation has not been confined to the government funding of family mediation. Similar pressures, for example, to demonstrate competence and to measure and achieve outcome success come from external donors who fund those working as international mediators. Here, where the unique circumstances of practice (painstaking and long-term, often 'behind the scenes'; working in teams, etc.) impose unique constraints, the problem of practicability in respect of regulation and its implementation is acute. Reliance on personal reputation and first-hand experience of an individual's professional and personal *attributes* is therefore the preferred means of assessing quality and competence in this field.

On the other hand, regulation is problematic for different reasons for community mediators who, on the whole, resist 'professionalisation' in principle on the grounds that it brings control of entry into a field, the defining ethos of which is one of grass-roots, volunteer, lay and community empowerment.

These concerns highlight the most powerful of questions about the nature of mediation itself – whether it is an ancient craft accessible to all with aptitude and ability, or a discrete professional discipline with its own hallmarks. Notwithstanding some quality assurance progress, hazards continue to exist both in the proliferation of commercial training of mediators regardless of demand, and in unregulated practice.

KEY TEXTS

- Council of Europe (1998) European Recommendation No R (98) 1 on Family Mediation.
- National Organisation for Training and Standards Setting in Advice, Advocacy, Counselling, Guidance, Mediation and Psychotherapy (CAMPAG) (October 1998) *Mediation Standards* (London: CAMPAG)
- Ogus, A. (1998) 'Re-thinking Self-Regulation' in R. Baldwin, C. Scott and C. Hood (eds), *A Reader in Regulation* (Oxford: Oxford University Press)
- Legal Services Commission (2002) *Quality Mark Standard for Mediation,* December (London: Community Legal Service)
- Roberts, M. (2005) 'Family Mediation: The Development of the Regulatory Framework in the United Kingdom', *Conflict Resolution Quarterly,* 22 (4): pp. 509–526
- Roberts, M. (2005, republished 2012) 'Family Mediation: The Development of the Regulatory Framework in the United Kingdom' in C. Menkel-Meadow (ed), *Foundations of Dispute Resolution,* Vol. 1 (Aldershot, Hants: Ashgate Publishing Ltd)
- Society of Professionals in Dispute Resolution (SPIDR) (1989) 'Report of the SPIDR Commission on Qualifications, 1989. Ensuring Competence and Quality in Dispute Resolution Practice.' (Report No. 2) (Washington, DC: SPIDR Commission on Qualifications, 1995)

q

quality assurance (includes standards)

SEE ALSO ethics of mediation; professional regulation; supervision and UK College of Family Mediators

Mediation has been no different from other professional activities in having had to meet the demands of the 'new accountability' that has characterized government trends toward quality assurance over the past decade, particularly *family mediation* where public funding as been available since 1996 (O'Neill, 2002).

Quality assurance is composed of three main components (Power, 1994):

- **quality control**, consisting of mechanisms within an organization for maintaining and enhancing quality of provision;
- **quality audit**, consisting of the external scrutiny of quality control mechanisms and processes in place to support quality, and their monitoring against stated objectives; and
- **quality assessment**, consisting of the external review and judgment about the quality of provision.

Quality control has long been practised by mediation providers and has taken different forms and implemented to different degrees. These include selection procedures for determining aptitude of mediators; accreditation of practitioners on the basis of experience and competence; peer mentoring and consultancy; continuing professional development; and, perhaps unique to family mediation, requirements for supervised practice (also termed professional practice consultancy).

'Audits are needed when accountability can no longer be sustained by informal relations of trust alone but must be formalised, made visible and subject to independent validation' (Power, 1994, p. 11).

The audit requires that performance be defined in terms of quantifiable effectiveness, namely Value For Money (VFM). Values of service, care and quality are displaced by rule-setting and the requirements of detailed adherence to procedures, record-keeping and protocols. The problematic implications of the 'audit explosion' – transporting the audit approach from its original financial context to non-financial processes – are exemplified in its application to *mediation* where important indices of effectiveness (for example, the personal attributes of the mediator) and success (the 'process' benefits of reduced conflict and stress, improved communication, and enhanced capacity of the parties to negotiate together in the future) are more elusive and not easily quantifiable for purposes of measuring cost-effectiveness.

In the UK, a focus on assessment has informed standard-setting initiatives. This is manifest not only across different fields of *alternative dispute resolution* (*ADR*) but also across the formal justice system, for example, family, civil and criminal (see standards for the Bar Standards Board, the Solicitors' Regulatory Authority and ILEX Professional Standards, 2010). What unites these diverse initiatives is their common competence-based approach to assessment, an approach in line with that in the USA. This involves an identification of mediator practice competencies based on empirical evidence of what mediators *actually* do rather than on what they *say* they do (see SPIDR, 1995; Della Noce, 2009). Defining quality standards in terms of performance-based practice competency may be contrasted with another North American approach which claims to evaluate mediation practice from a transformative perspective. Here the intended *purpose* of the intervention is what is decisive for assessment purposes – 'the actual activities of the mediator as less important than the reason for engaging in the activity' (Antes and Saul, 2001, p. 314).

Official consensus that national standards of quality should define good practice of mediation (Council of Europe Recommendation No R (98)1, 1998 on Family Mediation; Legal Services Commission Quality Mark Standard for Mediation, 2002) has resulted in two linked initiatives with respect to the development of standards relating to the major fields of mediation practice namely community, commercial, family, industrial and environment. First, in the 1990s, all these fields participated in a government-sponsored project to devise generic standards for mediation plus a specific 'evidence route' to apply the particular knowledge and skill requirements to each field. This resulted in an agreed common, performance-based mediation standard upon which a mediation qualification is based (CAMPAG Standards in Mediation, 1998). These standards inform both the government-supported competence assessment method for all mediators doing publicly funded work and the Quality Mark Standard for Mediation 2002 (the official kite – mark available for all services providing privately funded and publicly funded family and community mediation).

Also in the 1990s, mediators from different fields joined the Joint Mediation Forum (JMF) to work together to promote mediation, to exchange ideas, to lobby government, and to establish and maintain high standards of training and service provision including a common code of practice – the Model Code of Conduct covering the role of the mediator, the conduct of mediation and mediator standards (Richbell, 1999). Its more ambitious objective, the achievement of an over-arching, umbrella organization, kite-marking standards of competency for the emerging profession of mediators, met with such serious opposition from mediation providers fearing backdoor regulation that the JMF itself was fatally undermined.

The tensions that beset the JMF (for example, the conflict between the commercial interests of provider bodies and high standard-setting; risks of lawyer domination of mediation, etc.) resonate in contemporary efforts to ensure an effective quality assurance regime for mediation practice. In the private sector and in the court, mediation can be conducted without recognized mediation training or qualifications of any kind, and without adhering to a code of practice. Only publicly funded family mediation provision currently meets stringent quality assured standards. Yet external funding, while addressing demands for accountability and consistency and uniformity of high standards, is not unproblematic, bringing with it concerns about the risks of loss of professional autonomy, flexibility and creativity.

KEY TEXTS
- Council of Europe (2004) 'Directive of the European Parliament and of the Council: COM (2004) 718 Final' (Strasbourg, France: Council of Europe)

- Legal Services Commission (2002) *Quality Mark Standard for Mediation* (London: Community Legal Service)
- National Institute for Dispute Resolution (NIDR) (1993) 'Interim Guidelines for Selecting Mediators' (Washington, D.C.: NIDR)
- Power, M. (1994) *The Audit Explosion* (London: Demos)
- Society of Professionals in Dispute Resolution (SPIDR) Commission (1995) *Report of The SPIDR Commission on Qualifications, 1989, Ensuring Competence and Quality in Dispute Resolution Practice* (Report no.2) (Washington DC: SPIDR Commission on Qualifications)

r

representative negotiations (includes lawyer negotiation and litigation)

SEE ALSO adudication; dispute resolution; law and negotiations

The three main functions of lawyers are advice-giving, *advocacy* and *negotiation* and it is negotiation that occupies most of lawyers' time, solicitors in particular, when they are involved in *dispute resolution*. Representative negotiations refer to the bi-lateral or multi-lateral exchanges between legal professionals themselves, acting as partisan champions on behalf of their clients with a view to reaching a compromise and the settlement of the issues in dispute. The parties are not present and do not participate directly, having delegated the conduct of negotiations to these representatives. Because negotiations between lawyers cover both intra-party and inter-party exchanges, they are necessarily complex. Lawyer representatives seek to manage this complexity by maintaining full control over the negotiation, its substance, pace, and tone – transforming the dispute into legal discourse and discouraging direct communication between the parties in the process.

Representative negotiations by lawyers, with the exception of those occurring within the practice of *collaborative law*, are distinctive because they occur within the framework of the litigation process, even those under Pre-Action/Application Protocols taking place as an early stage in the path towards adjudication. The prospect of a trial, with its win/lose outcome, inevitably exerts a powerful influence on the progress and shape of representative negotiations (Roberts and Palmer, 2005). Even where an environment of legal settlement-seeking prevails, 'the shadow of the law' (the likely outcome of a judicial determination, in particular) is cast over negotiations (Mnookin and Kornhauser, 1979). Family solicitors in England who are members of *Resolution* subscribe to a code of practice which reflects an awareness of the impact that lawyers can have on relations between their clients and recognizes the need for solicitors to adopt conciliatory and settlement-seeking approaches in the interests of all the parties, including their children. This constructive approach in dealing with family law matters has been incorporated in the Law Society's Family Law Protocol and endorsed by the courts.

So many variables affect the negotiating process conducted by lawyer representatives – the nature of the dispute, the parties, and the kind of practice and individual negotiating style of the lawyer – that it is difficult to generalize about this activity (Roberts and Palmer, 2005). Empirical research on lawyer negotiation is also limited, most studies being based on self-reports by lawyers (often self-serving) following completed negotiations. Observational studies of actual negotiations are rare. North American research on divorce negotiations has found these to be 'depressingly consistent' with negotiations in a variety of legal contexts (Menkel-Meadow, 1993, p. 369). Findings showed that lawyer representative negotiations reflected a desire not to bargain too hard and to settle cases quickly for the 'going rate'. This was the case especially where they were 'repeat players' with each other and sought to reach 'standardized solutions' with little evidence of problem-solving or focussing on the individual needs and interests of particular clients. Cases settled quickly with little 'negotiation intensity' or bargaining, of either a principled or unprincipled nature, as both sides tried 'to cut a quick deal' that was often 'fairer' to the lawyers' payment incentives than to particular clients (ibid., p. 371; see also Genn, 1987; Condlin, 1985).

Mediation must be distinguished from this form of intervention. Neither negotiations conducted by legal professionals on behalf of their clients, however conciliatory, nor 'collaborative law' negotiations can be compared with those negotiations that occur in mediation. In mediation it is the parties themselves who are the negotiators, engaging directly with one another in a communication process structured and managed by an impartial third-party intervener, *the mediator*. The mediator does not give advice, does not negotiate and does not make a determination.

KEY TEXTS
- Condlin, R. (1985) '"Cases on Both Sides": Patterns of Argument in Legal-Dispute Negotiation', *Maryland Law Review*, 44: pp. 65–136
- Genn, H. (1987) *Hard Bargaining: Out of Court Settlement in Personal Injury Actions* (Oxford: Clarendon Press)

RESEARCH

- Ingleby, R. (1992) *Solicitors and Divorce* (Oxford; Clarendon Press)
- Menkel-Meadow, C. (1993) 'Lawyer Negotiations: Theories and Realities – What We Learn from Mediation' in 'Dispute Resolution: Civil Justice and Its Alternatives', *Modern Law Review*, 56 (3) (Special Issue): pp. 361–379
- Mnookin, R.H. and Gibson, R.J. (1994) 'Disputing through Agents: Co-operation and Conflict between Lawyers in Litigation', *Columbia Law Review*, 94: p. 509
- Mnookin, R.H. and Kornhauser, L. (1979) 'Bargaining in the Shadow of the Law: The Case of Divorce', *Yale Law Journal*, 88: pp. 950–997

research

SEE ALSO **Alternative Dispute Resolution (ADR); informal justice; knowledge and theory**

The field of *alternative dispute resolution (ADR)*, and *mediation* in particular, is acknowledged to have been the subject of extensive research study since its modern emergence in the early 1980's. A large, cross-disciplinary body of literature, much of it North American, valuably informs understandings of the field drawing on the literature of anthropology, sociology, psychology, law and systems theory. Research findings encompass a range of perspectives and conclusions about, for example, the political implications of *informal justice*; *power, neutrality* and coercion; styles and *models of practice*; consumer views; and assessment of effectiveness.

Some commentary has been critical of contemporary mediation training programmes (for example, in being exclusively skills and technique-based and devoid of explicit theories of practice) and of practice (arising from concerns relating to *justice*, gender imbalances, claims to neutrality, etc.). As a result, the relationship between researchers and practitioners has been characterized as a problematic one, with interaction between researchers and practitioners limited and perceived to be threatening (Rifkin, 1994). In addition, research findings (empirical and theoretical) tend to refer to aspects of understanding actors' *and* observers' templates that are usually distinguished from the domain of 'practice'. Some researchers also dismiss as rhetoric, advanced to promote the expansion of an 'occupational jurisdiction', the value of what practitioners themselves contribute to their own knowledge base of policy and practice. This practitioner perspective is regarded as self-serving, to be contrasted with the objective 'social scientific analysis' of the field by social scientists (Dingwall and Greatbatch, 1993, p. 367).

An alternative perspective acknowledges a less oppositional experience in a field recognized to be 'experiential' and exemplifying the concepts and practices of the 'theories-in-use' approach (see Schon, 1983; Menkel-Meadow *et al.*, 2005). The significance of 'grounded theory' highlights too the recognition that good practice and the reflections of experienced practitioners constitute a rich resource for the development of the best models and theories (Jones, 2001, p. 133).

In the field of *family mediation*, early research conducted in the West, largely focussed on settlement rates, cost effectiveness, process benefits and client satisfaction, constitutes the largest body of empirical research of all the mediation fields (for example, Pearson and Thoennes, 1989; Walker *et al.*, 1994; Emery, 2001, 2005; Kelly, 2004). Acknowledged methodological and other difficulties (for example, variations in research populations, measures and dispute settings, and the proliferation of practice styles, models and approaches) have made generalized findings or reliance on single studies problematic. Notwithstanding, convergence has emerged on many questions over two decades of research, indicating the robustness of some major findings in this field of mediation. Such findings show, for example, success in mediation as a function both of the pre-existing characteristics of the dispute and the disputants, as well as the degree to which the disputants perceive the mediators to have accomplished the primary tasks of mediation; that settlement-seeking pressures negatively affect the experience of mediation and the quality of outcomes; that the less judicial control and coercion of the court there is, the better the outcome; and that addressing underlying tensions and obstacles to agreement in high conflict family disputes is more likely to achieve improved co-operation between parents and better outcomes for children. Above all, what is essential for success is the skill, knowledge and experience of the mediator (Thoennes and Pearson, 1985; Kelly, 2004; Trinder, 2006; Walker, 2012).

More particularly, developments in family mediation in the UK and in Europe demonstrate the value of the close collaboration of researchers and practitioners in joint working groups constructing a range of policies and practice guidelines including selection criteria and procedures for determining aptitude for mediation, domestic abuse, the role of children in mediation, cross cultural mediation, and international family mediation.

The impact of research findings on policy formation in the UK is complex but unclear, particularly in respect of the degree to which research actually informs policy decision-making – for example, in the fields of civil and family mediation where research has been concentrated (see Walker, 2000; Davis *et al.*, 2000; Walker *et al.*, 2004; Genn *et al.*, 2007).

KEY TEXTS

- Bondy, V. and Mulcahy, L. with Doyle, M. and Reid, V. (2009) 'Mediation and Judicial Review: An Empirical Research Study', *Public Law Project* (London: Nuffield Foundation)
- De Girolamo, D. (2013) *The Fugitive Identity of Mediation: Negotiations, Shift Changes and Allusionary Action* (London: Routledge)
- Emery, R.E. *et al.* (2001) 'Child Custody Mediation and Litigation: Custody, Contact and Co-Parenting Twelve Years after Initial Dispute Resolution', *Journal of Consulting and Clinical Psychology*, 59: pp. 410–418
- Kelly, J.B. (2004) 'Family Mediation Research: Is There Empirical Support for the Field?' *Conflict Resolution Quarterly*, 22: pp. 1–2, 3–35
- Menkel-Meadow, C. *et al.* (2005) *Dispute Resolution: Beyond the Adversarial Model* (New York: Aspen Publishers)
- Roberts, S. (2009) '"Listing Concentrates the Mind": The English Civil Court as an Arena for Structured Negotiation', *Oxford Journal of Legal Studies*, 29 (1): pp. 1–23

For information on recent research studies see: http.www.adrnow.org.uk

restorative justice (includes victim/offender mediation)

SEE ALSO community mediation; elder mediation; informal justice; justice and youth mediation

The aims of restorative justice may be contrasted with those associated with the old paradigm of retributive justice of the traditional criminal justice system, namely, crime defined as a violation of the state and an adversarial and punitive approach (Zehr, 1985). These different aims shift the focus explicitly from the offender and their need for punishment and rehabilitation to that of the victim of crime, and their material and emotional needs. Restorative justice seeks ideally therefore to restore the balance disturbed by crime and to make good, wherever possible, the social and individual harm caused to those concerned – the victim, their family, friends and the community. In this way restorative justice embodies the principle that crime is fundamentally against people not just against the state (Umbreit, 1995).

Mediation, applied in this context in a variety of hybrid manifestations, is termed *'Victim-Offender Mediation'* (*VOM*). It is deployed to further the broad objectives of restorative justice. By means of the process of mediator-facilitated communication, those most affected by the crime are given the opportunity to become actively involved with their offenders in order to bring home to them the 'human reality' of their victimization and to hold them personally accountable for their behaviour (Smith *et al.*, 1988, p. 137). VOM, both face-to-face and indirect, enables victims themselves to explore issues wider than those that can be raised in court in order to better understand what occurred as well as to secure compensation and reparation, both material and psychological. This approach may be contrasted with victims' usually negative experience of the criminal justice system associated with feelings of passivity, marginalization, powerlessness and vulnerability. For offenders, this process can provide the opportunity to take responsibility for their actions, to apologize for the harm they have caused and to make amends, whether by virtue of their participating in the process itself, and/or by voluntarily agreeing to carry out specific activities as a form of reparation. Restorative justice is incorporated in law in New Zealand, Australia and the USA and in criminal and civil legislation in the UK (for example, in the youth justice reforms incorporated in The Crime and Disorder Act, 1998).

In theory restorative justice aims to meet the needs of all those affected, seeking both to assist the victim's recovery and to re-integrate the offender into society. However, the characteristics and purposes of VOM (associated as they are with criminal policy goals), and the nature and derivation of its cases (offences, rather than *disputes*, derived from criminal justice agencies) have generated serious doubts distinct from those associated with the general critique of informal justice. Concerns highlight, for example, the tensions associated with the ambiguous location of VOM between the public and the private sphere, and the hazards arising from actual and potential conflicts of interest amongst those involved – the victim, the offender, and the public officials representing the interests of the state (such as probation officers).

These circumstances, including the timing of victim–offender mediation (whether taking place between conviction and sentence or after sentence) require that safeguards need to be in place for mediation to be effective and fair to those participating rather than serving criminal justice ends of restriction of access to the law (for victims) and diversion from custody (for certain offenders).

This is an area of practice where the mediator has to be carefully trained and highly skilled in order to orchestrate a difficult, complex and delicate process sensitively, within clear boundaries. This involves balancing competing objectives and interests and managing multiple responsibilities, in order to ensure a confidential and non-coercive environment for constructive exchange. Research shows, amongst a range of positive findings, that although the possibility of receiving restitution appears to motivate victims to enter the mediation process, following their participation they indicate that meeting the offenders and being able to talk about what happened was more satisfying than receiving restitution. Offenders involved in mediation indicated that although anxious about a confrontation with the victim, meeting the victim and being able to talk about what happened was the most satisfying aspect of the process (see Umbreit, 1995).

KEY TEXTS

- Bolitho, J., Bruce, J. and Mason, G. (2012) *Restorative Justice: Adults and Emerging Practice* (Sydney: Institute of Criminology Series)
- Braithwaite, J. (2002) *Restorative Justice and Responsive Regulation* (New York: Oxford University Press)
- Graef, R. (2001) *Why Restorative Justice? Repairing the Harm Caused by Crime* (Calouste Gulbenkian Foundation, UK)

- Rossner, M. (2011) 'Emotions and Interaction Ritual: A Micro Analysis of Restorative Justice', *British Journal of Criminology*, 51: pp. 95–119
- Umbreit, M.S. (1995) *Mediating Interpersonal Conflicts: A Pathway to Peace* (West Concord, Minnesota: CPI Publishing)
- Zehr, H. and Toews, B. (eds) (2004) *Critical Issues in Restorative Justice* (Monsey, NY: Criminal Justice Press)

S

Special Educational Needs (SEN) mediation (includes education mediation)

SEE ALSO community mediation; medical mediation and youth mediation

Mediation is formally recognized to have particular potential for addressing disagreements between parents, schools (staff and/or governing bodies) and local education authorities (LEA's) in respect of a child's special educational needs. Legislation in this field officially recommends consideration of mediation by requiring each local education authority to arrange for independent mediation to be available to parents of children with SEN with a view to avoiding or resolving any disagreement over the special educational provision for that child. The arrangements made by a LEA must provide for the appointment of independent persons with the function of facilitating the avoidance of such disagreements. Local authorities and the Special Educational Needs and Disability Tribunal (SEND) are required to inform parents of the availability of independent mediation as part of the SEN dispute resolution process. These requirements are applicable to all pupils with special educational needs, not just those with statements of SEN and provide for mediation to be used at any time during the SEN process and about any aspect of SEN provision (Education Act, 1996 s.332 B; DfES/581/2001 The Special Educational Needs Code of Practice para. 2.23; Special Educational Needs and Disability Act, 2001).

The primary aim of mediation in this context is to resolve disagreements in a way that enables relationships between all the parties involved – parents, school staff, the governing body, and the LEA – to be as constructive as possible (Huff, 2010). The core principles of mediation – *confidentiality, voluntary participation,* mediator *impartiality* and procedural flexibility – are protected. SEN mediation can play a positive role in the following ways:

- It can prevent conflict becoming entrenched and communication breaking down both by facilitating early confidential exchanges with all parties and by providing the opportunity for the parties to engage genuinely both in the discussion of their concerns and in the participation of their resolution.
- It can lead to improved understanding by the parents of the barriers that might be preventing the achievement of their desired outcome thereby improving 'the disagreement journey' for parents – for example, where the education authority cannot or is unable to negotiate on a particular key issue or when the desired outcome is not achievable (Tennant, *et al.*, 2008).
- In those circumstances too, mediation can generate the creation of alternative solutions or new outcomes acceptable to the parties.
- Mediation can avoid resort to Tribunal appeals by resolving disagreements beforehand. Mediation can be initiated at any stage, even after an appeal has been lodged and before the hearing date without prejudice to the right to appeal.
- Mediation can, at least, assist in clarifying issues prior to Tribunal hearings.
- It can assist too in the implementation of Tribunal decisions.
- Mediation can facilitate good case management by enhancing more informed participation.

It is not envisaged that the legal representation of parties in mediation will be helpful in the field of SEN mediation. This is perceived as being 'contrary to the spirit of informal disagreement resolution…. The purpose of disagreement resolution is not to apportion blame but to achieve a solution to a difference of view in the best interest of the child' (SEN Code of Practice, 2001, para. 2.27). As in other fields where mediation occurs between authorities ('repeat players') and individuals or families ('one-stoppers'), there is much debate in this context too, about the potential for unfairness arising from the unequal power endowments of the parties.

Notwithstanding government support for and provision of mediation, the numbers of registered appeals, and figures that show a high success rate of mediated cases (the vast majority resulting in the resolution of some or all of the disagreements), surprisingly few requests for independent mediation are, in fact, received. One reason posited for this low take-up of mediation is that, despite the legal requirements, neither the parents nor the local authorities receive information from Tribunals about alternative dispute resolution options once an appeal is registered (Huff, 2010).

KEY TEXTS

- Huff, A. (2010) 'SEN Mediation – Why Not Give It a Go?' *Ace Education Now* (London: Advisory Centre of Education)
- Lamb, B. (December 2009) *Inquiry on Special Educational Needs and Parental Confidence* (London: DCSF-01143)
- Penfold, C. *et al.* (2009) *Parental Confidence in the Special Educational Needs Assessment, Statementing and Tribunal System* (National Centre for Social Research, Research Report No. DCSF – RR117, London: DCSF)
- Silbey, S.S. (1994) 'Patrick Davis: "To Bring Out the Best...To Undo a Little Pain" in Special Education Mediation' in D.M. Kolb and Associates *When Talk Works: Profiles of Mediators* (San Francisco: Jossey-Bass)
- *Special Education Needs (SEN) – A Guide for Parents and Carers* (2009) (London: Department for Children, Schools and Families (DCSF))
- Tennant, R. *et al.* (2008) *Special Educational Needs Disagreement Resolution Services: National Evaluation* (National Centre for Social Research, Research Report No, DCSF – RR054. London: DCSF)

Specialist Child Care Mediation (SCCM) (includes family group conferences and public law mediation)

SEE ALSO **children and mediation; family mediation and third persons in mediation**

Specialist Child Care Mediation has been developed as a new form of intervention designed to provide impartial third-party assistance to enable social workers and parents to reach agreed solutions designed to protect children without, at the same time, destroying the trust and understanding which is necessary to form the basis of the effective social worker–parent relationship.

Several influences converged towards the development of this new application of *mediation*. North American studies had testified, initially in theory (for example, Mayer, 1985) but later following over a decade of practice, to the advantages of mediation as a less disruptive form of intervention than litigation and *adjudication* in the context of child protection cases. In such cases the child care professional faces the difficult task of having to intervene in families in order to protect the child and at the same time preserve the integrity of the family by minimizing the involvement of local authorities and the courts. These studies have found that a positive relationship between the social worker and the parents can be the most important means of protecting the child. This requires the co-operation of the parents. Establishing this essential co-operation, yet confronting parents with the harm that their conduct may be causing their *children*, is one of the central and difficult tasks of the child care professional. The situation is further complicated because social workers find themselves having to act in several, often conflicting, roles in relation to their clients, namely, combining both statutory, investigative and adjudicative roles with therapeutic objectives. Not only does occupying these contradictory roles result in great stress for the professional, but the actions that may need to be taken to protect children (such as their removal from their parents) also generate powerful reactions from those parents.

Studies in the UK have confirmed those of North America showing that resort to the adversarial legal system as the only or the main forum for protecting and promoting the welfare of children in these circumstances can have deleterious effects for many children. Notwithstanding the principle of the primacy of the welfare of the child in law, children's interests can become subsumed in the adversarial contest between local authority and parents (King and Trowell, 1992).

Mediation in public law cases can provide a voluntary and confidential forum for exchange in which the worker's role in relation to the family can be clarified and, paradoxically, made more acceptable to the family. Conflicting interests (frequently common in these circumstances) can be established explicitly and alternative options, focussed on the needs and welfare of the children, can be explored with the objective of setting up an effective working partnership between the professionals and the parents as the best means of protecting the children. One of the first tasks in such cases is not only to identify the appropriate criteria for the suitability of cases (the child cannot be in immediate danger, for example) but also the necessity of separating what is negotiable (for example, placement plans, contact arrangements, treatment or therapy, implementation of court orders, etc.) from what is non-negotiable (abuse, removal of a child from a harmful or potentially harmful situation, etc).

The limited focus, on the task and on the future, makes mediation as a process more suitable in these circumstances than the competitive and judgmental impact of adjudication. Parental collaboration in the *decision-making* process can be the means of enabling parents to experience greater control in their own, often problematic, lives. This approach also can assist disputing parents in becoming more child-focussed and therefore being able to accept more easily, difficult and painful outcomes (ADR Project Final Report, 1998).

The first inter-disciplinary pilot project in the UK, the ADR Joint Project, was set up in 1993 by National Family Mediation (NFM) and the Tavistock Clinic (Child and Family Department) and funded by the Department of Health (1993–1997) Its aims were both to identify the knowledge and skills applicable for the application of ADR involving public law child protection and child welfare case, as well as to prepare a specialist training programme for this work (cf. *family mediation* in private law cases involving parental separation and divorce).

The specific description of this intervention as *Specialist Child Care Mediation* was carefully chosen to reflect the common understanding reached by the project's inter-disciplinary team which recognized the necessity of combining complementary expertise – both mental health (child mental health experience in particular) and mediation expertise – in respect of this new practice. The limits and boundaries were clearly delineated. Where there was severe mental illness or where the parties lacked decision-making capacity, mediation became unsuitable. However mediation could be effective where there were mental health concerns such as depressive illness, obsessive behaviour or child developmental difficulties. The fact that there were mediators present with mental health expertise enabled these problems to be recognized and sensitively managed, resulting in increased understanding as well as the lessening of conflict.

The question that the project had to address was how the complementary contributions of both disciplines could best be utilized in a new and yet untried (in the UK) intervention. The description *Specialist Child Care Mediation* was adopted therefore, not only because it embodied this combination of expertise (exemplified in co-working mediation pairs) but also could be of benefit in clarifying its remit to potential referrers and families unfamiliar with the term '*ADR*'.

Specialist Child Care Mediation should not be conceived of as just the extension of family mediation to a new area of conflict. It is distinguished by its content (of greater complexity, often complicated by mental health problems); context (the direct interest of the state in the process and the outcome); the multi-party nature of participation, both parties with decision-making authority and those with a direct interest in the outcome (this could mean up to ten or more participants such as social work team leaders, childcare professionals, guardians-ad-litem, foster parents, natural parents, other family members); the nature and circumstances of the disputes (disputes either between social workers and team leaders, between families and foster parents or between families and local authorities); and the inherent power imbalances associated with the circumstances (institutional, cultural, social and racial). The direct consultation of willing older children (aged 11–15) by the mediators was possible and desirable in appropriate circumstances but required careful planning and execution and was separate from the mediation session involving the adults.

These kinds of cases, therefore, are significantly different from those public law cases which are already being referred to family mediation services increasingly. There will be a public law component in those cases that is limited to the kinds of issues that family mediation services customarily address – an example could be a social worker referral to family mediation service of a case involving a child on the 'at risk' register and where the issue relates to a need to restore or improve contact arrangements or to mitigate a breakdown of communication between parents or foster parents.

Specialist Child Care Mediation and *Family Group Conferences* (FGC) share features of their operation but there are also important differences. Social workers do not participate in FGC planning for the child. Such plans are bound, in any event, by the prior decisions of social workers as to what is and what is not negotiable. A mediation service is completely independent of social services while the FGC is not. Nor is dispute resolution between families and social service departments a function of the FGC (for a full discussion of the differences between mediation and the FGC see ADR Project Final Report, 1998; King, 1999).

Findings show that mediation in public law child protection and child welfare cases, despite the lateness of referrals and their associated high conflict, could achieve high levels of client satisfaction (with the fairness of the process and the impartiality of the mediators, in particular) and could enhance the benefits to children. Participants reported a reduction in hostility and improved understanding and communication in complex and difficult circumstances. They considered that mediation had afforded them a valuable opportunity to come together at a time when communication had broken down and felt they had been listened to. They considered SCCM preferable to going to court and less stressful (ADR Project Final Report, 1998; King, 1999).

However the very circumstances of these cases also create barriers to its use. These include the need for deeply entrenched professional interests and traditional attitudes to be overcome, including authoritarian and adversarial approaches to complex public law situations; perceived resistance to the idea of any possibility of 'partnership' between vulnerable families and social workers (especially where there is a threat that children could be removed from their parents); late referrals of cases manifesting severe and intractable conflict and therefore least likely to be successful; and a considerable reluctance in practice, of legal and social work professionals (despite their theoretical endorsement of mediation), to refer cases to mediation or to encourage their clients to take part in mediation. This is likely to reflect an unwillingness to relinquish professional control and decision-making authority over cases, as well as a reluctance to accept a fundamental change of role – from dominant professional expert to that of equal party in the negotiation process – in an innovative endeavour to seek an outcome in the best interests of the child.

KEY TEXTS

- *Alternative Dispute Resolution Project Final Report* (1998) (London: Department of Health)
- King, M. (1999) 'The Future of Specialist Child Care Mediation', *Child and Family Law Quarterly*, 11: pp. 137–149

- King, M. and Trowell, J. (1992) *Children's Welfare and the Law: The Limits of Legal Intervention* (London: Sage Publications)
- Mayer, B. (1985) 'Conflict Resolution in Child Protection and Adoption', *Conflict Resolution Quarterly*, 7: pp. 69–81 (published online in 2008)
- Mayer, B. (1989) 'Mediation in Child Protection Cases: the Impact of Third Party Intervention on Parental Compliance Attitudes', *Mediation Quarterly*, 24
- Roberts, M. (June 2013) 'Specialist Child Care Mediation: Mediation in Public Law Cases', *Family Law*, 43 (6)
- Thoennes, N. (1997) 'Child Protection Mediation. Where We Started', *Family Conciliation Courts Review*, 35: p. 136

strategies (includes negative positioning and questioning)

SEE ALSO **the mediation process; the mediator; negotiation; styles of mediation and the zero-sum game**

In the context of *mediation* practice, strategies usually refer to the ways in which skills are applied intentionally and purposely by *the mediator* to achieve a particular objective (Whatling, 2012). North American definitions convey the same understanding: 'A mediator employs strategies – plans – to conduct the mediation. And he [*sic*] uses techniques – particular moves or behaviours – to effectuate those strategies.' (Riskin, 1994, p. 111). Whatever strategies a mediator deploys – for example, active listening, conflict management, *questioning* or summarizing – these are bound to reflect their assumptions about the following:

- the nature and goals of the process in which they are engaged (*see negotiation and mediation and the mediation process*);
- orientations/beliefs about the appropriate focus of mediation – for example, an evaluative orientation will differ fundamentally from a facilitative orientation (*see styles of mediation*);
- the qualities of the 'ideal' mediator (see *attributes of the mediator*);
- the efficacy of different *models of practice*, for example, whether or not the mediator brings the parties together in direct face-to face negotiations or, on the other hand, acts as a conduit or 'go-between' between the parties who remain physically apart (see *the caucus*);
- the nature and function of *conflict* – whether it be regarded as a pathological phenomenon or as a 'normal' even constructive

response to the need to restore or re-order relationships (*see conflict*).

The strategies mediators deploy will reflect their understanding about what is happening in mediation – namely, the inter-relationship between the developmental stages of the mediation process and the cyclical exchanges that propel those stages forwards towards an outcome (*see the mediation process*).

Whatever strategies are employed by the mediator, these will be operating in two main directions – towards facilitating communication and learning between the parties (the more they understand of each other's predicament, objectives, reasons and feelings, the better their chances of co-ordination and of reaching a mutually agreed outcome); and towards instructing the parties (implicitly or explicitly) in the norms and methods of negotiation (*see negotiation*). Learning how to negotiate together involves learning how to talk to one another and how to improve negotiating capacity for the future.

The skill and judgement required for the effective use of strategies are best developed through experience of the process itself. Different strategies will be required at different stages of the process. The kind of information exchanged therefore needs to be related to the appropriate stage in the negotiation process. The same message may carry different information at a different phase. The strategy of the mediator will be highly dependent on its timing within the process so that what may be appropriate at an early stage may be inappropriate at a later stage, and vice versa. An understanding of the meaning of the strategy can only occur within an understanding of the context of the process it serves. For these reasons therefore, effective interventions – their timing, their manner and their strength – should be consonant with the phase reached in the negotiation process. For example, for the mediator to emphasize common interests before the parties have fully explored the extent of their differences, could be useless or worse, harmful. Similarly, where the parties have begun to communicate directly and constructively with one another, strongly interventionist strategies by the mediator, rather than minimal ones, could prejudice progress.

The main constellations of strategies relate to the phases of *the mediation process*, overlapping inevitably in accordance with the dynamic of the interaction. Real life mediated *negotiations*, unique and unpredictable as they are, are obviously more variable and complex than can be conveyed by the analytically distinct phases identified in the literature (see Gulliver's processual delineation of mediation, 1979). Overall this is a process of discovery and clarification, the essence of which is learning through a series of exchanges of information. It is the task of the mediator to understand and manage this process by setting up a proper structure for the communication arrangements and making sure these are understood and used properly by the parties. This is achieved by means of strategies that advance the intrinsic logic of the process and therefore of orderly and progressive movement towards a settlement of the dispute.

Strategies that facilitate the communication exchanges of the parties include those that not only increase the flow of information between the parties, but also those that monitor the accuracy and 'non belligerence' of that information (Kressel, 1985). Too much information (in volume and complexity) can be as problematic as too little or conflicting information.

The strategy of active listening (being both empathetic and sceptical at the same time) is recognized to be an important means of encouraging information exchange. Some mediators (for example, Haynes, 1993) strongly advocate the use of *questioning* as a primary strategic approach for ensuring party ownership of the answers and therefore of control over both the content of communication and of the outcome. The questioning strategy can promote a number of mediation objectives – providing clarification and insight, focussing on core concerns, encouraging explanation, stimulating fresh thinking, offsetting imbalances, and exploring alternatives, amongst others. Silence too can be used strategically as a powerful questioning technique, culturally determined in respect of its impact and meaning – conveying assent, or uncertainty, or non-acquiescence depending on the cultural context (Gulliver, 1979).

The efficacy of the mediator's strategies depends not only on their content and purpose, their manner, and their timing, but also on how they inter-relate with the strategies that the parties themselves deploy. These combine in a fluid and dynamic situation of 'reciprocal influence' (Kressel and Pruitt, 1985, p. 196).

Whatever repertoire of strategies may be available to the mediator, their use will depend both on what the parties will require or tolerate and on what strategies they will seek to promote themselves, individually or in concert – for example, in order to use the mediator as a scapegoat or to win him/her over to the justice of their cause (Gulliver, 1977).

Special problems of strategy can challenge the mediator. Overcoming transitions between phases, for example, especially in moving from the phase of entrenched opposition, mistrust and hostility, to the phase where differences are narrowed and mistrust lessened, may require stronger, more interventionist strategies, for example. In situations of impasse, the mediator has power to make a dramatic suggestion or provide an opportunity for graceful retreat. Mediators have to face squarely, therefore, their potential to exercise *power* over the communication process in such a way that the substance of the communication is affected. Where strategies are introduced into mediation from other professional interventions (for example, the importation into family mediation of systemic family therapy techniques) in covert attempts to manipulate the parties' perceptions and preferences or their dynamic behaviour, these concerns are magnified. There has to be vigilance therefore in ensuring that the complex and subtle ways in which it is acknowledged that the mediators' strategies can exert influence within the process, do not exceed the proper authority of the mediator and undermine party control.

KEY TEXTS

- Gulliver, P.H. (1977) 'On Mediators' in I. Hamnett (ed), *Social Anthropology and Law* (London: Academic Press)
- Haynes, J. (January 1985) 'Matching Readiness and Willingness to the Mediators' Strategies', *Negotiation Journal*, 1 (1): pp. 79–92
- Kolb, D.M. (1985) *The Mediators* (Boston, Mass.: MIT Press)
- Kressel, K. and Pruitt, D.G. (1985) 'Themes in the Mediation of Social Conflict', *Journal of Social Issues*, 41 (2): pp. 179–198
- Riskin, L.L. (1994) 'Mediator Orientations, Strategies and Techniques', *Alternatives to High Cost Litigation*, 12 (9): pp. 111–114
- Silbey, S.S. and Merry, S.E. (1986) 'Mediator Settlement Strategies', *Law and Policy*, 8 (1): pp. 7–32

stress

SEE ALSO conflict; disputes; mediation and supervision

Many factors conspire to impose stress in *mediation*, whatever the field of practice.

Inherent sources of tension derive from the mediator role itself – its lofty, at times contradictory and ambiguous demands; the intermediate position occupied by *the mediator* between the parties; and the objectively difficult circumstances in which *negotiations* typically occur (Kressel, 1985). The mediator is expected to maintain a calm, rational, disinterested and impartial, yet empathic and creative presence in the midst of often open *conflict* and hostility, distress and insecurity. Another source of stress can arise too from the mediator's own, self-imposed expectation to resolve conflict themselves (see C. Marzotto in Roberts, 2007).

Each context of mediation practice imposes its unique forms of stress. *International mediators*, for example, have to work long distances away from home, for long hours, in special conditions of uncertainty and danger, having to ensure that core concerns, psychological needs, fears, past and present suffering (often associated with terrible circumstances of brutality, torture and killing) are fully acknowledged and that emotive exchanges surrounding these are *used* rather than discouraged, if substantive issues are to be adequately addressed (Princen, 1992).

Family mediation is acknowledged to exemplify most powerfully (though not exclusively) the emotional intensity of *disputes* arising from the breakdown of close personal relationships – 'The deepest hatred grows out of broken love....' (Simmel, 1908a, p. 93). *Commercial, labour, environmental, elder* and *neighbourhood mediation* also reveal experiences of powerful emotional content where a great deal, other than money, can be at stake, such as self esteem and a sense of justice and fairness (Roberts, 2007).

In addition, working often with limited information and under time constraints can be like 'stepping lightly across a minefield. If [the mediator] accidentally steps in the wrong place the entire process can blow up in his face' (Saposnek, 1983, p. 27).

Stress is largely accepted as an inevitable aspect of the task of mediating and is not necessarily experienced negatively. On the contrary, it can stimulate as a challenge, both strenuous and energizing.

Mediators in all fields have devised personal and professional ways of managing the consequences of stress arising from their work – whether 'switching off'; taking care of themselves with careful preparation and a balance of other activities; drawing on the support of friends, partners and family; devising informal support networks of peer colleagues (such as The Committee of Conflict Transformation Support for international mediators, and the trainee co-working and debriefing mechanisms in *ACAS* labour mediation); as well as participating in the formal professional organization of support by means of *supervision/professional practice consultancy* as required in the professionally regulated practice of family mediation (see Legal Services Commission Quality Mark Requirement D4 for family and community mediation, 2002).

KEY TEXTS

- Princen, T. (1992) *Intermediaries in International Conflict* (Princeton NJ: Princeton University Press)
- Roberts, M. (2007) *Developing the Craft of Mediation: Reflections on Theory and Practice* (London: Jessica Kingsley Publishers)
- Saposnek, D.T. (1983) *Mediating Child Custody Disputes* (San Francisco: Jossey-Bass)

styles of mediation

SEE ALSO attributes; the mediator; models of mediation; strategies and therapeutic mediation

A description of the style of *mediation* involves defining an individuality of practice approach which cannot be separated from other factors – the perceived purpose and management of the process; the parties (their needs and wishes) and other participants including lawyer representatives; the context and subject matter of the *negotiation*; the statutory framework; the personality, gender and profession of origin of the mediator and their level of experience; and the structural arrangements framing the organization of the session (the *model of practice*).

In the theoretical endeavour to address disparate and ambiguous forms of mediation practice approaches, different schemes of categorization have been constructed – for example, the 'bargaining' and 'therapeutic' conceptualizations of Silbey and Merry (1986). Riskin

(1994, 2003) devised his famous grid of descriptors of key 'mediator orientations' as a system of classification based on the two principal questions, one of problem definition and the other of mediator role – that is, whether *the mediator* defines the problem narrowly or broadly, and also whether *the mediator's* primary objective is either to evaluate, assess and predict the grounds for settlement, or to facilitate the parties' negotiations without evaluating. These two questions incorporate the approach to the outcome, whether seeking settlement, that is disposal of the legal issues, or consensual resolution of *all* the parties' issues (legal, ethical and psychological).

A well documented continuum representing the range of approaches has been identified cross-culturally in the literature (for example, Gulliver, 1979). These extend, in respect of strength of intervention, from virtual passivity to 'chairman' to 'enunciator' to 'prompter' to 'leader' to virtual arbitrator:

> These terms are not proposed as principally typological of interventions but rather as useful indices along that continuum: Actual roles and associated strategies can be displayed as more or less resembling, more or less near to, one or other of these indices. This, of course, states nothing about the effectiveness of the strategies. (Gulliver, 1979, pp. 220–221)

As the 'ownership' of mediation became the new and controversial focus of debate, a hierarchy of practice approaches was constructed, particularly in North America where differences of style were asserted to reflect fundamental contrasts of value, principle and philosophy (Charbonneau, 2001). One approach to practice, for example, the Transformative Mediation Framework, has laid claim to being 'a qualitatively distinct approach' to mediation in comparison with others, the 'problem-solving' approach, in particular. In contrast, the variety and scope of the professional and personal practice paradigms represented in Europe and the UK appear more rich, contradictory and more modest compared to the paradigms represented in the North American literature which tend to define practice styles in terms of rigid, either/or dichotomies (see, for example, Bush and Folger, 1994, 2005; Lang and Taylor, 2000).

These 'simplistic taxonomies' do not appear to constrain thinking in the UK or Europe in respect of the complexity and multi-layered textures of practice experience (Menkel-Meadow, 2001, p. 126).

An express reluctance to label or classify their style of practice seems to characterize responses of practitioners in the UK and Europe (Roberts, 2007). Mediators' reflections on their practice suggest that they regard the adoption of a combination of styles, adapted to meet the contingencies of the situation, context, stage in the process, and, above all, the parties' needs, as a positive option. Adopting a 'directive' style assumes different forms associated with a range of purposes and meanings and a readiness to assert a greater strength of intervention where necessary – for example, in managing difficult transitions, adopting a business-like approach, or contributing ideas about options. This is not seen to involve any departure from good practice principles, such as pressurization, manipulation or coercion. On the other hand, an unobtrusive style, termed variously as elicitive (in the international context), facilitative, 'laid back' or minimalist, conveys a different, 'low profile' mediator style. Some mediators adopt different styles sometimes in the same session, changing their approach to enhance effective practice especially with greater experience (Roberts, 2007).

The attempt to analyse and conceptualize the messy world of mediation practice inevitably involves the construction of convenient typologies designed to clarify practice approaches. This project, valuable as it is, should not diminish an understanding of the complexity, variety, ambiguity, contradiction and unpredictability of actual practice. No empirical research reveals any consensus on what exactly constitutes 'style' and questions remain about the relevance of the style of the mediator to their effectiveness.

One recent North American multi-dimensional analysis of conflict mediator style finds that observational data does not bear out mediators' own description of their style as 'eclectic' and that while there was clear stylistic variation within the sample, the major stylistic division was between a large, *settlement -oriented* group of mediators and a much smaller, *relationally oriented* group (Kressel *et al.*, 2012). Qualitative analysis identified facilitative and evaluative variants of the settlement orientation and transformative and diagnostic variants of the relational orientation. Findings show that disputing parties are more satisfied with a facilitative approach than a more evaluative approach and that facilitative and diagnostic mediators performed more successfully than the evaluative and transformative mediators (Kressel *et al.*, 2012). These findings are consistent with other studies that demonstrate how stylistic choice functions – namely, in a way that enables mediators to deal with inherent tensions (the need to settle and the lack of power to do so; keeping both a task and relational focus; the intermediate position of the mediator, etc) and ambiguity (the contradictory and 'lofty' demands; the objectively difficult circumstances, etc.) in the role of the third-party intervener (Kressel, 1985, p. 203; Kressel and Pruitt, 1985, Charkoudian *et al.*, 2009).

What empirical studies show is that success in mediation depends, not on the superiority of some stylistic approaches over others, but on the substantive expertise and the competence of the mediator in manifesting the attributes of the good mediator (a non-judgmental stance, optimism, warmth, sensitivity, patience, etc.) in realizing all the goals of the process (Kressel *et al.*, 2012; Thoennes and Pearson, 1985).

KEY TEXTS

- Bush, R.A.B. and Folger, J.P. (2005) *The Promise of Mediation: The Transformative Approach to Conflict.* 2nd edn (San Francisco: Jossey-Bass)
- Kressel, K. *et al.* (Winter 2012) 'Multidimensional Analysis of Conflict Mediator Style', *Conflict Resolution Quarterly,* 30 (2)
- Lang, M.D. and Taylor, A. (2000) *The Making of a Mediator: Developing Artistry in Practice* (San Francisco: Jossey-Bass)
- Riskin, L.L. (2003) 'Decision-Making in Mediation: The New Old Grid and the New New Grid System', *Notre Dame Law Review,* 79 (1): pp. 1–54
- Thoennes, N.A. and Pearson, J. (1985) 'Predicting Outcomes in Divorce Mediation: the Influence of People and Process', *Journal of Social Issues,* 41 (2): pp. 115–126

supervision (includes professional practice consultancy)

SEE ALSO **professional regulation; quality assurance and stress**

Supervision fulfils three main functions generally – support and professional guidance; professional development; and monitoring, assessment of and accountability for the quality of practice. The task of supervision was redefined as '*professional practice consultancy*' with the advent of the *UK College of Family Mediators* in 1996 in order to achieve its greater acceptability for mediators with a legal background.

Supervision has been the primary approach to the quality control of *family mediation* since the first services were established in the late 1970s (Allport 2005). Supervision was officially endorsed on the introduction of public funding for family mediation in 1996 as set out in the Quality Mark Standard for Mediation (Legal Services Commission, 2002, p. 155. D4.2) which states:

> Effective systems of supervision are critical to quality service provision, as they ensure that proper support is available to all staff to help them to deliver a consistently high-quality service, and because they should allow you to identify problems before they become significant or systemic.

The direct observation of practice by the supervisor, while not a requirement of the Quality Mark Standard for Mediation, is considered to be an objective, independent and one of the most effective means of fulfilling the quality control function of the supervisor (Legal Services Commission, 2002, p. 155, D4.2).

Supervision is further mandated for all mediators (both publicly and privately funded) in the standards of the professional body for family mediators (The UK College of Family Mediators [now the College of Mediators], 2000, 2003), and by all the family mediation provider bodies recognized by the Family Mediation Council (FMC Constitution, 2007, 5.4).

Fields other than family mediation do not have official supervisory requirements or arrangements in place for its provision. However, the support and professional guidance function of supervision is provided by peer support networks that have developed informally in these fields, for example, the Committee of Conflict Transformation Support for international mediators.

The professional development function is also provided across fields of mediation practice in the informal peer networks that foster exchanges and learning in a spirit of collegiality. This reflects the manner in which mediation expertise is predominantly gained through working in the guildhall mode, in particular, the apprenticeship model for acquiring skills and experience, and continuing professional and educational development. This craftsmanship approach inspires a model for quality assuring mediation practice

that lays emphasis on the value of regular exposure to peer practitioners as a source of effective learning rather than on more formal
procedure of regulation, such as accreditation and certification
(Sennett, 2006).

KEY TEXTS
- Allport, L. (2005) *Supervision in Mediation: Linking Practice and Quality*
  (Sion: Institut Universitaire Kurt Bosch)
- Coletta, C. and DiDomenico, A. (2000) 'Thoughts on Mediators as
  Craftspeople', *Alternative Dispute Resolution Reporter*, 4 (7)
- UK College of Family Mediators (2003) *Professional Practice Consultancy
  for Family Mediators: A Guide to Roles and Responsibilities* (Bristol:
  College of Mediators)
- Wilson, B. (2004) 'Towards a Theoretical Model of Professional
  Practice Consultancy', *Mediation in Practice,* April: pp. 14–20

t

theory (includes narrative mediation and problem solving mediation)

SEE ALSO informal justice; knowledge; research and the zero-sum game

Mediation has been richly theorized since the beginning of the twentieth century and a distinguished body of mediation knowledge exists as an autonomous theoretical source of understanding (for example, Simmel, 1908a; Douglas, 1962; Gulliver, 1979). This resource is distinct from the academic literature that also informs the broader study of *conflict* and *dispute resolution* – derived from anthropology, sociology, political science, social psychology, international relations, socio-legal studies, peace studies, systems theory, etc.

Notwithstanding this valuable theoretical heritage, mediation has often been described as a practice in search of a theory. As many analyses of mediation are pragmatic and descriptive, this can give rise to the view that it is a practice that self-consciously lacks any framework of theoretical understanding (Stevens, 1963). Yet, it can also be argued that all practice is inevitably informed by ideas, frames of reference or suppositions that provide understandings of what is going on so that the relationship between theory and the practice of mediation has been characterized as a problematic one (Rifkin, 1994).Various reasons have been cited to explain this:

- that theoretical studies (raising concerns about *justice* and *power*, for example) can be perceived to be threatening to practitioners;
- that training programmes focus on skill building and practice techniques at the expense of theoretical understanding;
- that the professionalization project can create resistance to theoretical approaches, especially if innovative, arising from fears about change or a lack of consensus about what might constitute good practice; and

- that vested interests, in seeking to appropriate mediation as part of, or as an adjunct to, an existing professional activity (legal practice, for example), deny its identity as a discrete and autonomous intervention.

An alternative view posits a less oppositional experience of the interaction between theory and practice in mediation. This is a field acknowledged to be 'experiential', where 'grounded theory' highlights the recognition that understanding of *what* one does as a practitioner and *why* one does it is as necessary to good practice as knowing *how* to do it (Schon, 1983; Menkel-Meadow *et al.*, 2005). This involves recognition too that the reflections of practitioners constitute a rich resource for the development of the best models and theories (Jones, 2001).

North American theories of mediation abound and have had an influence in the UK – for example, the Haynes approach (Haynes, 1993; Haynes *et al.*, 2004); *transformative mediation* (Bush and Folger, 2005: see also entry on *transformative mediation*); the interest-based approach (Fisher and Ury, 1981); *therapeutic family mediation* (Irving and Benjamin, 2002); the 'insight' approach to mediation (Picard *et al.*, 2004); and *narrative mediation* (Winslade and Monk, 2001). The narrative viewpoint for understanding conflict and its strategic approach to mediation, reflecting Western cultural influences, is set out as follows:

> The narrative perception is that people tend to organize their experiences in story form. The narrative metaphor draws attention to the ways in which we use stories to make sense of our lives and relationships ... Descriptions of problems are typically told in narrative terms. Such problem narratives have often been rehearsed and elaborated over and over again by participants in a conflict ... One of the major tasks of the mediator is to destablize the totalizing descriptions of conflict so as to undermine the rigid and negative motivations that the conflicted parties ascribe to each other. A variety of strategies can be employed by a mediator to loosen these negative attributions. These strategies help to create a context from which a preferred story line can be developed. (Winslade and Monk, 2001, pp. 3, 5)

The variety of sources and forms of theory incorporate a wide range of perspectives, research findings (empirical and theoretical), scholarship and academic studies. This rich body of theory (in comparison with 'theory' conceived in more narrow terms such as an academic text) can be of value in influencing, informing and advancing understanding and therefore practice experience. Teaching, training and peer exchange can generate processes of explication and conceptualization that result in knowledge, including self-knowledge, as well as skill building. It can be argued too, that the greater the theoretical range, the more adaptable and flexible can be the response of the mediator to the needs of the parties (Schaffer, 2004).

It would be misleading to postulate the notion that a conceptual, let alone practical, opposition need exist between the spheres of empirical and pragmatic knowledge, and of theoretical knowledge. Theory, in its many forms, can interweave constructively with practice in a recursive relationship of mutual influence and significance – 'there is nothing so practical as good theory' (anon).

KEY TEXTS

- Burton, J. (ed) (1990) *Conflict: Human Needs Theory* (London: Macmillan)
- Gulliver, P.H. (1979) *Disputes and Negotiations: A Cross-Cultural Perspective* (New York: Academic Press)
- Palmer, M. and Roberts, S. (forthcoming 2014) *Dispute Processes: ADR and the Primary Forms of Decision-Making*. 3rd edn (Cambridge: Cambridge University Press)
- Schon, D. (1983) *The Reflective Practitioner: How Professional Think in Action* (New York: Basic Books)
- Simmel, G. (1908a) *The Sociology of Georg Simme,* trans. K.H. Wolff (1955) (New York: Free Press)
- Winslade, J. and Monk, G. (2001) *Narrative Mediation: A New Approach to Conflict Resolution* (San Francisco: Jossey-Bass)

therapeutic mediation (includes systems theory)

SEE ALSO **family mediation; models of mediation; styles of mediation and theory**

In the theoretical endeavour to conceptualize disparate, complex and often ambiguous forms of mediation practice, different schemes of categorization have been constructed (Silbey and Merry,

1986; Riskin, 1994). This largely North American project has seen, therefore, the construction of convenient typologies of practice approaches – for example, the 'bargaining', 'problem-solving', 'transformative' or 'therapeutic' conceptualization of *mediation* practice. However, the attempt to distinguish *practice models, styles* and approaches by the creation of these 'simplistic taxonomies' (see Menkel-Meadow, 2001, p. 126), has resulted, not only in a tendency to dichotomize, even polarize, approaches to practice, but has also led to claims of qualitative superiority being asserted over other mediation approaches, as in the case of the *Transformative Mediation* Framework (Charbonneau, 2001).

In Europe and the UK, by contrast, these classifications do not appear to constrain thinking or practice. Not only does there appear to be an express reluctance to categorize or label mediation practice approaches, but, in most cases, *mediators*, across fields of practice, consider a flexible mix of approaches, styles and models to be preferable in order to be able to respond appropriately to the particular circumstances, wishes and needs of the parties (Roberts, 2007). It is acknowledged that there can be therapeutic benefits, in the widest sense, in the expression of strong feeling and concerns in mediation, where this results in the reduction or relief of anxiety, anger, stress and hostility.

'Therapeutic' mediation is contrasted in North American terms with 'legal mediation' as a function of the profession of origin, the training and the experience of the mediator rather than any other factor (Goldberg, Green and Sander, 2007). Therapeutic mediators would have a mental health professional background in psychotherapy, family therapy or other psychological disciplines where they are trained to address the underlying causes of personal and inter-personal conflict. Their specialist skills would make them more likely to focus in *mediation* on the emotional dimensions of the dispute, on past experience, and on the interpersonal dynamics rather than on the negotiating dynamics of exchanges or the resolution of the actual issues in dispute. These would be interpreted as 'the presenting problems'. The goal of therapeutic mediation would be, therefore, to concentrate less on the manifest dispute and more on resolving the internal conflicts that might underlie the dispute, in order to address and resolve the psychological and emotional aspects of the relationship of the parties. Inevitably therapeutic mediation would require many sessions, both joint and individual – more than other mediation approaches.

Mediation as a *dispute resolution* process differs in a number of fundamental respects – objectives, rationale, process, methods and theoretical assumptions – from the spectrum of therapeutic treatment interventions that range from the brief, task-centred intervention to the more extended interventions of counselling, psychotherapy and family therapy. In the UK the need to clarify and distinguish mediation and therapy became pressing when the danger emerged, in the 1980s, of the typologies of family therapy (family systems thinking, in particular) and its manipulative techniques (such as positive connotation and some reframing techniques) being imported into family mediation practice approaches (see Roberts, 1992; Haynes, 1992; Walker and Robinson, 1992; Amundson and Fong, 1993). The greatest dangers of distortion to the *mediation process* exist where family therapy techniques are used in the course of *in-court mediation*. This can result in the parties being subjected, unknowingly and involuntarily, both to the coercive pressures of the court and to the covert controls of 'treatment'.

Some practitioners have drawn a distinction between the use of family therapy techniques in *therapy,* and their deployment in *mediation* (Haynes, 1992).The main concern, however, is that the boundaries between mediation, in the context of family disputes, and family therapy could become blurred and that the competence-based, *decision-making* rationale of mediation could become tainted with the notions of dysfunction and treatment (by professional experts) that are associated with family therapy.

Even as an advocate of the therapeutic orientation in mediation, Kressel cautions against its application in practice

- because of the demands it places on the diagnostic competence of the mediator;
- because of the complications to the already difficult role of the mediator;
- because of the risks it runs of alienating the parties;
- because it is likely to be ineffective: long-standing patterns of relating cannot easily be changed by a short-term, 'task focussed' intervention (Kressel, 1985, pp. 275–278).

In this context Kressel (1985, p. 277) cites the advantages of the clarity, simplicity and 'time honoured interpretation of the mediator's role' – the modest profile of the mediator, the encouragement of party control, and the avoidance of the adoption of standards of settlement foreign to the parties.

KEY TEXTS

- Amundson, J.K. and Fong, L. (1993) 'She Prefers Her Aesthetics; He Prefers His Pragmatics: A Response to Roberts and Haynes', *Mediation Quarterly*, 11 (2): pp. 199–205
- Haynes, J. (1992) 'Mediation and Therapy: An Alternative View', *Mediation Quarterly*, 10 (1): pp. 21–34
- Irving, H. and Benjamin, M. (2002) *Therapeutic Family Mediation* (London: Sage Publications)
- Menkel-Meadow, C.J. (2001) 'Ethics in ADR: The Many C's of Professional Responsibility and Dispute Resolution', *Fordham Urban Law Journal*, 28 (4): pp. 979–990
- Roberts, M. (1992) 'Systems or Selves? Some Ethical Issues in Family Mediation', *Mediation Quarterly*, 10 (1): pp. 3–19
- Silbey, S.S. and Merry, S.E. (1986) 'Mediator Settlement Strategies', *Law and Policy*, 8 (1): pp. 7–32

third persons in mediation (includes translators)

SEE ALSO **children in mediation; cross cultural mediation; lawyers in mediation; models of mediation and Specialist Child Care Mediation**

Those who participate in *mediation* as decision-makers are commonly referred to as *the parties*. There may be two main parties, as is usual in *family*, *commercial* or *workplace mediation*, or there may be a number of parties as is more likely in the mediation of *international* and *environmental disputes*. In addition to the parties, there can be participants in mediation who do not have decision-making authority but whose presence fulfils important functions nonetheless. They may or may not be directly affected by the outcome of mediation. For purposes of terminological clarification, these participants in mediation can be distinguished from those with decision-making authority by being described as *third persons*. Third persons can act in the mediation process in several different capacities depending on the purpose of their presence. A preliminary typology categorizes four types of third-person participation according to their role and function (Roberts, 2003):

1. Partisan third persons present to support and/or represent each party:
   a) Unofficial partisan third persons such as a family member or friend. This support may be either an active or a passive one.
   b) Official partisan third persons such as a representative lawyer or a specially trained mediation advocate representing each party. This role could involve taking on the main negotiating function on behalf of their client (as occurs in many civil and commercial mediations).
2. Third persons with an independent interest in the subject matter and/or outcome of mediation – such as a step-parent, grandparent or birthparent.
3. Third persons with an official separate and independent interest – such as a social worker representing the state's interest in protecting the child.
4. Third persons whose function is to ensure, on behalf of one or more of the parties, accessibility to and effective participation in the mediation process – such as a translator. The status, role and function of the translator becomes central in consideration of cross cultural aspects of mediation.

Involvement of the third person in mediation gives rise generally to a number of additional important considerations – in respect of definitions, terminology, ethics and theoretical and professional issues. Practice models of mediation can be flexibly structured to accommodate the complicating, yet often beneficial, additional presence of a third person according to their role and function. Practice guidelines and procedures, devised to ensure high standards, clarity, safety and fairness, and the integrity of the mediation process, need to be in place. Careful advance planning will need to cover a number of professional and practice matters – securing consent and ensuring safeguards; suitability of facilities (separate waiting areas, room size, accessibility, etc.); use of co-mediators; seating arrangements; joint or shuttle sessions; length of session; time and cost implications; respect for cultural diversity; management of numerical, *power* and gender imbalances; management of independent professionals in the session; balancing different, possibly conflicting ethical and professional imperatives (for example, between social work and mediation approaches).

As *children* do not as a rule participate directly in the mediation session itself, their participation in the mediation process is neither as a party nor as a third person in the sense defined here (see *children in mediation* and *Specialist Child Care Mediation* for the ways in which children or young persons participate in family mediation by being consulted, directly or indirectly).

KEY TEXTS

- Roberts, M. (2003) 'Third Persons in Family Mediation: Towards a Typology of Practice', *Mediation in Practice* (Bristol: UK College of Family Mediators pp. 33–40).
- Guidelines for Lawyers (nd) (SCMA) website@mediationadvocates. co, UK

training

SEE ALSO **professional regulation; quality assurance and supervision**

All codes of practice and directives on *mediation* affirm the fundamental requirement for training for mediation. This is to ensure that mediators shall be competent and knowledgeable and to promote public trust and confidence in mediators and *the mediation process* (for example, European Code of Conduct for Mediators. 1.1 2008; European Directive on cross-border aspects of civil and commercial mediation 2008, article 4 *Ensuring the quality of mediation*; Council of Europe Recommendation No. R (98)1, 1998 on Family Mediation, Principle II, 34, 35). Findings have identified inadequate training as responsible for failures of practice – for the mediator's failure both to recognize the problem and to do anything about it (Cobb and Rifkin, 1990).

Best practice in training includes the teaching of theoretical and specialist knowledge as well as the opportunity to practise under expert *supervision* (Council of Europe Recommendation No R (98) 1, 1998, 35). The training standards devised by the *UK College of Family Mediators* (now the College of Mediators) identify the required components of a best practice training course, with a focus, in this case, on training for *family mediation*. These comprise induction, observation, reading, a taught course including role play, and the requirement of a minimum of ten hours mediation practice linked to the course by professional practice consultation/supervision in order to integrate theory and practice. The content of a quality training course must cover, therefore, the *principles* and values, and the knowledge and skills of mediation. Such a course shall deploy too a mix of training methods to include both formal and appropriate expert input and experiential training (demonstration, simulation and active experimentation such as role play and feedback) (Standards and Guidelines for Mediators and Approved Bodies, 2000, pp. 14–16).

Training needs to include anti-discriminatory practice and the study of the impact of culture on disputes, both because mediation practice needs to fulfil its potential to the wider community by being accessible and by meeting specific cultural needs, and because of the increasing application of mediation in *cross-cultural* situations (for the importance of addressing the cultural and faith context of training for mediation, see Whatling, 2012).

One of the first tasks of training is to make clear in what way mediation differs from other interventions, particularly those that may appear, at first sight, to be similar, for example, bilateral settlement seeking by lawyers, conciliatory approaches by judges or welfare officers of the court, the therapeutic focus of family therapists, or the focus on personal and inter-personal dynamics of counsellors.

The main objectives of training are three-fold:

- to transmit knowledge relating to the nature of the mediation process (its principles and core characteristics) and the role of the mediator within that process; the relative merits of different *models of practice*; and the substantive subject matter for *negotiation*;
- to transmit understanding of the appropriate application of the skills, techniques and strategies of practice. Recognition that the practice of mediation requires experience is critical, for how and when a mediator intervenes is as important as what s/he does. That cannot be taught;
- to achieve the disassociation of assumptions and practices of the trainee's original profession. This requires understanding of the philosophical map of mediation which may cover the same

territory as the familiar professional map, but with new and different landmarks. This is training's most important task – ensuring that the trainee has made the necessary transformation to the new role of mediator.

KEY TEXTS

- Acland, A.F. (1995) *Resolving Conflict without Going to Court* (London: Random Century)
- Folger, J.P. and Bush, R.A.B. (eds) (2001) *Designing Mediation: Approaches to Training and Practice with a Transformative Framework* (New York: Institute for the Study of Conflict Transformation)
- Haynes, J.M. (1982) 'A Conceptual Model of the Process of Family Mediation: Implications for Training', *American Journal of Family Therapy*, 10 (4): pp. 5–16
- Moore, C.W. (1996) *The Mediation Process: Practical Strategies for Resolving Conflict* (San Francisco: Jossey-Bass)
- Whatling, T. (2012) *Mediation Skills and Strategies: A Practical Guide* (London: Jessica Kingsley Publishers)

transformative mediation

SEE ALSO **models of mediation; styles of mediation; therapeutic mediation and theories**

The Transformative Mediation Framework is a relatively recent North American practice approach to *mediation* that has generated much interest amongst some mediators. It lays claim to being a 'qualitatively distinct' approach that reflects fundamental differences of value, principle and philosophy in comparison with other approaches to mediation, the *'problem-solving' approach* in particular (Charbonneau, 2001, p. 39). This framework, it is postulated, has the potential for generating transformative effects (that is, moral and more ethical ways of being) both in the parties and in society but only if mediators concentrate on the opportunities for party 'empowerment' and inter-party 'recognition' that arise in the process (Folger and Bush, 2001; Charbonneau, 2001, p. 42).

This approach is in line with the North American endeavour that seeks to address disparate and ambiguous forms of mediation practice by devising schemes of categorization (see Silbey and Merry, 1986; Riskin, 1994). This process can create false polarities, a risk perpetuated by the Transformative Mediation Framework which, in assuming the mantle of a superior practice model, not only appropriates traditionally acknowledged hallmarks of good practice as its own, but also premises their exclusive realization on a transformative 'mindset' (Folger and Bush, 2001, p. 23).

No account is taken here of the universal, empirically substantiated, cross-cultural body of knowledge on the nature and process of mediation that both confounds the divisive dualities inherent in the transformative framework of mediation (and other dichotomous approaches), and celebrates the heterogeneity and eclecticism, as well as the coherence, of the theory and the practice of mediation.

KEY TEXTS

- Bush, R.A.B. and Folger, J.P. (2005) *The Promise of Mediation: The Transformative Approach to Conflict.* 2nd edn (San Francisco: Jossey-Bass)
- Folger, J.P. and Bush, R.A.B. (2001) 'Transformative Mediation and Third Party Intervention: Ten Hallmarks of Transformative Mediation Practice' in J.P. Folger and R.A.B. Bush (eds), *Designing Mediation: Approaches to Training and Practice within a Transformative Framework* (New York: Institute for the Study of Conflict Transformation)

UK College of Family Mediators (includes College of Mediators)

SEE family mediation; quality assurance and professional regulation

As the first and only *mediation* regulatory body of its kind in the United Kingdom, the UK College of Family Mediators has occupied a unique institutional position amongst other mediation bodies. What distinguishes it is its sole focus on the standard-setting and monitoring of both mediation training and of mediation conduct and practice.

Its establishment was the culmination of a series of developments in family mediation over the last decade of the twentieth century, in particular, the rapid growth in the market of a number of mediation training and provider bodies. This proliferation of commercial training brought associated problems, the most serious of which was the risk of unregulated practice in the delicate area of *conflict* involving families and their children. There was also concern about the confusion and inconsistency inherent in a multiplicity of different accreditation schemes and the need to ensure that a proper balance was maintained between the demand for and the supply of mediators. The introduction of public funding for *family mediation* highlighted too, in the interests of protecting the public, the need for a uniform framework of national standards for all practitioners (whatever their sector of provision – private, not-for-profit and statutory). With official encouragement and financial support from government, intent on the promotion of mediation as part of legislative reform, the UK College of Family Mediators was set up in 1996 to be a single, national professional membership body for family mediators. Its three main objectives were:

- to advance the education of the public in the skills and practice of family mediation;

- to set, promote, improve and maintain the highest standards of professional conduct and training for those practising in the field of family mediation;
- to make available the details of registered mediators qualified to provide family mediation (UK College of Family Mediators, 1997, p. A3).

The UK College affirmed too the principle that that mediation should be accessible to all members of the community regardless of their cultural, religious or ethnic background.

In addition to setting standards for entry for individual practitioner members (based on the demonstration of professional practice competence), the UK College of Family Mediators also approved independent providers ('approved bodies') to carry out the functions of recruitment, selection, training (including continuing professional development courses),consultation and supervision, according to standards set and monitored by regular audits.

In this way, the requisite separation of functions – of standard setting and monitoring, on the one hand, and of selection, training and provision of mediation on the other –was secured (see Council of Europe Recommendation No. R (98) 1; ACLEC Report, 1999). Such an institutional separation of functions is seen to be essential if conflicts of interest (for example, commercial interests versus the public interest) and conflicts of function (standard setting and monitoring versus provision and delivery of services) are to be avoided.

An abiding achievement of the UK College has been its creation of a body of professional quality assurance material. Its Code of Practice and a range of policies and detailed training and practice guidelines embody requirements and recommendations covering significant areas of practice. These include the role of *children* and young persons in family mediation, screening for *domestic abuse*, conflicts of interest, *confidentiality* and *privilege*, recording and memoranda of understanding. All these currently determine the standards of good practice for family mediators.

The creation of the UK College of Family Mediators marked the formal arrival of family mediation as a new profession in that the three hallmarks characterizing the achievement of professional status were now officially in place – a recognized and distinct body of knowledge; mechanisms for the transmission of that body of knowledge; and mechanisms for self-regulation, evaluation and accountability (Abel, 1986). In establishing its own disciplinary and complaints committees, the UK College officially acknowledged the necessity for addressing bad practice by means of formal and transparent procedures.

Notwithstanding the withdrawal of their increasingly ambivalent support for the UK College by the provider bodies (reluctant to submit to the scrutiny and the cost involved in the independent audit, as well threatened by the risk of losing membership at a time of growing competition in a limited field of practice), the UK College, renamed in 2007 as the College of Mediators (to reflect its expanded membership of mediators from a wide range of fields of practice), retains its institutional singularity as a regulatory body for mediators set up solely for this purpose. Those training and services provider bodies which broke away from the UK College formed a new body, the Family Mediation Council (FMC), which replaced independent audit of training and provision with self-regulation by those bodies of themselves. (FMC Constitution, 2007, 4.4.) As regulatory independence is recognized to be the safest means to avoid the risk of prejudicing the public interest, the unacceptability of self-regulation under the FMC has been challenged officially (see the Family Justice Review Final Report, 2011, and the FMC Review Final Report, 2012, 15 and 16, para. 94):

> The existing arrangements for self-approval by Member Organisations of training course should end. A new system of independent approval and monitoring of all mediation training course should be introduced as soon as possible ... The FMC should appoint an independent panel to carry out this work (paras 95–99) ... A system of inspection or audit of Member Organisations should be introduced.

The FMC is now recognized by government as the umbrella representative body for family mediation (made up of Member Bodies including the College of Mediators). It is under government scrutiny as it sets about introducing proper procedures for independent audits and improved institutional arrangements for appropriate governance.

Not without struggle has family mediation emerged over 30 years as a distinct, discrete and autonomous professional activity, manifest in and upheld by its own regulatory apparatus. This trajectory is similar to that charted in Australia where four phases of development have been identified (NADRAC, 2001):

1. a period of pioneering work establishing ADR;
2. increasing adoption of ADR approaches and training of practitioners leading to an oversupply of mediators in a limited market;
3. development of rivalry among practitioners resulting in fragmentation, duplication and inconsistency of practice, and finally;
4. increasing co-ordination and collaboration.

The recent course of development in this country reflects aspects of phases three and four of the Australian experience (Astor and Chinkin, 2002).

KEY TEXTS

- Abel, R.L. (1986)'The Decline of Professionalism', *Modern Law Review*, 49 (1): pp. 1–46
- Astor, H. and Chinkin, C. (2002) *Dispute Resolution in Australia*. 2nd edn (Chatswood, Australia: Butterworth)
- Council of Europe (1998). *Recommendation No. R (98) 1 of the Committee of Ministers to Member States on Family Mediation* (Strasbourg, France. Council of Europe)
- Lord Chancellor's Advisory Committee on Legal Education and Conduct (ACLEC) (1999) *Mediating Family Disputes: Education and Conduct Standards for Mediators* (Report) (London: Lord Chancellor's Department)
- McEldowney, J. (2012) *Family Mediation in a Time of Change: FMC Review Final Report* (Family Mediation Council: London)
- National Alternative Dispute Resolution Advisory Council (NADRAC) (2001) 'Annual Report 2001–2002' (Australia: Canberra)
- Norgrove, D. (2011) *Family Justice System: Final Report* (London: Ministry of Justice)
- Roberts, M. (2005) 'The Development of the Regulatory Framework', *Conflict Resolution Quarterly*, 22 (4): pp. 509–526, republished

in C. Menkel-Meadow (ed) (2012), *Complex Dispute Resolution: Foundations of Dispute Resolution*, Vol. 1 (Hampshire: Ashgate)

United Nations mediation

SEE ALSO **conflict; impartiality; international mediation; third persons in mediation and the Ombudsman**

Mediation is one of a range of important interventions that the United Nations (UN) adopts in its efforts to prevent, manage and resolve *conflict* in the world.

> The United Nations Ombudsman and Mediation Services work to intervene in the intersection where creativity meets conflict and helps to channel these conflicts into productive solutions. We do this through conflict coaching, by giving feedback to UN offices, by using shuttle diplomacy, mediation and other tools of informal dispute resolution. We also seek to track the root causes to these difficulties and propose changes to minimize them in future and to create a more harmonious workplace at the UN. (Johnston Barkat, Assistant Secretary-General, UN Ombudsman and Mediation Services, 2011)

In this context mediation can be deployed at any stage of conflict both in internal conflicts and in inter-state disputes:

- prior to a conflict through preventive diplomacy to avoid conflict starting;
- during a conflict through peacemaking activities to prevent conflict continuing;
- after a conflict to promote the implementation of agreements;
- during the peace-building effort designed to consolidate peace and lay the foundations for sustainable development (Mediation in the United Nations, 2011).

Mediation can be requested by any party to a dispute or be referred by bodies such as the UN Dispute Tribunal, the UN Appeals Tribunal or other offices such as the Office of Staff Legal Assistance. When the United Nations is called upon to mediate in a conflict, the parties accept what is termed a 'mediation mandate' which embodies their acceptance of the terms of the intervention. The UN mediator has authority to meet and listen to all the parties to the conflict, consult all who are relevant to the resolution of the conflict and can propose ideas and solutions for facilitating an end to the conflict. In line with mediation practice in other contexts, all the parties involved must consent to participate if mediation is to proceed, and the mediation outcome is not legally binding unless the Security Council takes steps to enforce the agreement. The implementation of the mediated outcome rests upon the commitment of the parties.

The UN Guidance for Effective Mediation (2012), drawing on its own experience and best practice knowledge as well as that from Member States, identifies eight mediation 'fundamentals', namely:

- preparedness;
- consent;
- *impartiality;*
- inclusivity;
- national ownership;
- international law and normative frameworks;
- coherence, co-ordination and complementarity of the mediation effort;
- quality peace agreements.

The impartiality of the UN mediator does not involve any claim to mediator *neutrality*. The UN mediator is mandated to uphold certain universal principles and values and may need to make these known explicitly.

Inclusivity refers to the extent to which and the manner in which the perspectives and needs of all the parties and other stakeholders are represented and integrated into the process and outcome of mediation. This does not mean that all the stakeholders need to be included directly in the process. It does mean that mechanisms for incorporating all views need to be in place. An inclusive approach is more likely to identify and address the root causes of conflict and to ensure that the needs of all those affected are taken into account. Such an approach is more likely therefore to increase the legitimacy of any agreement and therefore to improve the chances of its effective implementation.

As well as identifying these key factors as fundamental for effective mediation practice, the Guidance also indicates how these might be applied in practice. Mediators need to make careful assessments, to engage in proper planning and to monitor and evaluate their efforts. With this expertise, professional support and a supportive external environment, their chances of achieving success are enhanced and the likelihood of mediator error is minimized. However, the Guidance makes clear that success or failure of the mediation effort will ultimately depend on whether all the parties to the conflict accept mediation and are genuinely committed to exploring the possibility of a negotiated solution to the conflict and to reaching an agreement. If so, the role of the mediator is invaluable (UN Guidance for Effective Mediation, 2012).

The UN Department of Political Affairs (DPA) provides support and resources (advisory, logistical and financial) to assist in its own mediation efforts as well as those of partner bodies. In 2006 the DPA established the Mediation Support Unit which in 2008 set up a Standby Team of Mediation Experts to assist, individually, in pairs or in groups, mediators in the field (for example, in Libya, Yemen, Somalia and Kyrgyzstan). Team members hold a wealth of relevant expertise – on power sharing; constitution-making; natural resources and conflict; ceasefires and other security arrangements; and gender issues as these relate to the conflict. The Team can provide assistance in the form of a Rapid Response, enabling a mediation start-up at short notice and can assist too with advance planning, support and resources, all key to effective mediation in critical situations. The DPA acts as a repository of policy, guidance and mediation knowledge, developing and maintaining an online mediation support database, *UN Peacemaker*, which provides information and guidance material to mediators (for example, data on the over 750 peace agreements already achieved, other support services of the UN, etc.). This database is crucial in assisting in the planning, support and co-ordination of mediation efforts as well as containing advisory information on strategic assessments and policy guidance. Lessons learned in mediation constitute a body of best practice guidance.

While UN political missions play an important role in addressing global conflict (for example, in supporting elections in Libya, in tackling coups in West Africa and in seeking to find solutions in Syria's civil war), the UN's mediation role gains increasing support (see the 2009 Report to the Security Council on UN Mediation

Efforts by the Secretary-General S/2009/189). Leaders from many countries (such as Finland, Turkey, Senegal and Nigeria) continue to stress the importance of strengthening the role of UN mediation in preventing and settling disputes before they become intractable. The Secretary General of the United Nations recently highlighted the particular advantages of mediation in both interstate but more commonly nowadays, intrastate conflict (civil wars predominantly in Third World Countries). In being both relatively inexpensive and yielding impressive results, mediation has been found to have the special capacity, through small-scale civilian operations, to adapt flexibly to the specific dynamics of each particular conflict situation (Report to the General Assembly 13/09/12).

KEY TEXTS

- Annan, K. (2012) *Interventions: A Life in War and Peace* (London: The Penguin Press)
- Bell, C. (2008) *On the Law of Peace: Peace Agreements and the Lex Pacifactoria* (Oxford: Oxford University Press)
- Park, J. (September 2010) 'Conflict Management and Mediation Theory: South Africa's Role in Burundi's Civil Conflict', *International Area Studies Review,* 13 (3): pp. 181–201
- Ramsbotham, O., Woodhouse, T. and Miall, H. (eds) (2011) *Contemporary Conflict Resolution.* 3rd edn (Cambridge: Polity Press)
- UN Guidance for Effective Mediation (2012) (New York: UN Department of Political Affairs)
- Zartman, I.W. (ed) (2007 revised edn) *Peacemaking in International Conflict: Methods and Techniques* (Washington DC: United States Institute of Peace)

W

workplace mediation (includes employment mediation)

SEE ALSO community mediation; conflict; disputes and industrial relations mediation

Workplace mediation involves the application of an informal yet structured process to assist those in disagreement or *dispute* over working relationships to reach mutually acceptable joint decisions to settle or resolve matters. The main objectives of workplace mediation are to promote a good management and organizational culture based on openness and trust; to respect the rights of individuals; to understand how relationships in the workplace break down and what their impact can be on people and on business; and to restore and maintain healthy relationships in the workplace (ACAS/TUC Mediation Guide, 2010).

The practice of workplace mediation is endorsed by current employment policy and legislation which encourages resort to early, more cost-effective and flexible mechanisms to resolve workplace *conflict* and disputes (see Gibbons Report, 2007, Recommendation 8; Equality Act, 2010, Employment Code of Practice, 17.101)

The workplace issues that are suitable for mediation are different from those that are dealt with by *industrial relations mediation* (such as dismissal, redundancy cases and employment disputes). The most suitable issues for workplace mediation issues include:

• bullying and harassment cases, where there is perceived discrimination or unfairness, personality clashes, and cases of relationship and communication breakdown between individuals or groups or individuals and their managers. [These are examples of the kinds of complex and delicate but less well defined problems that cannot easily be dealt with by formal procedures];

- where managers cannot themselves deal with the issues because they may be perceived as biased or party to the conflict;
- circumstances where *negotiations* between management and the unions have broken down and both parties agree to attempt mediation.

While formal procedures may be more appropriate in respect of some of these issues, depending on the individual circumstances, mediation is, however, clearly unsuitable in the sorts of situations set out below:

- when it is used to bypass or undermine agreed procedures (such as discipline or grievance procedures) for addressing a dispute or to avoid fulfilling managerial responsibilities. [Mediation should, it is recommended, be seen as a complement to and not as an alternative to agreed procedures and should be used only where these procedures have been exhausted or there is agreement by the parties to put them in abeyance (ACAS/TUC Mediation Guide, 2010)];
- where a judgement about right or wrong is necessary or where there could be serious criminal activity;
- where one or both parties have no power to settle the issue;
- where a party bringing a harassment or discrimination case wants it investigated;
- where one side is so intransigent that no positive outcome can reasonably be expected by resorting to mediation (ACAS/TUC Mediation Guide, 2010).

Unlike *commercial mediation*, the parties are not usually represented in mediation although there are circumstances when representation (by a lawyer, trade union representative or other support person) may be necessary – for example, in cases of bullying or harassment where an employee feels particularly vulnerable, or in cases of special need (such as a deaf employee).

Mediation outcomes are flexible, varied (compared to the limitations of tribunal outcomes even if successful, such as reinstatement or financial compensation) and determined by the parties themselves. They can include an apology; a commitment to change behaviour; an agreement to allocate work more fairly and to provide greater levels of responsibility; an agreement to review policies and procedures, etc. (ACAS/TUC Mediation Guide, 2010). Because workplace mediation is usually an early intervention, one of its main outcome benefits (in contrast to the win-lose outcome of tribunals) can be the prevention of the irretrievable breakdown of a relationship with the result that the employee is more likely to remain on in employment. Early intervention also limits escalation of the conflict and the parties becoming more entrenched. Mediation can also assist at a later stage, for example, following a disciplinary or grievance process, to restore or rebuild staff relationships.

Evidence suggests that the use of mediation can avoid unnecessary tribunal claims and considerably reduce the level of formal grievance, bullying and harassment complaints (Gibbons, 2007).

Those who mediate in respect of workplace issues can be either internal mediators such as employees who act as mediators, in addition to their day jobs, trade union representatives who act as mediators, or mediators provided by external mediation providers (such as TCM Solutions, Consensio, Globis Mediation, CMP Resolutions in the UK). Models of practice vary (see for example, the five types approach of CMP Resolutions).The European Code of Conduct for Mediators, ACAS, the Civil Mediation Council, the College of Mediators, and the Scottish Mediation Network set quality assurance standards for the training and conduct of workplace mediators.

KEY TEXTS

- Banks, L. and Saundry, R. (2010) 'Mediation-a Panacea for the Ills of Workplace Dispute Resolution? A Comprehensive Review of the Literature Examining Workplace Mediation', *iRowe Research Paper No. 1* (Institute for Research into Organisations, Work and Employment, University of Central Lancashire (UCLAN))
- Cloke, K. and Goldsmith, J. (2005) *Resolving Conflicts at Work: Eight Strategies for Everyone on the Job* (San Francisco, CA: Jossey-Bass)
- Crawley, J. and Graham, H. (2005) *Mediation for Managers: Resolving Conflict and Rebuilding Relationships at Work* (Boston and London: Nicholas Brearley Publishing)

- Gibbons, M. (2007) *Better Dispute Resolution: A Review of Employment Dispute Resolution in Great Britain* (London: Department of Trade and Industry)
- Latreille, P. (2010) *Mediation at Work: of Success, Failure and Fragility.* Research Paper Ref. 06/10, www.acas.org.uk/researchpapers.
- Lewis, C. (2009) *The Definitive Guide to Workplace Mediation and Managing Conflict at Work* (London: Bell and Bain Ltd)

y

youth mediation (includes gang, homelessness and peer mediation)

SEE ALSO community mediation; conflict; disputes; models of mediation and restorative justice

Mediation involving young people is most developed in the context of restorative approaches to addressing *conflict* and bullying in schools (see Hopkins, 2011, 2009, 2004). Peer mediation can involve the deployment of school children and young persons themselves, trained to mediate successfully in *disputes* between fellow students.

More recent initiatives have been pioneered in attempts to mediate between rival *gangs of youths*. This is an arena fraught not only with high conflict but also with extreme danger. The most likely motives for gang related violence relate to what are referred to the three 'r' s – 'Respect, Revenge and Revenue' (for example, from drug dealing). There will almost always be an overlapping impact of neighbourhood gang culture on local schools.

In London, the Metropolitan Police have identified more than 100 distinct street gangs consisting of 1,600 'high impact players' who display extreme, violent behaviour, and a further 2,000 'associates' closely linked to each gang's criminal activity (BBC News 17/02/2009). What sustains a gang is its tight coherence binding members who are either 'in' or 'out'. 'Once in – never out' is the de facto motto of many gangs which highlights the difficulties and risks attendant in attempts at extrication from gang life. Efforts to mediate in this context of gang, knife and gun crime, can be highly problematic, time consuming and complex. Mediators need to have knowledge of gangs and need to be trained in:

- how to bridge gang and school cultures;
- how to link in with community-based programmes (resettlement and housing support, training, advice and skills development, etc.) and with specialist groups (counselling, mentoring, etc.);

- how to assist with post-mediation follow-up support; and, especially;
- how to keep safe (including learning counter-surveillance techniques and being given stab-proof vests).

This arena of practice is not called 'threat to life' and 'high risk' mediation without reason. 'It works because 'kids don't want to die. Parents don't want them to die' (Kirk Dawes, West Midlands Mediation and Transformation Service).

Mediation of conflicts in this context can be between different kinds of parties – between gangs, and between gangs and authority figures. Mediation approaches and models of practice, whilst similar to those mediations involving multi-parties and large groups, have to be adapted to the unique environment of existing or pending violence. Extensive resort to preliminary private sessions is necessary, for example, to provide a safe forum for gang members or associates to discuss their concerns openly. Trust has to be built up slowly over time. Distrust of outsiders is compounded by the high level of social and economic deprivation that characterizes the communities in which gangs usually operate. Obtaining 'a license to operate' in the neighbourhood will therefore be essential. There has to be liaison with all stakeholders in the neighbourhood, even collaboration with insiders, and there also needs to be effective 'rumour control'. Mutual trust is essential to the viability of any mediation initiative. Mediation is best presented initially as an option only. The principle of *confidentiality* has to be explicit as do its limits. Gang members are more likely to change when approached as *people* worthy of respect rather than as gang members. Former gang members living in the community have specialist knowledge as community based 'gang specialists' and can provide invaluable assistance in engaging potential participants in mediation. Once mediation starts, *shuttle* and *caucus* approaches rather than joint meetings are more likely to be effective.

The primary focus of the mediator needs to be adjusted too, in order to address issues arising from the unique circumstances of youth crime and gang violence. The mediator's central task, of facilitating communication between the parties, becomes more complicated when people do not know how to communicate, find communication difficult, more so where they cannot be seen even to be seeking communication, or are forbidden to communicate. If parties are pre-occupied with their own survival at worst, or are highly charged with hostility at best, the usual objective of the mediator, in seeking to improve mutual understanding and in generating creative problem-solving, can seem highly unrealistic. Furthermore, reaching an 'agreement' may itself seem to be an impossible luxury. Rather, an accommodation, implicit even, resulting in an outcome that can, just, be lived with, even unhappily, may be all that is realistically feasible where parties may need to remain, or be seen to remain, enemies.

The significance of structural, social and personal *power* relations has import in the mediation of and between youth gangs particularly where authority figures are involved as parties in the intervention. The different and unequal forms of power and the consequent imbalances of bargaining power likely to arise need to be recognized – for example, the formal powers of the police, the power to use language, the power to make life difficult and cause disruption, the power to control the arena of conflict, etc. (*see power*). It is unlikely that one side will have all the power and control. The significance of power relations within the wider social context includes the norms, values, rules and beliefs that critically inform the behaviour and strategies of all parties – for example, in the importance that can be attached to respect in gangs, and the need to avoid actions that might threaten a neighbourhood's respect.

Mediation is but one of a range of interventions that are necessary in order to reduce and prevent serious youth crime and violence and to help vulnerable young people (for example, children in care, in foster homes, etc.) both to resist the pressures towards becoming gang members and to exit gang life, as well as to gain the necessary motivation for and means of re-entering education and employment. Mediating in this context cannot occur successfully without the collaboration of the local community, its resources, leaders, neighbourhood groups, and support and educational programmes.

Another quite different arena of youth involvement in mediation is in respect of homelessness. *Alone in London* was one of the first organizations to set up a mediation service to assist young people (under 26 years) alienated from their families, to re-establish communication and resolve disputes with their families. With family breakdown a major cause of youth homelessness, this organization aims both to prevent a young person running away or being ejected from their home, as well as to re-establish positive contact with family members (where this is safe and appropriate) where there is already homelessness or a young person has been in care. A main focus has been on the prevention of homelessness through awareness-raising in schools, etc.

Many local authorities have introduced mediation schemes, often contracted out to local, not-for-profit community and family mediation services, to address the linked problems of broken family relationships and homelessness. A Court of Appeal decision highlighted the dangers of local authorities using mediation to avoid their statutory housing responsibilities (*Robinson v Hammersmith and Fulham London Borough Council* [2006] 1 WLR 3295). As this case illustrates, mediation can be deployed to serve the interests of local authorities rather than the best interests of a young person.

There are other concerns about mediation in respect of homelessness – mediation may not be suitable where abuse is reported; funding by local authorities can compromise the independence of mediation services; and neutrality and confidentiality may be jeopardized where mediation services provide information in reports on outcomes made to local authorities (Advice Service Alliance, 2006).

KEY TEXTS

- Cohen, R. (1999) *The School Mediators' Field Guide: Prejudice, Sexual Harassment, Large Groups and Other Daily Challenges* (Watertown, MA: School Mediation Associates), Chapter 9 Mediating Conflicts Involving Youth Gangs
- Ferrara, J.M. (1996) *Peer Mediation: Finding a Way to Care* (Portland, Maine: Stenhouse Publishers)
- Garb, P. (no date) 'Meeting the Needs of Law Enforcement and Gang Intervention Mediators in Violent Environments' (UC Irvine's Centre of Citizen Diplomacy)
- Hopkins, B. (2011) *The Restorative Classroom: Using Restorative Approaches to Foster Effective Learning* (London: Optimus Education (Optimus Professional Publishing Ltd))
- Thorsborne, M. and Vinegrad, D. (2008) *Restorative Practices in Schools* (UK: Speechmark Publishing Ltd)

Z

the zero-sum game

SEE ALSO the mediation process; negotiation; strategies and theory

The zero-sum game is a mathematical representation, derived from game and economic theory, of the principle that for every winner there must be a loser. It is based on the assumption of a strictly competitive relationship between the parties (whether an individual or a group), the gains of one necessarily entailing the losses of the other.

Five forms of exchange have been identified along a spectrum ranging from altruism at one end (representing the most co-operative of exchanges) to 'winner takes all' at the other end (where competition prevails over co-operation) and 'the apex predator rules' (Sennett, 2012, p. 86). In the middle, co-operation and competition are most balanced in dialogic exchanges which differentiate individuals and groups. While zero-sum game exchanges lie at the adversarial, competitive end of the spectrum, co-operation and *negotiation*, are nevertheless still necessary – in order to both set and agree ground rules for the contest and the basic conventions for behaviour between the parties, and to keep exchanges going in order to continue competing. The loser must also be left with something, otherwise any incentive to compete would be destroyed. Also the willingness to take risks (in particular, the risk of losing) binds both winners and losers (Sennett, 2012). The zero-sum principle exists, therefore, largely in the domain of abstract game and economic theory rather than in the real world.

A zero-sum game definition, based on assumptions of competitive rivalry, the simplification of an issue, and the wish for a quick outcome, appears even more simplistic and inaccurate in its application to the *mediation* of *disputes*. Here actual negotiations involve many issues, with multiple attributes and complex interconnections, and are characterized by uncertainty, intricacy and incomparability (Gulliver, 1979). Gulliver's processual analysis of the mediation process entails an intrinsic change of orientation with the parties moving from the early phase of competition, conflict and difference through a process of clarification, exploration and expansion (including the consideration of new alternatives) towards the greater likelihood of a positive and an integrative outcome, based on qualitative and quantitative gains for both parties.

This occurs even in circumstances where the expectation of a zero-sum outcome might be assumed to be typical or, even unavoidable, for example, where there are limited, quantifiable material interests at stake, such as money or land (Gulliver, 1979). 'Money, in fact, is not necessarily just money ... it represents and can promote a variety of things ... valuable prestige, good will, improved labour relations, or increased productivity' (Gulliver, 1979, p. 149).

Furthermore, the dynamics of competitive rivalry of the zero-sum game contradict the fundamental ethic of co-operation and *respect* that lies at the core of the *principles* and practice of mediation – respect for the parties' perceptions and meanings, for their autonomy, and for their *decision-making* authority, and their capacity to co-operate in reaching their own, mutually acceptable agreements. (Davis, 1984; Sennett, 2003)

KEY TEXTS

- Binmore, K. (2007) *Playing for Real: A Text on Game Theory* (Oxford: Oxford University Press)
- Raghavan, T.E.S. (2003) 'Zero-Sum Two Person Games' in R.J. Aumann and S. Hart (eds), *Handbook of Game Theory with Economic Applications*, Vol. 2. 2nd edn (Amsterdam: Elsievier)
- Sennett, R. (2012) *Together: The Rituals, Pleasures and Politics of Cooperation* (London: Allen Lane/Penguin)
- Walton, R.E. and McKersie, R.B. (1965) *A Behavioural Theory of Labour Negotiating* (New York: McGraw Hill)

bibliography

Abdel Wahad, M.S., Katsh, E. and Rainey, D. (eds) (2012) *ODR: Theory and Practice* (The Hague: Eleven International Publishing)

Abel, R.L. (1982) 'The Contradictions of Informal Justice' in R. Abel (ed), *The Politics of Informal Justice* (New York: Academic Press)

Abel, R.L. (1986) 'The Decline of Professionalism', *Modern Law Review,* 49 (1): pp. 1–46

Abel, R.L. (1988) *The Legal Profession in England and Wales* (Oxford: Blackwell)

ACAS (2010) ACAS/TUC *Mediation: A Guide for Trade Union Representatives* (London: ACAS)

ACAS (2010) *Mediation: An Employer's Guide* (Acas/CIPD) www.acas.org. uk/index.aspx?articleid=1680

ACAS (n.d.) *The ACAS Role in Conciliation, Arbitration and Mediation* (London: Advisory, Conciliation and Arbitration Service)

Acland, A.F. (1990) *A Sudden Outbreak of Common Sense: Managing Conflict through Mediation* (London: Hutchinson Business Books)

Acland, A.F. (1995) *Resolving Disputes without Going to Court* (London: Random Century)

Acland, A.F. (2007) in Roberts, M. *Developing the Craft of Mediation: Reflections on Theory and Practice* (London: Jessica Kingsley Publishers), Chapters 5, 8 and 9

ADR Bibliography (n.d.) London: Standing Conference of Mediation Advocates (SCMA). website@mediationadvocates.co.uk.

Advice Services Alliance (2006) *Notes for Advisers* (London: Advice Services Alliance)

Age Concern, Action on Elder Abuse: www.elderabuse.org.uk

Allen, H. (2013) 'Confidentiality – A Guide for Mediators: How Significant Is Mediation Confidentiality in Practice?' *ADR Times,* 31 January (London: CEDR)

Allport, L. (2005) *Supervision in Mediation: Linking Practice and Quality* (Sion: Institut Universitaire Kurt Bosch)

Alternative Dispute Resolution Project Final Report (1998) (London: Department of Health)

Amundson, J.K. and Fong, L. (1993) 'She Prefers Her Aesthetics; He Prefers His Pragmatics: A Response to Roberts and Haynes', *Mediation Quarterly*, 11 (2): pp. 199–205

Annan, K. (2012) *Interventions: A Life in War and Peace* (London: The Penguin Press)

Antes, J.R. and Saul, J.A. (2001) 'Evaluating Mediating Practice from a Transformative Perspective', *Conflict Resolution Quarterly*, 18 (3): pp. 313–323

Ap Cynan, R. (2012) 'Mediating at a Distance – Making Use of ICT'. Unpublished paper

Astor, H. and Chinkin, C. (2002) *Dispute Resolution in Australia*. 2nd edn (Chatswood, Australia: Butterworth)

Auerbach, J.S. (1983) *Justice without Law? Resolving Disputes Without Lawyers* (Oxford: Oxford University Press)

Augsburger, D.W. (1992) *Conflict Mediation Across Cultures-Pathways and Patterns* (Kentucky: Westminster/John Knox Press)

Avruch, K. (1998) *Culture and Conflict Resolution* (Washington, DC: Institute of Peace Press)

Babbitt, E.F. (1994) 'Jimmy Carter: The Power of Moral Suasion in International Mediation' in D.M. Kolb and Associates, *When Talk Works: Profiles of Mediators* (San Francisco: Jossey-Bass Publishers)

Backaby, N., Partasides, C., Redfern, A. and Hunter, M. (eds) (2009) *Redfern & Hunter on International Arbitration*. 5th edn (Oxford: Oxford University Press)

Baldwin, J. (2008) 'Arbitration' in P. Cane and J. Conaghan (eds), *The New Oxford Companion to Law* (Oxford: Oxford University Press)

Banks, L. and Saundry, R, (2010) 'Mediation-a Panacea for the Ills of Workplace Dispute Resolution? A Comprehensive Review of the Literature Examining Workplace Mediation', *iRowe Research Paper No. 1* (Institute for Research into Organisations, Work and Employment, University of Central Lancashire (UCLAN))

Barlow, A. and Hunter, R. (2012) *Mapping Paths to Family Justice – Some Preliminary Findings* (London: ESRC)

Bar Tal, B. (1998) 'Societal Beliefs in Times of Intractable Conflict: The Israeli Case', *International Journal of Conflict Management*, 9 (1): pp. 22–50

Behrens. J. (2003) *Church Disputes Mediation* (Gracewing: London)

Beldam, Lord Justice (October 1991) *A Report of the Committee on Alternative Dispute Resolution* (London: General Council of the Bar)

Bell, C. (2008) *On the Law of Peace: Peace Agreements and the Lex Pacifactoria* (Oxford: Oxford University Press)

Bercovitch, D.J. (ed) (1996) *Resolving International Conflicts: The Theory and Practice of Mediation* (Boulder, CO: Lynne Rienner Publishers)

Bercovitch, D.J. and Rubin, J.G. (eds) (1992) *Mediation in International Relations* (Hampshire, UK and New York: Palgrave Macmillan)

Binmore, K. (2007) *Playing for Real: A Text on Game Theory* (Oxford: Oxford University Press)

Bird, A. (1994) 'Enhancing Patient Well-Being: Advocacy Or Negotiation?' *Journal of Medical Ethics*, 19: pp. 152–156

Blacklock, R. and Roberts, M. (1994) 'Professional Standards in the Selection of Family Mediators', *Family Law*, 24: p. 206

Bolitho, J., Bruce, J. and Mason, G. (2012) *Restorative Justice: Adults and Emerging Practice* (Sydney: Institute of Criminology Series)

Bondy, V. and Doyle, M. (2011) *Mediation in Judicial Review: a Practical Handbook for Lawyers* (London: The Public Law Project)

Bondy, V. *et al.* (2009) *Mediation and Judicial Review: An Empirical Research Study* (London: The Public Law Project, Nuffield Foundation)

Bordow, S. and Gibson, J. (1994) *Evaluation of the Family Court Mediation Service*, Research Report No. 12, (Melbourne: Family Court of Australia)

Bottomley, A. (1984) 'Resolving Family Disputes: A Critical View' in M.D.A. Freeman (ed), *State, Law and the Family* (London: Tavistock)

Bowling, D. and Hoffman, D. (2000) 'In Theory: Bringing Peace into the Room: The Personal Qualities of the Mediator and Their Impact on the Mediation', *Negotiation Journal*, 16: pp. 5, 5–27

Braithwaite, J. (2002) *Restorative Justice and Responsive Regulation* (New York: Oxford University Press)

Brazil, W. (1990) 'Special Master in Complex Case: Extending the Judiciary or Reshaping Adjudication?' *University of Chicago Law Review* 53: p. 394

Brown, H. and Marriott, A. (2011) *ADR: Principles and Practice*. 3rd edn (London: Sweet and Maxwell)

Buck, T. (2012) *An Evaluation of the Long-Term Effectiveness of Mediation in Cases of International Parental Child Abduction* (Leicester: Reunite International Child Abduction Centre)

Buck, T., Kirkham, R. and Thompson, B. (2011) *The Ombudsman Enterprise and Administrative Justice* (Aldershot, Hants: Ashgate)

Burger, W.E. (1982) 'Isn't there a Better Way', *American Bar Association Journal*, 68: pp. 274–277

Burton, J. (1990) (ed) *Conflict: Human Needs Theory* (London: Macmillan)

Bush, R.A.B. and Folger, J.P. (2005) *The Promise of Mediation: The Transformative Approach to Conflict*. 2nd edn (San Francisco: Jossey-Bass)

Campbell, T. (2001) *Justice* (London: Palgrave Macmillan)

Caplan, P. (1995) 'Anthropology and the Study of Disputes' in P. Caplan (ed), *Understanding Disputes: the Politics of Argument* (Oxford: Berg Publishers)

Cane, P. and Conaghan, J. (2008) (eds) *The New Oxford Companion to Law* (Oxford: Oxford University Press)

CEDR: www.cedr.com

Charbonneau, P. (2001) 'How Practical is Theory' in J.P. Folger and R.A.B. Bush (eds), *Designing Mediation: Approaches to Training and Practice within a Transformative Framework* (New York: Institute for the Study of Conflict Transformation)

Cloke, K. and Goldsmith, J. (2005) *Resolving Conflicts at Work: Eight Strategies for Everyone on the Job* (San Francisco, CA: Jossey-Bass)

Cobb, S. and Rifkin, J. (1991) 'Practice and Paradox: Deconstructing Neutrality in Mediation', *Law and Social Enquiry*, 16 (1): pp. 35–62

Cohen, R. (1999) *The School Mediators' Field Guide: Prejudice, Sexual Harassment, Large Groups and Other Daily Challenges* (Watertown, MA: School Mediation Associates), Chapter 9 Mediating Conflicts Involving Youth Gangs

Coletta, C. and DiDomenico, A. (2000) 'Thoughts on Mediators as Craftspeople', *Alternative Dispute Resolution Reporter*, 4: p. 17

Committee on the Rights of the Child's *General Comment No.12* (2009) 'The Right of the Child to Be Heard' CRC/C/CG/12. 20 July 2009, available at, http://www.2.ohchr.org/english/bodies/crc/comments.htm

Condlin, R. (1985) '"Cases on Both Sides": Patterns of Argument in Legal-Dispute Negotiation', *Maryland Law Review*, 44: pp. 65–136

Conneely, S. (2002) *Family Mediation in Ireland* (Aldershot, Hants. Ashgate Publishing Ltd)

Coogler, O.J. (1978) *Structured Mediation in Divorce* (Lexington, MA: Lexington Books/DC Heath)

Cormick, G.W. (1977) 'The Ethics of Mediation: Some Unexplored Territory', unpublished paper presented to The Society of Professionals in Dispute Resolution, Fifth Annual Meeting, October, Washington, DC.

Cormick, G.W. (Winter 1982) 'Intervention and Self-Determination in Environmental Disputes: a Mediator's Perspective', *Resolve*, Winter: pp. 260–265

Corry, G. (Fall 2012) 'Political Dialogue Workshops: Deepening the Peace Process in Northern Ireland', *Conflict Resolution Quarterly*, Colloquy on Dialogue Processes (Part 2), 30 (1): pp. 53–79

Council of Europe (1998) Recommendation no. R (98) 1 of the Committee of Ministers to Member States on Family Mediation (Strasbourg, France: Council of Europe), 5 February

Council of Europe (2004) 'Directive of the European Parliament and of the Council: COM (2004) 718 Final' (Strasbourg, France: Council of Europe)

Craig, Y. (1994) 'Elder Mediation: Can It Contribute to the Prevention of Elder Abuse and the Protection of the Rights of Elders and Their Carers?' *Journal of Elder Abuse and Neglect*, 6: pp. 83–95

Craig, Y. (1996) 'Patient Decision-Making: Medical Ethics and Mediation', *Journal of Medical Ethics*, 22: pp. 164–167

Craig, Y. (1997) *Elder Abuse and Mediation: Exploratory Studies in America, Britain and Europe* (Aldershot: Avebury)

Craig, Y. (1998) *Advocacy, Counselling and Mediation in Casework* (London: Jessica Kingsley Publishers)

Craig, Y. (1999) *Peacemaking for Churches* (London: SPCK)

Craig, Y. (2000) 'The Multicultural Elder Mediation Project EMP: Empowerment for Older, Disabled and Mentally Frail Persons' in M. Liebman (ed), *Mediation in Context* (London: Jessica Kingsley Publishers)

Craig, Y. (April 2003) 'The Complex Problem of Elder Abuse' *Mediation in Practice* (Bristol: UK College of Family Mediators/Mediation UK), pp. 18–21

Cranston, R. (2008) 'Ombudsmen' in P. Cane and J. Conaghan (ed), *The New Oxford Companion to Law* (Oxford: Oxford University Press)

Crawley, J. (2012a) *Argument to Agreement: Resolving Disputes Through Mediation.* Pocket Guide 1 (Cambridgeshire: Pocket Guides to Conflict Resolution)

Crawley, J. (2012b) *Creative Conflict Management: Talk It Out.* Pocket Guide 2 (Cambridgeshire: Pocket Guides to Conflict Resolution)

Crawley, J. and Graham, H. (2005) *Mediation for Managers: Resolving Conflict and Rebuilding Relationships at Work* (Boston and London: Nicholas Brearley Publishing)

Cross, R. and Tapper, C. (2007) *On Evidence.* 11th edn (Oxford: Oxford University Press)

Curle, A. (1971) *Making Peace* (London: Tavistock Publications)

Davis, A.M. (1984) 'Comment' in *A Study of Barriers to the Use of Alternative Methods of Dispute Resolution* (Vermont School of Law Dispute Resolution Project, South Royalton, VT: VLSDRP)

Davis, A.M. in Kolb, D.M. *et al.* (1994) *When Talk Works: Profiles of Mediators* (San Francisco: Jossey-Bass)

Davis, G. and Bader, K. (March and April 1985) 'In-court Mediation: The Consumer View', Parts 1 and 11, *Family Law*, 15 (3): pp. 42–49, 82–86

Davis, G. *et al.* (July 2000) 'Monitoring Publicly Funded Family Mediation', *Final Report to the Legal Services Commission*

De Girolamo, D. (2013) *The Fugitive Identity of Mediation: Negotiations, Shift Changes and Allusionary Action* (London: Routledge)

Della Noce, D.J. (2009) 'Evaluative Mediation: In Search of Practice Competencies', *Conflict Resolution Quarterly*, 27 (2): pp. 193–214

Department of Work and Pensions (DWP) (July 2011) *Government's response to the consultation on Strengthening Families, Promoting Parental*

Responsibility: The Future of Child Maintenance. Cm 8130 (London: DWP)

De Sousa Santos, B. (1982) 'Law and Community: the Changing Nature of State Power in Late Capitalism' in R. Abel (ed), *The Politics of Informal Justice* (New York: Academic Press)

Deutsch, M. (1973) *The Resolution of Conflict: Constructive and Destructive Processes* (New Haven, CT: Yale University Press)

Dingwall, R. and Greatbatch, D. (1988) 'Empowerment Or Enforcement? Some Questions about Power and Control in Divorce Mediation' in R. Dingwall and J. Eekelaar (eds), *Divorce Mediation and the Legal Process* (Oxford: Oxford University Press)

Dingwall, R. and Greatbatch, D. (1993) 'Whose in Charge? Rhetoric and Evidence in the Study of Mediation', *Journal of Social Welfare and Family Law*, 15: pp. 367–385

Dolder, C. (2008) 'Alternative Dispute Resolution' in P. Cane and J. Conaghan (eds), *The New Oxford Companion to Law* (Oxford: Oxford University Press)

Douglas, A. (1957) 'The Peaceful Settlement of Industrial and Intergroup Conflict', *The Journal of Conflict Resolution*, 1 (1): pp. 69–81

Douglas, A. (1962) *Industrial Peacemaking* (New York: Columbia University Press)

Doyle, M. (2001) 'Getting on Stream with Online Mediation', *Mediation Magazine*, February, p. 8 (Bristol: Mediation UK)

Durkheim, E. (1893, published in English 1947) *The Division of Labour in Society* (New York)

Dworkin, R. (1986) *Law's Empire* (London: Fontana)

Dworkin, R. (2005) *Taking Rights Seriously* (Boston: Harvard University Press)

Ebner, N. (2012) 'E-Mediation' in M.S. Abdel Wahab, E. Katsh, and D. Rainey (eds), *ODR: Theory and Practice* (The Hague: Eleven International Publishing)

Ebner, N. and Getz, C. (2012) 'ODR: The Next Green Giant', *Conflict Resolution Quarterly*, 29 (3): pp. 283–307

Eckhoff, T. (1969) 'The Mediator and the Judge' in V. Aubert (ed), *Sociology of Law* (Harmondsworth: Penguin)

Ellickson, R.C. (1994) *Order Without Law: How Neighbours Settle Disputes* (London: Harvard University Press)

Elliott, D.C. (1996) 'Med/arb: Fraught with Danger or Ripe with Opportunity', *Arbitration*, 62 (3): pp. 175–177

Ellis, J. (2012) 'Collaborative Law, a Waste of Time or the Way Forward?: A Critical Appraisal of the Use of Collaborative Lawyering in Family Law Disputes and Beyond', *Mediation in Ireland*, CPD Seminars, 11 February 2012

Emery, R.E. *et al.* (2001) 'Child Custody Mediation and Litigation: Custody, Contact and Co-Parenting Twelve Years after Initial Dispute Resolution', *Journal of Consulting and Clinical Psychology,* 59: pp. 410–418

European Commission (2002) European Union Green Paper on *Alternative Dispute Resolution in Civil and Commercial Law,* ref.com (2002) 196 final

European Mediation Directive 2008/52/EC of the European Parliament and of the Council of 21st May

European Mediation Directive (2008) of the European Parliament and of the Council of 21 May, 2008/52/EC

Falk Moore, S. (1995) 'Imperfect Communications' in P. Caplan (ed), *Understanding Disputes: The Politics of Argument* (Oxford: Berg)

Felstiner *et al.* (1980–1981) 'The Emergence and Transformation of Disputes: Naming, Blaming and Claiming ... ', *Law and Society Review,* 15 (3): pp. 631–654

Ferrara, J.M. (1996) *Peer Mediation: Finding a Way to Care* (Portland, Maine: Stenhouse Publishers)

Finer Report (1974) *Report of the Committee on One Parent Families.* Cm. 5629 (London: HMSO)

Fisher, R. and Ury, W. (1991) *Getting to YES: Negotiating Agreement Without Giving In.* 2nd edn (London: Business Books)

Fiss, O.M. (1984) 'Against Settlement', *Yale Law Journal,* 93: pp. 1073–1090

Fitzpatrick, P. (1993) 'The Impossibility of Popular Justice' in S. Engle Merry and N. Milner (eds), *The Possibility of Popular Justice: A Case Study of Community Mediation in the United States* (Ann Arbor: University of Michigan Press)

Folberg, J. and Milne, A. (eds) (1988) *Divorce Mediation: Theory and Practice* (New York: Guilford Press)

Folger, J.P. and Bush, R.A.B. (2001) 'Transformative Mediation and Third Party Intervention: Ten Hallmarks of Transformative Mediation Practice' in J.P. Folger and R.A.B. Bush (eds), *Designing Mediation: Approaches to Training and Practice within a Transformative Framework* (New York: Institute for the Study of Conflict Transformation)

Folger, J.P. and Bush, R.A.B. (eds) (2001) *Designing Mediation: Approaches to Training and Practice with a Transformative Framework* (New York: Institute for the Study of Conflict Transformation)

Folger, J.P. and Jones, T.S. (1994) *New Directions in Mediation* (London: Sage)

Fortin, J., Scanlan, L. and Hunt, J. (2013) 'Taking a Longer View of Contact: Perspectives of Young Adults Who Experienced Parental Separation', www.sussex.ac.uk/law/research/centreforresponsibilities/takingalongerviewofcontact

Francis, D. (2002) *People, Peace and Power: Conflict Transformation in Action* (London: Pluto Press)

Francis, D. (2010) *From Pacification to Peacebuilding: A Call to Global Transformation* (London: Pluto Press)

Freeman, M.D.A. (1984) 'Questioning the Delegalisation Movement in Family Law: Do We Really Want a Family Court?' in J.M. Eekelaar and S.N. Katz (eds), *The Resolution of Family Conflict: Comparative Legal Perspectives* (Toronto: Butterworths)

Fuller, L.L. (1963) 'Collective Bargaining and the Arbitration', *Wisconsin Law Review*, 18 (3): pp. 39–42

Fuller, L.L. (1971) 'Mediation –Its Forms and Functions', *Southern California Law Review*, 44: pp. 305–339

Gaetz, S. (1995) 'Youth-Development': Conflict and Negotiations in an Urban Irish Youth Club' in P. Caplan (ed.), *Understanding Disputes: the Politics of Argument* (Oxford: Berg)

Galanter, M. (1981) 'Justice in Many Rooms: Courts, Private Ordering, and Indigenous Law', *Journal of Legal Pluralism and Unofficial Law*, 19: pp. 1–47

Galanter, M. (1985) 'A Settlement Judge Is Not a Trial Judge": Judicial Mediation in the United States', *Journal of Law and Society*, 12 (1): pp. 1–18

Galanter, M. (1986) 'The Emergence of the Judge as a Mediator in Civil Case', *Judicature*, 69: pp. 257–262

Gale, J., Mowery, R.L., Hermann, M.S. and Hollett, N.L. (2002) 'Considering Effective Divorce Mediation: Three Potential Factors', *Conflict Resolution Quarterly*, 19: pp. 389–420.

Garb, P. (no date) 'Meeting the Needs of Law Enforcement and Gang Intervention Mediators in Violent Environments' (UC Irvine's Centre of Citizen Diplomacy)

Genn, H. (1987) *Hard Bargaining: Out of Court Settlement in Personal Injury Actions* (Oxford: Clarendon Press)

Genn, H. (1999a) *Paths to Justice: What People Do and Think about Going to Law* (Oxford: Hart)

Genn, H. (1999b) *Mediation in Action: Resolving Civil Disputes without Trial* (London: Calouste Gulbenkian Foundation)

Genn, H. *et al.* (2007) *Twisting Arms: Court Referred and Court Linked Mediation Under Judicial Pressure*, Vol. 1 (Ministry of Justice Research Series 1/07, May)

Getz, C. (2010) 'Evaluation of the Distance Mediation Project: Report on Phase II of the Technology-Assisted Family Mediation Project', http://www.mediatebc.com/PDFs1-2-Mediation-Services/Distance-Mediation-Project-Evaluation-Report. aspx (accessed 28 July 2011)

Gibson, K. (September 1999) 'Mediation in the Medical Field', *The Hastings Centre Report*, 29 (5)

Gibbons, M. (2007) *Better Dispute Resolution: A Review of Employment Dispute Resolution in Great Britain* (London: Department of Trade and Industry)

Giddens, A. (1984) *The Constitution of Society* (Cambridge: Polity Press)

Gilligan, C. (1982) *In a Different Voice* (Cambridge, MA: Harvard University Press)

Goethe von, J.W. (1809; trans., 1971) *Elective Affinities* (Harmonsworth: Penguin)

Goldberg, S.B. (1982) 'The Mediation of Grievances under a Collective Bargaining Contract: An Alternative to Arbitration', *Northwestern University Law Review*, 77 (270): pp. 281–284

Goldberg, S.B., Green, E.D. and Sander, F.E.A. (2007) *Dispute Resolution* (Boston: Little, Brown and Company)

Goldberg, S.B., Sander, F.E.A., Rogers, N.H. and Cole, S.R. (2007) *Dispute Resolution: Negotiation, Mediation and Other Processes.* 5th edn (New York: Aspen Law and Business Publishers)

Government White Paper (2004) *Transforming Public Services: Complaints, Redress and Tribunals*, Cm. 6243. Department for Constitutional Affairs (London: The Stationery Office)

Graef, R. (2001) *Why Restorative Justice? Repairing the Harm Caused by Crime* (Calouste Gulbenkian Foundation, UK)

Grillo, T. (1991) 'The Mediation Alternative: Process Dangers for Women', *Yale Law Journal*, 100 (6): pp. 1545–640

Guidelines for Lawyer Mediators. Standing Conference of Mediation Advocates. website@mediationadvocates.co.uk

Gulliver, P.H. (1979) *Disputes and Negotiations: A Cross-Cultural Perspective* (New York: Academic Press), Chapter 7

Gulliver, P.H. (1977) 'On Mediators' in I. Hamnett (ed), *Social Anthropology and Law* (London: Academic Press)

Hague Conference on Private International Law (2007) *Feasibility Study on Cross-Border Mediation in Family Matters*

Harlow, C. and Rawlings, R. (1997) *Law and Administration.* 2nd edn (London: Butterworths)

Harrington, C.B. (1985) *Shadow Justice: The Ideology and Institutionalisation of Alternatives to Court* (Westport CT: Greenwood Press)

Harrington, C.B. (1992) 'Delegalisation Reform Movements: A Historical Analysis' in Richard Abel (ed), *The Politics of Informal Justice, Volume 1: The American Experience* (New York: Academic Press)

Harrington, C.B. (1994) 'Howard Bellman: Using "Bundles of Input" to Negotiate an Environmental Dispute' in D. Kolb and Associates (ed), *When Talk Works: Profiles of Mediator* (San Francisco: Jossey-Bass)

Hart, H.L.A. (1961) *The Concept of Law* (Oxford: Clarendon Press)

Hay, C, McKenna, K. and Buck, T. (2010) Evaluation of Early Neutral Evaluation: Alternative Dispute Resolution in the Social Security and Child Support Tribunal (Ministry of Justice)

Haynes, J. (1985) 'Matching Readiness and Willingness to the Mediators' Strategies', *Negotiation Journal*, January: pp. 79–92

Haynes, J. (1992) 'Mediation and Therapy: An Alternative View', *Mediation Quarterly*, 10 (1): pp. 21–34

Haynes, J. (1993) *The Fundamentals of Family Mediation* (London: Old Bailey Press)

Haynes, J.M. (1982) 'A Conceptual Model of the Process of Family Mediation: Implications for Training', *American Journal of Family Therapy*, 10 (4): pp. 5–16

Haynes, J.M., Haynes, G.l. and Fong, L.S. (2004) *Mediation: Positive Conflict Management* (New York: State University of New York Press)

Hester, M. *et al.* (2007) *Making an Impact: Children and Domestic Violence* (London and Philadelphia: Jessica Kingsley Publishers)

Hoban, T.M. (1984) 'Alternative Dispute Resolution and Hazardous Waste Site Cleanup Cost Allocation', *A Study of Barriers to the Use of Alternative Methods of Dispute Resolution* (South Royalton VT: Vermont Law School Dispute Resolution Project)

Hodson, D. (2008) 'The EU Mediation Directive: The European Encouragement to Family Law ADR', *International Family Law*, December

Hoffman, M. (2004) 'Peace and Conflict Impact Assessment Methodology' in A. Austin, M. Fisher and N. Roper (eds), *Transforming Ethnopolitcal Conflict: The Berghof Handbook* (Wiesbaden, Germany: V.S. Verlag)

Home Office, (1994) *National Standards for Probation Service Family Court Welfare Work* (London: HMSO)

Hopkins, B. (2004) *Just Schools: A Whole School Approach to Restorative Justice* (London: Jessica Kingsley Publishers)

Hopkins, B. (2009) *Just Care: Restorative Approaches to Working with Children in Public Care* (London: Jessica Kingsley Publishers) Research and Evaluation: www.transformingconflict.org.

Hopkins, B. (2011) *The Restorative Classroom: Using Restorative Approaches to Foster Effective Learning* (London: Optimus Education (Optimus Professional Publishing Ltd)); *The Peer Mediation and Mentoring Manual* (London: Optimus Professional Publishing Ltd)

Hopkins, B. and Shah, S. (2003) 'Restorative Justice in Schools', *Mediation in Practice*, April: pp. 4–11.

Huff, A. (2010) 'SEN Mediation – Why Not Give it a Go?' *Ace Education Now* (London; Advisory Centre of Education)

Ilich, I. (1975) 'The Medicalisation of Life', *Journal of Medical Ethics*, 1: pp. 73–77

Ingleby, R. (1992) *Solicitors and Divorce* (Oxford: Clarendon Press)

Ingleby, R. (1993) 'Court Sponsored Mediation: the Case against Mandatory Participation', *Modern Law Review*, 56: pp. 441–451

Ingleby, R. (1994) 'The Legal Process in Family Disputes and the Alternatives' in J. Eekelaar and M. Maclean (eds), *Divorce Mediation and the Legal Process* (Oxford: Clarendon Press)

Irving, H. and Benjamin, M. (2002) *Therapeutic Family Mediation* (London: Sage Publications)

James, A.L. and Hay, W. (1993) *Court Welfare in Action: Practice and Theory* (Hemel Hempstead: Harvester Wheatsheaf)

Jones, T.S. (2001) 'Editor's Introduction', *Conflict Resolution Quarterly*, 19 (2): pp. 131–134

Johnston, J. (1993) 'Gender, Violent Conflict and Mediation', *Family Mediation*, 3 (2): pp. 9–13

Katsh, D. and Rifkin, J. (2001) *Online Dispute Resolution: Resolving Conflict in Cyberspace* (San Francisco: Jossey-Bass)

Kelly, J.B. (2004) 'Family Mediation Research: Is There Empirical Support for the Field?' *Conflict Resolution Quarterly*, 22: pp. 1–2, 3–35

Keshavjee, M.M. (2013) *Islam, Sharia and Alternative Dispute Resolution: Mechanisms for Legal Redress in the Muslim Community* (London: I.B. Tauris)

Keys Young (August 1996) *Research/Evaluation of Family Mediation Practice and the Issue of Violence* (NSW: Attorney General's Department)

King, M. (1999) 'The Future of Specialist Child Care Mediation', *Child and Family Law Quarterly*, 11: pp. 137–149

King, M.S. *et al.* (2009) *Non-Adversarial Justice* (Annandale, NSW, Australia: The Federation Press)

King, M. and Trowell, J. (1992) *Children's Welfare and the Law: The Limits of Legal Intervention* (London: Sage Publications)

Kirby, B. (2006) 'CAFCASS: Productive Conflict Management Research and the Impetus for Change', *Family Law*, November, 36: pp. 970–974

Kolb, D.M. (1985) *The Mediators* (Cambridge, Massachusetts; London: The MIT Press)

Kolb, D.M. (ed) (1994) *When Talk Works: Profiles of Mediators* (San Francisco: Jossey Bass)

Kressel, K. (1985) *The Process of Divorce* (New York: Basic Books)

Kressel, K. and Pruitt, D.G. (1985) 'Themes in the Mediation of Social Conflict', *Journal of Social Issues*, 41 (2): pp. 179–198

Kressel. K., Henderson, T., Reich, W. and Cohen, C. (2012) 'Multidimensional Analysis of Conflict Mediator Style', *Conflict Resolution Quarterly*, 30 (2): pp. 135–171

Lamb, B. (December 2009) *Inquiry on Special Educational Needs and Parental Confidence* (London: DCSF-01143)

Landsberger, H.A. (August 1956) 'Final Report on a Research Project in Mediation', *Labour Law Journal*, 7: pp. 501–510

Lang, M.D. and Taylor, A. (2000) *The Making of a Mediator: Developing Artistry in Practice* (San Francisco: Jossey-Bass)

Larsen, R. and Thorpe, C. (Spring 2006) 'Elder Mediation: Optimizing Major Family Transitions', *Marquette Elders Adviser*, 7 (2): pp. 293–312

Latreille, P. (2010) *Mediation at Work: Of Success, Failure and Fragility.* Research Paper Ref. 06/10, www.acas.org.uk/researchpapers

Latreille, P. (2011) *Mediation: A Thematic Review of the ACAS/CIPD Evidence.* Research Paper ACAS Ref. No 13/11. www.acas.org.uk/researchpapers

LeBaron, M. (1998) 'Mediation and Multi-cultural Reality', *Peace and Conflict Studies*, 5 (1): pp. 41–56

LeBaron, M. (2005) *Bridging Troubled Waters –Conflict Resolution from the Heart* (New York: Jossey-Bass)

LeBaron, M. and Pillay, V. (2006) *Conflict Across Cultures – A Unique Experience of Bridging Differences* (Boston, MA: Intercultural Press)

LeBaron, M. and Zumeta, Z.D. (2003) 'Lawyers, Culture and Mediation Practice', *Conflict Resolution Quarterly*, 20 (4): pp. 463–472

Lederach, J.P. (1995) *Preparing for Peace: Conflict Transformation Across Cultures* (New York: Syracuse University Press)

Lederach, J.P. (2003) *The Little Book of Conflict Transformation* (Intercourse, PA: Good Books)

Legal Services Commission (2002) *Quality Mark Standard for Mediation* (London: Community Legal Service)

Lewis, C. (2009) *The Definitive Guide to Workplace Mediation and Managing Conflict at Work* (London: Bell and Bain Ltd)

Lewis, C. (2011) *Win-Win: Resolving Workplace Conflict: 12 Stories* (London: Bell & Bain Ltd)

Lewis, R. and Clark, J. (1993) *Employment Rights, Industrial Tribunals and Arbitration: The Case of Alternative Dispute Resolution* (Liverpool: Institute of Employment Rights)

Liebmann, M. (2000) *Mediation in Context* (London: Jessica Kingsley Publishers)

Lombard, N. and McMillan, L. (eds) (2012) *Violence Against Women: Current Theory and Practice in Domestic Abuse, Sexual Violence and Exploitation* (London: Jessica Kingsley Publishers)

Lord Chancellor's Advisory Committee on Legal Education and Conduct (ACLEC) (1999) *Mediating Family Disputes: Education and Conduct Standards for Mediators* (Report) (London: Lord Chancellor's Department)

Lubman, S. (1967) 'Mao and Mediation: Policy and Dispute Resolution in Communist China', *California Law Review*, 55

Lukes, S. (1973) *Individualism* (Oxford: Basil Blackwell)

Lukes, S. (1974) *Power: A Radical View* (Basingstoke: Macmillan Education)

Mackie, K. (ed) (2002) *A Handbook of Dispute Resolution: ADR in Action.* 2nd edn (London and New York: Routledge and Sweet and Maxwell)

Mackie K. *et al.* (2000) *The ADR Practice Guide: Commercial Dispute Resolution* (London: Butterworths)

Mackie, K. *et al.* (2007) *The ADR Practice Guide: Commercial Dispute Resolution.* 3rd edn (London: Bloomsbury Professional)

Marcus, L.J. with Dorn, B. and McNulty, E. (2011) *Renegotiating Health Care: Resolving Conflict to Build Collaboration.* 2nd edn (Sand Francisco: Jossey-Bass Publishers)

Marcus, L.J. and Roover, J.E. (2003) 'Healing the Conflicts That Divide Us: Health Care and Mediation', *AC Resolution*, Spring: pp. 17–19

McCrearey, B. (2008) *Elder Mediation Annotated Resource Library.* (Ann Arbor, Michigan: Centre for Social Gerontology, Inc)

McCrory, J.P. (1981) 'Environmental Mediation-Another Piece for the Puzzle', *Vermont Law Review*, 6 (1): pp. 49–84

McCrory, J.P. (1985) 'The Mediation Process', paper delivered at the Bromley Conference, April (Bromley, Kent: SE London Family Mediation Bureau)

McCrory, J.P. (1988) 'Confidentiality in Mediation of Matrimonial Disputes', *Modern Law Review*, 51 (4): pp. 442–66

McDermott, F.E. (1975) 'Against the Persuasive Definition of Self-Determination' in F.E. McDermott (ed.), *Self-Determination in Social Work* (London: Routledge and Kegan Paul)

McEldowney, J. (2012) *Family Mediation in a Time of Change: FMC Review Final Report* (Family Mediation Council: London)

McFarlane, J. (2005) 'The Emerging Phenomenon of Collaborative Family Law (CFL): A Qualitative Study of CFL Cases' (Canada: Departments of Justice)

McIntosh, J. (2000) 'Child Inclusive Mediation: Report on a Qualitative Research Study', *Mediation Quarterly*, 18 (1): pp. 55–69

McVeagh, N. (2006) 'Mediation in Clinical Negligence Cases and NHS Complaints – a Way Forward?' www.restorativejustice.org.uk/ Health_Sector/MediationJournalJune06

Marshall, T. (1988) 'Informal Justice: The British Experience' in R. Matthews (ed), *Informal Justice?* (London: Sage Publications)

Mather, L., Maiman, R.J. and McEven, C.A. (1995) 'The Passenger Decides on the Destination and i Decide on the Route: Are Divorce Lawyers Expensive Cab Drivers?' *International Journal of Law and the Family*, 9: pp. 286–310

Matthews, R. (ed) (1988) *Informal Justice?*(London: Sage Publications)

Mayer, B. (1985) 'Conflict Resolution in Child Protection and Adoption', *Conflict Resolution Quarterly*, 7: pp. 69–81 (published online in 2008)

Mayer, B. (1989) 'Mediation in Child Protection Cases: The Impact of Third Party Intervention on Parental Compliance Attitudes', *Mediation Quarterly*, 24

McEldowney, J. (2012) *Independent Review of the Family Mediation Council* (London: FMC)

McGuigan, R. and McMechan, S. (2005) 'Integral Conflict Analysis: a Comprehensive Quadrant Analysis of An Organizational Conflict', *Conflict Resolution Quarterly*, 22 (3): pp. 349–363

3rd Mediation Symposium (2010) *Creating Confidence in Mediators* (London: Chartered Institute of Arbitrators)

Mediation in the Rochester Diocese Leaflet,(nd) (Rochester: Diocesan Office) mediation@rochester.anglican.org

Mediation UK (1995) *Training Manuel in Community Mediation* (Bristol: Mediation UK)

Menkel-Meadow, C. (1985) 'Portia in a Different Voice: Speculation on a Women's Lawyering Process', *Berkeley Woman's Law Journal*, 1 (1): pp. 39–63

Menkel-Meadow, C. (9 May 1993) 'Lawyer Negotiations: Theories and Realities – What We Learn from Mediation', in 'Special Issue – Dispute Resolution: Civil Justice and Its Alternatives', *Modern Law Review*, 56 (3): pp. 361–379

Menkel-Meadow, C. (ed) (1995) *Mediation Theory, Policy and Practice* (Dartmouth, Aldershot: Ashgate)

Menkel-Meadow, C. (2001) 'Ethics in ADR: The Many C's of Professional Responsibility and Dispute Resolution', *Fordham Urban Law Journal*, 28 (4): pp. 979–990

Menkel-Meadow, C. (2007) 'Restorative Justice: What Is It and Does It Work?' *Annual Review of Law and Social Science*, 3 (10): pp. 161–187

Menkel-Meadow, C. (ed) (2012) *Complex Dispute Resolution. Foundations of Dispute Resolution*, Vol. I; *Multi-Party Dispute Resolution, Democracy and Decision-Making*, Vol. II; *International Dispute Resolution*, Vol. III (London: Ashgate)

Menkel-Meadow, C.J. *et al.* (2005) *Dispute Resolution: Beyond the Adversarial Model* (New York: Aspen Publishers)

Menkel-Meadow *et al.* (2007) *On the Requirements for Structural Fairness*, Chapter 7

Merrills, J.G. (Summer 1985) 'International Mediation: Conflict Resolution and Power Politics', *Journal of Social Issues*, 41 (2): pp. 27–45 [First published online on 14 April 2010]

Merrills, J.G. (2005) *International Dispute Settlement*. 4th edn (Cambridge: CUP)

Merry, S.E. (2002) 'Moving Beyond Ideology Critique to the Analysis of Practice', *Law and Social Inquiry*,27 (3): pp. 602–612 (Published online 28 July 2006)

Merry, S.E. and Milner, N. (eds) (1993) *The Possibility of Popular Justice: A Case Study of Community Mediation in the United States* (Ann Arbor: University of Michigan Press)

Mnookin, R.H. (1984) 'Divorce Bargaining: The Limits on Private Ordering', in J. Eekelaar and S.N. Katz (eds), *The Resolution of Family Conflict: Comparative Legal Perspectives* (Toronto: Butterworths)

Mnookin, R.H. and Gibson, R.J. (1994) 'Disputing through Agents: Co-operation and Conflict between Lawyers in Litigation', *Columbia Law Review*, 94: p. 509

Mnookin, R.H. and Kornhauser, L. (1979) 'Bargaining in the Shadow of the Law: The Case of Divorce', *Yale Law Journal*, 88: pp. 950–997

Moody, H. (1992) *Ethics in an Aging Society* (Baltimore: John Hopkins University Press)

Moore, C.W. (1996) *The Mediation Process: Practical Strategies for Resolving Conflict* (San Francisco: Jossey-Bass)

Moses, M. (2012) *The Principles and Practice of International Commercial Arbitration*. 2nd edn (Cambridge: CUP)

Mulcahy, L. *et al.* (2000) *Mediating Medical Negligence Claims: An Option for the Future?* University of London (London: The Stationery Office)

Murray, J.S., Rau, A.S. and Sherman, E.F. (1996) *Processes of Dispute Resolution: The Role of Lawyers*. 2nd edn (Westbury, New York: Foundation Press)

Nader, L. (2002) *The Life of the Law: Anthropological Projects* (Berkeley, CA: University of California Press)

National Alternative Dispute Resolution Advisory Council (NADRAC) (2001) 'Annual Report 2001–2002' (Australia: Canberra)

National Audit Office (NAO) (2007) *Legal Services Commission: Legal Aid and Mediation for People Involved in Family Breakdown* (Report by the Comptroller and Auditor General. London: NAO)

National Family Mediation (1998) *Cross Cultural Policy and Practice Guidelines*

National Institute for Dispute Resolution (NIDR) (1993) 'Interim Guidelines for Selecting Mediators' (Washington, D.C.: NIDR)

National Organisation for Training and Standards Setting in Advice, Advocacy, Counselling, Guidance, Mediation and Psychotherapy (CAMPAG), (October 1998) *Mediation Standards* (London: CAMPAG)

Neilson, L.S. and English, P. (2001) 'The Role of Interest –Based Facilitation in Designing Accreditation Standards: The Canadian Experience', *Mediation Quarterly*, 18 (3): pp. 221–248

Newman, P. (1994) 'Mediation-Arbitration (MedArb): Can It Work Legally?' *Arbitration*, 60 (3): pp. 174–176

Norgrove, D. (2011) *Family Justice Review Final Report* (London: Ministry of Justice)

Ogus, A. (1998) 'Re-Thinking Self-Regulation', in R. Baldwin, C. Scott and C. Hood (eds) *A Reader in Regulation* (Oxford: Oxford University Press)

Ogus, A. (2002) *Quality Mark Standard for Mediation* (London: Legal Services Commission)

O'Neill, O. (2002) 'A Question of Trust', *Reith Lectures*, bbc, Radio 4.

Palmer, M. and Roberts, S. (forthcoming 2014) *Dispute Processes: ADR and the Primary Forms of Decision-Making*. 3rd edn (Cambridge: CUP), Chapter 8

Park, J. (September 2010) 'Conflict Management and Mediation Theory: South Africa's Role in Burundi's Civil Conflict', *International Area Studies Review*, 13 (3): pp. 181–201

Parkinson, L. (2011) *Family Mediation: Appropriate Dispute Resolution in a New Family Justice System* (Bristol: Jordans/Family Law)

Patterson, C. and McKay, A. (2012) *Making Mediation Work in the Church of England* (Bridge Builders Ministries: London)

Paul, C. and Kiesewetter, S. (2011) *Cross –Border Family Mediation: International Parental Child Abduction, Custody and Access Cases. Frankfurt* (Germany, Wolfgang Metzner Verlag)

Paul, C. and Walker, J. (2008) 'Family Mediation in International Child Custody Conflicts: The Role of Consulting Attorneys', *American Journal of Family Law*, 22 (1), Spring: pp. 42–45

Paulsson, J. (2013) *The Idea of Arbitration*. 2nd edn (Oxford: Clarendon Law Series)

Penfold, C. *et al.* (2009) *Parental Confidence in the Special Educational Needs Assessment, Statementing and Tribunal System*. National Centre for Social Research, Research Report No. DCSF – RR117 (London: DCSF)

Picard, C., Bishop, P., Ramkay, R. and Sargent, N. (2004) *The Art and Science of Mediation* (Toronto: Emond Montgomery Publications Ltd)

Power, M. (1994) *The Audit Explosion* (London: Demos)

Practice Direction 3A-Pre-Application Protocol for Mediation Information and Assessment, April 2011 (London: Ministry of Justice)

Pre-Action Protocol for the Resolution of Clinical Disputes (1998) Department of Constitutional Affairs (London: Stationery Office), www.justice.gov.uk/civil/prorules

Princen, T. (1992) *Intermediaries in International Conflict* (Princeton, NJ: Princeton University Press)

Princen, T. (1994) 'Joseph Elder: Quiet Peacemaking in a Civil War' in D.M. Kolb and Associates *When Talk Works: Profiles of Mediators* (San Francisco: Jossey-Bass Publishers)

Pruitt, D.G. (1981) *Negotiation Behaviour* (New York: Academic Press)

Quality Mark Standard for Mediation (2002) London: Legal Services Commission, December 2002

Raiffa, H. (1982) *The Art and Science of Negotiation* (Cambridge MA: Belknap, Harvard University Press)

Raghavan, T.E.S. (2003) 'Zero-Sum Two Person Games' in R.J. Aumann and S. Hart (eds), *Handbook of Game Theory with Economic Applications*, Vol. 2. 2nd edn (Amsterdam: Elsievier)

Ramsbotham, O., Woodhouse, T. and Miall, H. (eds) (2011) *Contemporary Conflict Resolution*. 3rd edn (Cambridge: Polity Press)

Relationships Australia (2011) 'Development and Evaluation of Online Family Dispute Resolution Capabilities.' Final Report. *Commonwealth of Australia (Attorney General's Department) and Relationships Australia (QLD)*

Research Series 2/10, January 2010 (London: Ministry of Justice Brazil, W. (1990)) 'Special Master in Complex Case: Extending the Judiciary or Reshaping Adjudication?' *University of Chicago Law Review*, 53: p. 394

ResoLex: www.resolex.com

Richbell, D. (1999) 'National Standards for Mediation', *Family Mediation*, 9 (2): pp. 15–17

Richbell, D. (2008) *The Mediation of Construction Disputes* (Oxford: Blackwell Publishing)

Rifkin, J. (1994) 'The Practitioner's Dilemma' in J.P. Folger and T.S. Jones (eds), *New Directions in Mediation* (London: Sage)

Riskin, L.L. (1984) 'Towards New Standards for the Neutral Lawyer in Mediation', *Arizona Law Review*, 26: pp. 330–362

Riskin, L.L. (1994) 'Mediator Orientations, Strategies and Techniques', *Alternatives to High Cost Litigation*, 12 (9): pp. 111–114

Riskin, L.L. (2003) 'Decision-Making in Mediation: the New Old Grid and the New New Grid System', *Notre Dame Law Review*, 79 (1): pp. 1–54

Roberts, M. (1992) 'Systems or Selves? Some Ethical Issues in Family Mediation', *Mediation Quarterly*, 10 (1): pp. 3–19

Roberts, M. (1994) 'Who Is in Charge? Effecting a Productive Exchange between Researchers and Practitioners in the Field of Family Mediation', *Journal of Social Welfare and Family Law*, 4: pp. 439–454

Roberts, M. (April 1996) 'Family Mediation and the Interests of Women – Facts and Fears', *Family Law*, 26: pp. 239–241

Roberts, M. (2003) 'Third Persons in Family Mediation: Towards a Typology of Practice', *Mediation in Practice* (Bristol: UK College of Family Mediators), pp. 33–40. Guidelines for Lawyers in Mediation (SCMA), website@mediationadvocates.co, uk

Roberts, M. (2005) 'Hearing Both Sides: Structural Safeguards for Protecting Fairness in Family Mediation', *Mediation in Practice*, May: pp. 23–32

Roberts, M. (2005) 'The Development of the Regulatory Framework', *Conflict Resolution Quarterly*, 22 (4): pp. 509–526, republished in C. Menkel-Meadow (ed) (2012), *Complex Dispute Resolution: Foundations of Dispute Resolution*, 1 (Hampshire: Ashgate)

Roberts, M. (2007) *Developing the Craft of Mediation: Reflections on Theory and Practice* (London: Jessica Kingsley Publishers), Chapter 8

Roberts, M. (2008) *Mediation in Family Disputes: Principles of Practice.* 3rd edn (Aldershot, Hants: Ashgate), Chapter 6

Roberts, M. (December 2008) 'International Family Mediation and Recommendation No R (98)1: A Chronicle of Expansion Foretold', *International Family Law*: pp. 217–220

Roberts, M. (2010) 'Quality Standards for Family Mediation Practice', *Family Law*, 40: pp. 661–666

Roberts, M. (republished 2012) in C. Menkel-Meadow (ed), *Foundations of Dispute Resolution*, Vol. 1 (Aldershot, Hants: Ashgate Publishing Ltd)

Roberts, M. (June 2013) 'Specialist Child Care Mediation: Mediation in Public Law Cases', *Family Law*, 43 (6): pp. 749–752

Roberts, M. (2014) *Mediation in Family Disputes: Principles of Practice.* 4th edn (Aldershot, Hampshire: Ashgate Publishing Limited)

Roberts, S.A. (1983) 'The Study of Dispute: Anthropological Perspectives' in J.A. Bossy (ed) *Disputes and Settlements: Law and Human Relations in the West* (Cambridge: CUP)

Roberts, S. (1983) 'Mediation in Family Disputes', *Modern Law Review*, 46: pp. 337–357

Roberts, S. (2005) 'After Government?' Chorley Lecture published in the *Modern Law Review*, 68 (1): pp. 1–24

Roberts, S. (2008) 'Mediation', *The New Oxford Companion to Law* (Oxford: Oxford University Press)

Roberts, S. (2009) 'Listing Concentrates the Mind': The English Civil Court as an Arena for Structured Negotiation', *Oxford Journal of Legal Studies*, 29 (1): pp. 1–23

Roberts, S. (2013) *Order and Dispute: An Introduction to Legal Anthropology in the Classics of Law and Society Series.* 2nd edn (New Orleans, Louisiana: Quid Pro Books)

Roberts, S. and Palmer, M. (2005) *Dispute Processes: ADR and the Primary Forms of Decision-Making.* 2nd edn (Cambridge UK: CUP)

Roebuck, D. (2001) *Ancient Greek Arbitration* (Oxford: Oxford University Press)

Rosenberg, J.D. and Folberg, H.J. (1994) 'Alternative Dispute Resolution: An Empirical Analysis', *Stanford Law Review*, 46: p. 1487

Rossner, M. (2011) 'Emotions and Interaction Ritual: A Micro Analysis of Restorative Justice', *British Journal of Criminology*, 51: pp. 95–119

Rossner, M. and Tait, D. (2011) 'Contested Emotions: Adversarial Rituals in Non-Adversarial Justice Procedures', *Monash University Law Review*, 37 (1): pp. 241–258

Rubin, J.Z. and Brown, B.R. (1975) *The Social Psychology of Bargaining and Negotiation* (New York: Academic Press)

Rule, C. and Friedberg, T. (2006) 'The Appropriate Role of Dispute Resolution in Building Trust Online', *Artificial Intelligence and Law*, 13 (2): pp. 193–205

Sander, F.E.A. (1976) 'Varieties of Dispute Processing', *Federal Rules Decisions*, 70: pp. 11–134

Sander, F.E.A. (1985a) 'Alternative Methods of Dispute Resolution: An Overview', 37 *University of Florida Law Review*, 1: pp. 11–13

Sander, F.E.A. (1985b) 'Alternative Dispute Resolution in the United States: An Overview' in American Bar Association (ed), *Justice for a Generation* (St. Paul, Minnesota: West Publishing Company), pp. 253–261

Saposnek, D.T. (1983) *Mediating Child Custody Disputes* (San Francisco: Jossey-Bass)

Schaffer, L. (2004) 'Why Mediators Need Theory', *Mediation Matters* 77: pp. 14–15

Schelling, T.C. (1960) *The Strategy of Conflict* (Cambridge, MA: Harvard University Press)

Schon, D.A. (1983) *The Reflective Practitioner: How Professionals Think in Action* (New York: Academic Press)

Seidenberg, R. (1973) *Marriage between Equals: Studies from Life and Literature* (New York: Doubleday Anchor Press)

Sen, A. (2007) *Identity and Violence: The Illusion of Destiny* (London: Penguin)

Sen, A. (2009) *The Idea of Justice* (London: Penguin/Allen Lane)

Sennett, R. (2003) *Respect: The Formation of Character in an Age of Inequality* (London: Allen Lane)

Sennett, R. (2006) *The Culture of the New Capitalism* (New Haven and London: Yale University Press)

Sennett, R. (2008) *The Craftsman* (London: Allen Lane)

Sennett, R. (2012) *Together: The Rituals, Pleasures and Politics of Co-operation* (London: Allen Lane)

Shah-Kazemi, S.N. (2000) 'Cross-Cultural Mediation: A Critical View of the Dynamics of Culture in Family Disputes', *International Journal of Law, Policy and the Family*, 14: pp. 302–325

Shapiro, D. (2000) 'Pushing the Envelope – Selective Techniques in Tough Mediations', *The Arbitration and Dispute Resolution Law Journal*, 2/Junio: pp. 117–142

Shapiro, M. (1981) *Courts: A Comparative and Political Analysis* (Chicago: University of Chicago Press)

Silbey, S.S. (1994) 'Patrick Davis: "to Bring Out the Best ... to Undo a Little Pain" in Special Education Mediation' in D.M. Kolb and Associates *When Talk Works: Profiles of Mediators* (San Francisco: Jossey-Bass)

Silbey, S.S. and Merry, S.E. (1986) 'Mediator Settlement Strategies', *Law and Policy*, 8 (1): pp. 7–32

Simmel, G. (1908a) *Soziologie, trans. in The Sociology of Georg Simmel*, trans. K.H. Wolff (1955) (New York: Free Press)

Simmel, G. (1908b) *On Individuality and Social Forms*, in D.N. Levine (ed) (Chicago: University of Chicago Press, 1971)

Singer, J. (2004) *The EU Mediation Atlas: Practice and Regulation* (London: LexisNexis)

Smith. D., Blagg, H. and Derricourt, N. (1988) 'Mediation in the Shadow of the Law' in R. Matthews (ed), *Informal Justice?* (London: Sage Publications)

Society of Professionals in Dispute Resolution (SPIDR) (1989) *Qualifying Neutrals: The Basic Principles* (Washington, D. C.: National Institute for Dispute Resolution)

Society of Professionals in Dispute Resolution (SPIDR) Commission (1995) *Report of the SPIDR Commission on Qualifications, 1989, Ensuring Competence and Quality in Dispute Resolution Practice* (Report no. 2) (Washington D. C.: SPIDR Commission on Qualifications)

Special Education Needs (SEN) – A Guide for Parents and Carers (2009) (London: Department for Children, Schools and Families (DCSF))

Spencer, J.M. and Zammit, J.P. (1976) 'Mediation-Arbitration: A Proposal for Private Resolution of Disputes between Divorced or Separated Parents', *Duke Law Journal*, 911: pp. 932–938

St John Sutton, D., Gill J. and Gearing, M. (forthcoming) *Russell on Arbitration.* 24th edn (London: Sweet and Maxwell)

Stenelo, L-G. (1972) *Mediation in International Negotiations* (Malmö, Sweden: Nordens Boktryckeri)

Stevens, C.M. (1963) *Strategy and Collective Bargaining Negotiation* (New York: McGraw Hill)

Stulberg, J. (1981) 'The Theory and Practice of Mediation: A Reply to Professor Susskind' reprinted in S.B. Goldberg, E.D. Green and F.E.A. Sander (eds), *Dispute Resolution* (Boston and Toronto: Little, Brown)

Stulberg, J. (1987) *Taking Charge/Managing Conflict* (Lexington, MA: Lexington Books)

Summers Raines, S. (2006) 'Mediating in Your Pajamas: The Benefits and Challenges for ODR Practitioners', *Conflict Resolution Quarterly*, 22 (4): pp. 437–451

Tennant, R. *et al.* (2008) *Special Educational Needs Disagreement Resolution Services: National Evaluation* (National Centre for Social Research, Research Report No, DCSF – RR054, London: DCSF)

Tesler, P. (2003) 'Collaborative Family Law', *Pepperdine Dispute Resolution Law Journal*, 4: p. 317

Tesler, P. (2008) 'Collaborative Family Law, the New Lawyer and Deep Resolution of Divorce-Related Conflict', *Journal of Dispute Resolution*, 1: p. 83

Thoennes, N. (1997) 'Child Protection Mediation. Where we started', *Family Conciliation Courts Review*, 35: p. 136

Thoennes, N.A. and Pearson, J. (1985) 'Predicting Outcomes in Divorce Mediation: The Influence of People and Process', *Journal of Social Issues*, 41 (2): pp. 115–126

Thorsborne, M. and Vinegrad, D. (2008) *Restorative Practices in Schools* (UK: Speechmark Publishing Ltd)

Trinder, L. *et al.* (2006) *Making Contact Happen or Making Contact Work? The Process and Outcomes of In-Court Conciliation*. DCA Research Series 3/06, March (London DCA)

Touval, S. and Zartman, I.W. (eds) (1985) *International Mediation in Theory and Practice* (Boulder CO: Westview Press)

UK College of Family Mediators (2000) *Domestic Abuse Screening Policy* (London: UKCFM)

UK College of Family Mediators (2003) *Professional Practice Consultancy for Family Mediators: A Guide to Roles and Responsibilities* (Bristol: College of Mediators)

Umbreit, M.S. (1995) *Mediating Interpersonal Conflicts: A Pathway to Peace* (West Concord, Minnesota: CPI Publishing)

UN Convention on the Rights of the Child (1989)

UN Department of Peacekeeping. www.un.org/Depts/dpko/

United Nations Guidance for Mediators (2012) *Addressing Conflict-Related Sexual Violence in Cease-fire and Peace Agreements* (New York: UN Department of Political Affairs)

Urwin, P. *et al.* (2010) *Evaluating the Use of Judicial Mediation in Employment Tribunals*, Ministry of Justice Research Series 7/10, March, 2010

Verkuil, P.R. (1975) 'The Ombudsman and the Limits of the Adversary System', Columbia Law Review, 75: pp. 845–846

Walker, J. (April 2012) 'What Does the Research Tell Us?' *Presentation to Family Mediation Symposium: Improving the Client Experience of*

Mediation (London: Law Society) [check later Family Law publication details]

Walker, J. and Robinson, M. (1992) 'Conciliation and Family Therapy' in T. Fisher (ed), *Family Conciliation within the UK: Policy and Practice* (Bristol: Jordan and Sons Limited)

Walker, J. *et al.* (2004) *Picking up the Pieces: Marriage and Divorce Two Years After Information Provision* (London: DCA)

Wall, J.A. and Rude, D.E. (Summer 1985) 'Judicial Mediation: Techniques, Strategies and Situational Effects', *Journal of Social Issues*, 41 (2): pp. 47–63

Walsh, E. (2006) *Working in the Family Justice System: The Official Handbook of the Family Justice.* 2nd edn (Bristol: Family Law)

Walton, R.E. and McKersie, R.B. (1965) *A Behavioural Theory of Labour Negotiating* (New York: McGraw Hill)

Weber, M. ([1917] 1978) *Economy and Society*, G. Roth and C. Wittich (eds), E. Fischoff *et al.* (trans) (New York: Bedminster Press)

Whatling, T. (May 2008) 'Conflict and Diversity Matters: When You Are in Contact with the Other You Learn More', *Newsletter of the College of Mediators*, 2: pp. 11–15

Whatling, T. (2012) *Mediation Skills and Strategies: A Practical Guide* (London: Jessica Kingsley Publishers)

Whatling, T. and Kesavjee, M.M. (2005) 'Reflective Learning from the Training Programmes of the Ismaili Muslim Conciliation and Arbitration Boards Globally', *Mediation in Practice*, 23

White, J.J. (1980) 'Machiavelli and the Bar: Ethical Limitations on Lying in Negotiation', *American Bar Foundation Research Journal*, 4: pp. 926–938

Wiegand, S.A. (1996) 'A Just and Lasting Peace: Supplanting Mediation with the Ombuds Model', *Ohio State Journal on Dispute Resolution*, 12 (1): pp. 95–144

Wilson, B. (2004) 'Towards a Theoretical Model of Professional Practice Consultancy', *Mediation in Practice*, April: pp. 14–20

Winslade, J. and Monk, G. (2001) *Narrative Mediation: A New Approach to Conflict Resolution* (San Francisco: Jossey-Bass)

Woolf, Lord (1995) *Access to Justice: Interim Report to the Lord Chancellor on the Civil Justice System of England and Wales* (London: HMSO)

Wright, W.A. (2000) *Cultural Issues in Mediation: Individualist and Collectivist Paradigms*, available at www.mediate.com/articles/Wright.cfm

Zaidel, S. (2008) 'How Collaborative Is Collaborative Divorce?', *Family Mediation News*, 4

Zartman, I.W. (ed) (2007 revised edn) *Peacemaking in International Conflict: Methods and Techniques* (Washington DC: United States Institute of Peace

Zehr, H. (1985) *Retributive Justice: Restorative Justice* (Elkhart, Indiana: MCC US Office of Criminal justice) Occasional Paper 4.

Zehr, H. and Toews, B. (eds) (2004) *Critical Issues in Restorative Justice* (Monsey, NY: Criminal Justice Press)

index